By the Same Author

State-Specific ADA Compliance Manuals

Arizona - Arizona w/CD-ROM - CD-ROM Only
California - California w/CD-ROM - CD-ROM Only
Connecticut - Connecticut w/CD-ROM - CD-ROM Only

Florida - Florida w/CD-ROM - CD-ROM Only
Georgia - Georgia w/CD-ROM - CD-ROM Only
Illinois - Illinois w/CD-ROM - CD-ROM Only

Indiana - Indiana w/CD-ROM - CD-ROM Only
Maryland - Maryland w/CD-ROM - CD-ROM Only
Massachusetts - Massachusetts w/CD-ROM - CD-ROM Only

Michigan - Michigan w/CD-ROM - CD-ROM Only
Minnesota - Minnesota w/CD-ROM - CD-ROM Only
New Jersey - New Jersey w/CD-ROM - CD-ROM Only

New York State - New York State w/CD-ROM - CD-ROM Only
Ohio - Ohio w/CD-ROM - CD-ROM Only
Oregon - Oregon w/CD-ROM - CD-ROM Only

Pennsylvania - Pennsylvania w/CD-ROM - CD-ROM Only
South Carolina - South Carolina w/CD-ROM - CD-ROM Only
Texas - Texas w/CD-ROM - CD-ROM Only

Virginia - Virginia w/CD-ROM - CD-ROM Only
Washington - Washington w/CD-ROM - CD-ROM Only
Wisconsin - Wisconsin w/CD-ROM - CD-ROM Only

City-Specific ADA Compliance Manual

New York City - New York City w/CD-ROM - CD-ROM Only

For information, contact:

Jordan Publishing - 2475 Short Spur Trail - Prescott, AZ - 86305
Phone: (800)657-9881 - Fax: (928)708-9874
Email: jim@jordanpublishing.net - Website: www.jordanpublishing.net

ADA

AMERICANS WITH DISABILITIES ACT ARCHITECTURAL BARRIER REMOVAL AND COMPLIANCE MANUAL

A Simplified Approach to Accessibility

Based on:

Washington State Building Code with 2005 and 2006 Amendments

International Buiding Code

ICC/ANSI A117.1

FHAG - Fair Housing Accessibility Guidelines

Recreation Facilities - Federal Final Rule

WASHINGTON

©2006 James E. Jordan. All Rights Reserved.
Printed in the United States of America.

Copyright ©May 1, 2006 By James E. Jordan
Used by permission.
All rights reserved. No part of this publication may be reproduced, stored in a retrieval system, or transmitted, in any form or by any means, electronic, mechanical, photocopying, recording, or otherwise, without the prior permission of the author.

Book - ISBN: 1-932730-65-6
Book with CD/ROM - ISBN: 1-932730-66-4
CD/ROM only - ISBN: 1-932730-67-2

Graphic Design - Amy M. Jordan

"Portions of this document reproduce text, tables and figures from the 2003 International Building Code, International Code Council, Inc., Falls Church, Virginia. Reproduced with permission. All rights reserved."

The International Code Council (ICC) and International Conference of Building Officials (ICBO) assumes no responsibility for the accuracy or the completion of summaries provided herein.

This book is designed to help eliminate potential sources of liability that may result from non-compliance with the Americans with Disabilities Act (ADA). This book is designed only as an aid to identify barriers and does not express or imply guaranteed compliance.

FOREWORD

This book was conceived and written to help professionals and non-professionals recognize architectural barriers to persons with disabilities.

Its aim is to offer solutions to barrier removal and barrier-free design considerations.

As a reference book, it states in a clear concise form, using a step by step format, exact requirements to help with compliance with the ADA.

Architects, real estate persons, insurance adjusters, interior design professionals and property owners should find its easy to use format useful.

Building contractors can use it as an aid to estimating the costs of projects, and its thoroughness will save much confusion.

Service groups can use it as a source to help in the dissemination of information.

Every attempt has been made to be as thorough, complete and accurate as possible.

However, from the Federal, State, City or County levels of government, changes in codes can occur at anytime.

Check with your local building official for compliance.

James E. Jordan
May, 2006

INTRODUCTION

The 2003 International Building Code excerpts have been printed in normal type.

<u>Washington State Building Code Amendments (WAC) have been underlined.</u>

ICC/ANSI A117.1-2003 codes have been italicized.

Reference points and directional information have been printed in bold italic type.

TABLE OF CONTENTS

Foreword ii
Introduction iii
Tables and Diagrams viii

International Building Code - Accessibility

Chapter 1:   General - (1101.1)
                WAC - (1101.2 through 1101.2.11) 1
Chapter 2:   Definitions - (1102) 4
Chapter 3:   Scoping Requirements - (1103)
                WAC - (1103.2.15) 6
Chapter 4:   Accessible Route - (1104)
                ICC/ANSI A117.1
                Accessible Routes - (402) Walking Surfaces - (403)
                WAC - (1101.2.1) (1101.2.2) (1104.4) 9
Chapter 5:   Accessible Entrances - (1105)
                WAC - (1105.1) 16
Chapter 6:   Parking - (1106)
                ICC/ANSI A117.1 - Parking Spaces - (502)
                WAC - (1106.3) (1106.4) (1106.6) 18
Chapter 7:   Passenger Loading Zones - (1106.7)
                ICC/ANSI A117.1 - Passenger Loading Zones - (503)
                WAC - (1106.7.4) 24

International Building Code - Dwelling Units and Sleeping Units

Chapter 8:   Dwelling Units and Sleeping Units - (1107) 27
Chapter 9:   Group I Occupancies - (1107.5) 29
Chapter 10:   Group R Occupancies - (1107.6)
                WAC - (1107.6) (1107.6.2.1.1) 32
Chapter 11:   General Exceptions - (1107.7) 36

ICC/ANSI A117.1 - Dwelling Units and Sleeping Units

Chapter 12:   *Accessible Units - (1002)* 39
Chapter 13:   *Type A Units - (1003)* 43
Chapter 14:   *Type B Units - (1004)* 55
Chapter 15:   *Units with Accessible Communication Features - (1005)* 66

International Building Code - Means of Egress

Chapter 16:   Ramps - (1010)
                WAC - (1024.11) - *ICC/ANSI A117.1 - Ramps - (405)* 69
Chapter 17:   Handrails - (1009) (1607.7)
                WAC - (1010.8) (1024.13) 77

TABLE OF CONTENTS

International Building Code - Fire Protection Systems
Chapter 18:   Alarms - (907.9)
                         ICC/ANSI A117.1 - Alarms - (702) 81

International Building Code - Special Occupancies
Chapter 19:   Special Occupancies - (1108) (1108.1) 84
Chapter 20:   Assembly Area Seating - (1108.2)
                         ICC/ANSI A117.1 - Assembly Areas - (802) 85
Chapter 21:   Dining Areas - (1108.2.9)
                         ICC/ANSI A117.1 - Dining Surfaces and Work Surfaces - (902) 95
Chapter 22:   Self-Service Storage Facilities - (1108.3) 98
Chapter 23:   Judicial Facilities - (1108.4)
                         ICC/ANSI A117.1
                         Holding Cells and Housing Cells - (806) Courtrooms - (807) 99

International Building Code - Other Features and Facilities
Chapter 24:   Other Features and Facilities - (1109) (1109.1) 103
Chapter 25:   Toilet and Bathing Facilities - (1109.2)
                         ICC/ANSI A117.1 - Toilet and Bathing Rooms - (603)
                         WAC - (1101.2.5) 104
Chapter 26:   Unisex Toilet and Bathing Rooms - (1109.2.1) 107
Chapter 27:   Water Closet Compartment - (1109.2.2)
                         ICC/ANSI A117.1
                         Water Closets and Toilet Compartments - (604)
                         Wheelchair Accessible Compartments - (604.8)
                         Ambulatory Accessible Compartments - (604.9)
                         WAC - (1101.2.5) (1101.2.6) 109
Chapter 28:   Sinks - (1109.3)
                         ICC/ANSI A117.1 - Lavatories and Sinks - (606) 118
Chapter 29:   Kitchens and Kitchenettes - (1109.4)
                         ICC/ANSI A117.1 - Kitchens and Kitchenettes - (804) 121
Chapter 30:   Drinking Fountains - (1109.5)
                         ICC/ANSI A117.1 - Drinking Fountains and Water Coolers - (602)
                         WAC - (1109.5) 125
Chapter 31:   Elevators - (1109.6)
                         ICC/ANSI A117.1 - Elevators - (407)
                         WAC - (1101.2.4) (1109.6) 128

ICC/ANSI A117.1
Chapter 32:   Limited-Use/Limited-Application Elevators - (408) *142*
Chapter 33:   Private Residence Elevators - (409) *145*

TABLE OF CONTENTS

International Building Code - Other Features and Facilities

Chapter 34:	Lifts - (1109.7)	
	ICC/ANSI A117.1 - Platform Lifts - (410)	149
Chapter 35:	Storage - (1109.8)	
	ICC/ANSI A117.1 - Storage Facilities - (905)	152
Chapter 36:	Detectable Warnings - (1109.9)	
	ICC/ANSI A117.1 - Detectable Warnings - (705)	
	WAC - (1109.9)	154
Chapter 37:	Assembly Area Seating - (1109.10)	156
Chapter 38:	Seating at Tables - Counters - Work Surfaces - (1109.11)	157
Chapter 39:	Service Facilities - (1109.12)	
	ICC/ANSI A117.1	
	Dressing - Fitting - Locker Rooms - (803)	
	Benches - (903)	
	Sales and Service Counters - (904)	158
Chapter 40:	Controls - Operating Mechanisms - Hardware - (1109.13)	164
Chapter 41:	Operable Windows - (1109.13.1)	
	ICC/ANSI A117.1 - Windows - (506)	165
Chapter 42:	Recreational Facilities - (1109.14)	
	WAC - (1109.14.3)	166
Chapter 43:	Stairways - (1109.15)	
	ICC/ANSI A117.1 - Stairways - (504)	167

International Building Code - Signage

Chapter 44:	Signage - (1110) (1007) (1011)	
	ICC/ANSI A117.1 - Signs - (703)	
	WAC - (1101.2.9)	170

International Building Code - Supplementary Accessibility Requirements

Chapter 45:	Appendix (E107) (E108) (E109) (E110) - Signage	184

International Building Code - Accessibility for Existing Buildings

Chapter 46:	Accessibility for Existing Buildings - (3409) Appendix (E104.3.4)	
	WAC - (3409.5) (3409.6) (3409.7) (3409.7.2) (3409.7.3) (3409.7.7) (3409.7.9)	187
Chapter 47:	Historic Buildings - (3409.8)	193

ICC/ANSI A117.1

Chapter 48:	*Floor Surfaces - (302)*	*195*
Chapter 49:	*Changes in Level - (303)*	*197*
Chapter 50:	*Turning Space - (304)*	*198*
Chapter 51:	*Clear Floor Space - (305)*	*200*
Chapter 52:	*Knee and Toe Clearance - (306)*	*202*
Chapter 53:	*Protruding Objects - (307)*	*204*

TABLE OF CONTENTS

Chapter 54:   *Reach Ranges - (308)* *206*
Chapter 55:   *Operable Parts - (309)* *208*

Chapter 56:   *Doors and Doorways - (404)*
                          WAC - (1101.2.3) (1101.2.11) *209*
Chapter 57:   *Curb Ramps - (406)* *217*

Chapter 58:   *Water Closets and Toilet Compartments for Children's Use - (604.10)* . . . *221*
Chapter 59:   *Urinals - (605)* *223*
Chapter 60:   *Bathtubs - (607)* *224*
Chapter 61:   *Shower Compartments - (608)* *228*
Chapter 62:   *Grab Bars - (609)* *234*
Chapter 63:   *Seats - (610)* *237*
Chapter 64:   *Washing Machines and Clothes Dryers - (611)* *239*

Chapter 65:   *Telephones - (704)* *240*
Chapter 66:   *Assistive Listening Systems - (706)* *243*
Chapter 67:   *Automatic Teller Machines (ATMs) and Fare Machines - (707)* *244*
Chapter 68:   *Two-Way Communication Systems - (708)* *249*

Chapter 69:   *Transportation Facilities - (805)* *250*

Chapter 70:   **Fair Housing Accessibility Guidelines (FHAG)** **254**

Chapter 71:   **Recreation Facilities - Federal Final Rule - (15)** **267**
                          Amusement Rides - (15.1) 267
                          Boating Facilities - (15.2) 272
                          Fishing Piers and Platforms - (15.3) 276
                          Golf - (15.4) 278
                          Miniature Golf - (15.5) 280
                          Play Areas - (15.6) 282
                          Appendix - Play Areas - Children - (A15.6) 291
                          Exercise Equipment and Machines
                               Bowling Lanes - Shooting Facilities - (15.7) 297
                          Swimming Pools - Wading Pools - Spas - (15.8) 297

Diagrams 306

Bibliography 442

Index 443

TABLES AND DIAGRAMS

TABLES

Table	Description	Page
A	Clear Width of an Accessible Route	14
B	Accessible Parking Spaces	19
C	Accessible Dwelling and Sleeping Units	33
D	Allowable Ramp Dimensions for Construction in Existing Sites - Buildings and Facilities	74
E	Visible and Audible Alarms	82
F	Accessible Wheelchair Spaces	86
G	Receivers for Assistive Listening Systems	88
H	Required Wheelchair Space Location Elevation over Standing Spectators	93
I	Accessible Self-Service Storage Facilities	98
J	Maximum Reach Depth and Height	120
K	Minimum Dimensions of Elevator Cars	135
L	Accessible Check-out Aisles	159
M	Visual Character Height	174
N	Braille Dimensions	179
O	Ramps - (Existing Buildings)	191
P	Maneuvering Clearances at Manual Swinging Doors	211
Q	Maneuvering Clearances at Sliding and Folding Doors	212
R	Maneuvering Clearances for Doorways without Doors	245
S	Tactile Symbols	234
T	Boat Slips - Minimum Number	274
U	Number and Types of Ground Level Play Components Required to be on Accessible Route	284
V	Children's Reach Ranges	295

DIAGRAMS

Diagram	Description	Page
1	Clear Width of an Accessible Route	306
2	Clear Width at Turn	307
3	Size of Wheelchair Turning Space	308
4	Vehicle Parking Space Size	309
5	Parking Space Access Aisles	310
6	Passenger Loading Zone Access Aisle	311
7	Water Closets in Type A Units	312
8	Clearance for Bathtubs in Type A Units	313
9	Standard Roll-in-Type Shower Compartment in Type A Units	314
10	Minimum Kitchen Clearance in Type A Units	315

TABLES AND DIAGRAMS

Diagram	Description	
11	U-Shaped Kitchen Clearance in Type A Units	316
12(a)	Work Surface in Kitchen for Type A Units	
12(b)	Kitchen Sink for Type A Units	317
13	Lavatory in Type B Units - Option A Bathrooms	318
14	Water Closets in Type B Units	319
15	Parallel Approach Bathtub in Type B Units - Option A Bathrooms	320
16	Forward Approach Bathtub in Type B Units - Option A Bathrooms	321
17	Transfer-Type Shower Compartment in Type B Units	322
18	Lavatory in Type B Units - Option B Bathrooms	323
19	Bathtub Clearance in Type B Units - Option B Bathrooms	324
20	Minimum Kitchen Clearance in Type B Units	325
21	U-Shaped Kitchen Clearance in Type B Units	326
22	Ramp Landings	327
23	Ramp Edge Protection	328
24(a)	Handrail Height	
24(b)	Handrail Clearance	
24(c)	Circular Cross Section	
24(d)	Non-Circular Cross Section	329
25(a)	Top and Bottom Handrail Extensions at Ramps	
25(b)	Top Handrail Extensions at Stairs	
25(c)	Bottom Handrail Extensions at Stairs	330
26(a)	Width of a Wheelchair Space in Auditorium and Assembly Areas	
26(b)	Depth of a Wheelchair Space in Auditorium and Assembly Areas	331
27(a)	Lines of Sight over the Heads of Seated Spectators	
27(b)	Lines of Sight between the Heads of Seated Spectators	332
28	Wheelchair Space Elevation	333
29	Water Closet Location	334
30(a)	Size of Clearance for Water Closet	
30(b)	Water Closet Height	335
31(a)	Side Wall Grab Bar for Water Closet	
31(b)	Rear Wall Grab Bar for Water Closet	336
32	Swing-up Grab Bar for Water Closet	337
33	Dispenser Location	338
34	Wheelchair Accessible Toilet Compartments	339
35	Wheelchair Accessible Compartment Doors	340
36	Wheelchair Accessible Compartment Toe Clearance	341
37	Ambulatory Accessible Compartment	342
38	Height of Lavatories and Sinks	343
39	Pass-through Kitchen Clearance	344
40	U-Shaped Kitchen Clearance	345
41	Drinking Fountain Spout Location	346
42	Height of Elevator Call Buttons	347

TABLES AND DIAGRAMS

Diagram   *Description*

Diagram	Description	Page
43	Destination-Oriented Elevator Indication	348
44	Elevator Visible Signals	349
45	Elevator Floor Designation	350
46	Destination-Oriented Elevator Car Identification	351
47	Inside Dimensions of Elevator Cars	352
48	Elevator Car Control Buttons	353
49	Control Button Identification	354
50	Inside Dimensions of Limited Use/Limited-Application (LULA) Elevator Cars	355
51	Location of Controls in Private Residence Elevators	356
52	Platform Lift Doors and Gates	357
53	Truncated Dome Size and Spacing	358
54	Benches	359
55	Height of Checkout Counters	360
56	Treads and Risers for Accessible Stairways	361
57	Stair Nosings	362
58(a)	International Symbol of Accessibility	
58(b)	International TTY Symbol	
58(c)	Volume-Controlled Telephone	
58(d)	International Symbol of Access for Hearing Loss	363
59	Character Height	364
60	Height of Tactile Characters above Floor or Ground	365
61	Location of Tactile Signs at Doors	366
62	Braille Measurement	367
63	Position of Braille	368
64	Pictogram Field	369
65(a)	Carpet on Floor Surfaces	
65(b)	Openings in Floor Surfaces	370
66	Vertical Changes in Level	371
67	Beveled Changes in Level	372
68	Size of Clear Floor Space	373
69	Position of Clear Floor Space	374
70	Maneuvering Clearance in an Alcove	375
71	Toe Clearance	376
72	Knee Clearance	377
73	Limits of Protruding Objects	378
74	Post-Mounted Protruding Objects	379
75	Reduced Vertical Clearance	380
76	Unobstructed Forward Reach	381
77	Obstructed High Forward Reach	382
78	Unobstructed Side Reach	383
79	Obstructed High Side Reach	384

TABLES AND DIAGRAMS

Diagram   *Description*

Diagram	Description	Page
80	Clear Width of Doorways	385
81	Maneuvering Clearance at Manual Swinging Doors	386
82	Maneuvering Clearance at Sliding and Folding Doors	387
83	Maneuvering Clearance at Doorways without Doors	388
84	Maneuvering Clearance at Recessed Doors	389
85	Two Doors in Series	390
86	Counter Slope of Surfaces Adjacent to Curb Ramps	391
87	Sides of Curb Ramps	392
88	Diagonal Curb Ramps	393
89	Islands	394
90	Children's Water Closet Location	395
91(a)	Children's Water Closet Height	
91(b)	Children's Dispenser Location	396
92	Urinals	397
93	Clearance for Bathtubs	398
94	Grab Bars for Bathtubs with Permanent Seats	399
95	Grab Bars for Bathtubs without Permanent Seats	400
96	Location of Bathtub Controls	401
97	Transfer-Type Shower Compartment Size and Clearance	402
98	Standard Roll-in-Type Shower Compartment Size and Clearance	403
99	Alternate Roll-in-Type Shower Compartment Size and Clearance	404
100	Grab Bars in Transfer-Type Showers	405
101	Grab Bars in Standard Roll-in-Type Showers	406
102	Grab Bars in Alternate Roll-in-Type Showers	407
103	Transfer-Type Shower Controls and Hand Shower Location	408
104	Standard Roll-in-Type Shower Control and Hand Shower Location	409
105	Alternate Roll-in-Type Shower Control and Hand Shower Location	410
106	Size and Spacing of Grab Bars	411
107	Bathtub Seats	412
108	Shower Compartment Seats	413
109	Height of Laundry Equipment	414
110	Clear Floor Space for Telephones	415
111	Numeric Key Layout	416
112	Size of Bus Boarding and Alighting Areas	417
113	Bus Shelters	418
114	Track Crossings	419
115	Reach Ranges - FHAG	420
116	Maximum Side Reach over an Obstruction - FHAG	421
117	Water Closets in Adaptable Bathrooms - FHAG	422
118	Grab Bar Reinforcements for Adaptable Bathtubs - FHAG	423
119	Grab Bar Reinforcements for Adaptable Showers - FHAG	424
120	Clear Floor Space for Adaptable Bathrooms - FHAG	425

TABLES AND DIAGRAMS

Diagram	Description	
121	Clear Floor Space at Lavatories - FHAG	426
122	Clear Floor Space at Showers and Bathtubs - FHAG	427
123	Protrusions in Wheelchair Spaces	428
124	Pier Clearances	429
125(a)	Pier Clear Space Reduction	
125(b)	Edge Protection at Pier	430
126	Edge Protection at Fishing Piers	431
127	Golf Club Reach Range	432
128	Transfer Platforms	433
129	Transfer Steps	434
130	Pool Lifts	435
131	Pool Lift and Sloped Entry - Submerged Depth	436
132	Sloped Entry Handrails	437
133	Clear Deck Space at Transfer Walls	438
134(a)	Transfer Wall Height	
134(b)	Transfer Wall Depth and Length	
134(c)	Grab Bars at Transfer Walls	439
135(a)	Transfer System Platform	
135(b)	Clear Deck Space at Transfer Systems	440
136	Transfer Systems	441

Chapter 1:

IBC - WAC
GENERAL

IBC - Chapter 11   **Accessibility**

1101   **General**

1101.1   **Scope**

The provisions of the 2003 International Building Code - Chapter 11, shall control the design and construction of facilities for accessibility to physically disabled persons.

WAC - 7/01/06

1101.2   **Design**

Buildings and facilities shall be designed and constructed to be accessible in accordance with the 2003 International Building Code and ICC/ANSI A117.1, except those portions of ICC/ANSI A117.1 amended by this chapter.

1101.2.1   **ICC/ANSI A117.1 - Section 403**
(Chapter 4: Accessible Route - 403 - pp. 13-15)

Landings for Walking Surfaces

The maximum rise for any run is 30 inches (762mm).

Landings shall be provided at the top and bottom of any run.

Landings shall be level and have a minimum dimension measured in the direction of travel of not less than 60 inches (1524mm).

1101.2.2   **ICC/ANSI A117.1 - Section 403.5**
(Chapter 4: Accessible Route - 403.5 - pp. 13-15)

Clear Width of Accessible Route

Clear width of an accessible route shall comply with ***Chapter 4: Accessible Route - Table A - p. 14.***

For exterior routes of travel, the minimum clear width shall be 44 inches (1118mm).

Chapter 1: IBC - WAC - General (continued)

1101.2.3   **ICC/ANSI A117.1 - Section 404.2.8**
(Chapter 56: Doors and Doorways - 404.2.8 - p. 214)

Door-Opening Force

Fire doors shall have the minimum opening force allowable by the appropriate administrative authority.

The maximum force for pushing open or pulling open doors other than fire doors shall be as follows:

    Interior hinged door: 5.0 pounds (22.2N)

    Sliding or folding doors: 5.0 pounds (22.2N)

At exterior doors where environmental conditions require a closing pressure greater than 8.5 pounds (37.8N), power-operated doors shall be used within the accessible route of travel.

These forces do not apply to the force required to retract latch bolts or disengage other devices that hold the door in a closed position.

1101.2.4   **ICC/ANSI A117.1 - Section 407.4.6.2.2**
(Chapter 31: Elevators - 407.4.6.2.2 - p. 137)

Arrangement

This section is not adopted.

1101.2.5   **ICC/ANSI A117.1 - Section 603.4 and 604.11**
(Chapter 25: Toilet and Bathing Facilities - 603.4 - p. 106)
(Chapter 27: Water Closet Compartment - 604.11 - p. 117)

Coat Hooks - Shelves - Dispensers - Other Fixtures

Coat hooks provided shall accommodate a forward reach or side reach complying with *Chapter 54: Reach Ranges - 308 - pp. 206 & 207.*

Where provided, shelves shall be installed so that the top of the shelf is 40 inches (1016mm) maximum above the floor or ground.

Drying equipment, towel or other dispensers, and disposal fixtures shall be located 40 inches (1016mm) maximum above the floor or ground to any rack, operating controls, receptacle or dispenser.

Chapter 1: IBC - WAC - General (continued)

1101.2.6   **ICC/ANSI A117.1 - Section 604.6**
(Chapter 27: Water Closet Compartment - 604.6 - p. 113)

Flush Controls

Hand-operated flush controls for water closets shall be mounted not more than 44 inches (1118mm) above the floor.

1101.2.7   **Reserved.**

1101.2.8   **Reserved.**

1101.2.9   **ICC/ANSI A117.1 - Section 703.6.3.1**
(Chapter 44: Signage - 703.6.3.1 - p. 181)

International Symbol of Accessibility

Where the International Symbol of Accessibility is required, it shall be proportioned complying with *Diagram 58(a) - p. 363*.

All interior and exterior signs depicting the International Symbol of Accessibility shall be white on a blue background.

1101.2.10   **Reserved.**

1101.2.11   **ICC/ANSI A117.1 - Section 404.3.5**
(Chapter 56: Doors and Doorways - 404.3.5 - p. 216)

Control Switches

Controls switches shall be mounted 32 inches to 40 inches (813mm to 1016mm) above the floor and not less than 18 inches (457mm) nor more than 36 inches (914mm) horizontally from the nearest point of travel of the moving doors.

Chapter 2:

INTERNATIONAL BUILDING CODE DEFINITIONS

IBC - Chapter 11　　　　　　　　　　　**Accessibility**

1102 - 1102.1　　　　　　　　　　　　**Definitions**

The following words and terms shall, for the purposes of the 2003 International Building Code - Chapter 11 and as used elsewhere in the 2003 International Building Code, have the following meanings:

Accessible
A site, building, facility or portion thereof, that complies with the 2003 International Building Code - Chapter 11.

Accessible Route
A continuous, unobstructed path that complies with the 2003 International Building Code - Chapter 11.

Accessible Unit
A dwelling unit or sleeping unit that complies with the 2003 International Building Code and Chapters 1 through 9 of ICC A117.1.

Circulation Path
An exterior or interior way of passage from one place to another for pedestrians.

Common Use
Interior or exterior circulation paths, rooms, spaces or elements that are not for public use and are made available for the shared use of two or more people.

Detectable Warning
A standardized surface feature built in or applied to walking surfaces or other elements to warn visually impaired persons of hazards on a circulation path.

Dwelling Unit or Sleeping Unit - Multistory
A dwelling unit or sleeping unit with habitable space located on more than one story.

Dwelling Unit or Sleeping Unit - Type A
A dwelling unit or sleeping unit designed and constructed for accessibility in accordance with ICC A117.1.

Chapter 2: IBC - Definitions (continued)

Dwelling Unit or Sleeping Unit - Type B
A dwelling unit or sleeping unit designed and constructed for accessibility in accordance with ICC A117.1, consistent with the design and construction requirements of the Federal Fair Housing Act.

Employee Work Area
All or any portion of a space used only by employees and only for work.

Corridors, toilet rooms, kitchenettes and break rooms are not employee work areas.

Facility
All or any portion of buildings, structures, site improvements, elements and pedestrian or vehicular routes located on a site.

Intended to be Occupied as a Residence
This refers to a dwelling unit or sleeping unit that can or will be used all or part of the time as the occupant's place of abode.

Multilevel Assembly Seating
Seating that is arranged in distinct levels where each level is comprised of either multiple rows, or a single row of box seats accessed from a separate level.

Public Entrance
An entrance that is not a service entrance or a restricted entrance.

Public-Use Areas
Interior or exterior rooms or spaces that are made available to the general public.

Restricted Entrance
An entrance that is made available for common use on a controlled basis, but not public use, and that is not a service entrance.

Self-Service Storage Facility
Real property designed and used for the purpose of renting or leasing individual storage spaces to customers for the purpose of storing and removing personal property on a self-service basis.

Service Entrance
An entrance intended primarily for delivery of goods or services.

Site
A parcel of land bounded by a property line or a designated portion of a public right-of-way.

Wheelchair Space
A space for a single wheelchair and its occupant.

Chapter 3:

IBC - WAC
SCOPING REQUIREMENTS

IBC - Chapter 11   **Accessibility**

1103   **Scoping Requirements**

1103.1   **Where Required**

Buildings and structures, temporary or permanent, including their associated sites and facilities, shall be accessible to persons with physical disabilities.

1103.2   **General Exceptions**

Sites, buildings, facilities and elements shall be exempt from the 2003 International Building Code - Chapter 11, to the extent specified in this chapter.

1103.2.1   **Specific Requirements**

Accessibility is not required in buildings and facilities, or portions thereof, to the extent permitted by *Chapters 4-11 - 1104 through 1107.7 - pp. 9-38 and Chapters 19-44 - 1108 through 1110 - pp. 84-183.*

1103.2.2   **Existing Buildings**

Existing buildings shall comply with *Chapter 46: Accessibility for Existing Buildings - 3409 - pp. 187-192 and Chapter 47: Historic Buildings - 3409.8 - pp. 193 & 194.*

1103.2.3   **Employee Work Areas**

Spaces and elements within employee work areas shall only be required to comply with *Chapter 18: Fire Protection Systems - Alarms - 907.9.1.2 - p. 81, Chapter 4: Accessible Route - 1104.3.1 - p. 10* and Section 1007 of the 2003 International Building Code and shall be designed and constructed so that individuals with disabilities can approach, enter and exit the work area.

Work areas, or portions of work areas, that are less than 150 square feet (14 m^2) in area and elevated 7 inches (178mm) or more above the ground or finish floor where the elevation is essential to the function of the space shall be exempt from all requirements.

Chapter 3: IBC - WAC - Scoping Requirements (continued)

1103.2.4 **Detached Dwellings**

Detached one- and two-family dwellings and accessory structures, and their associated sites and facilities as applicable in the 2003 International Building Code - Section 101.2, are not required to be accessible.

1103.2.5 **Utility Buildings**

Occupancies in Group U are exempt from the requirements of the 2003 International Building Code - Chapter 11, other than the following:

1. In agricultural buildings, access is required to paved work areas and areas open to the general public.

2. Private garages or carports that contain required accessible parking.

1103.2.6 **Construction Sites**

Structures, sites and equipment directly associated with the actual processes of construction including, but not limited to, scaffolding, bridging, materials hoists, materials storage, or construction trailers are not required to be accessible.

1103.2.7 **Raised Areas**

Raised areas used primarily for purposes of security, life safety, or fire safety including, but not limited to, observation galleries, prison guard towers, fire towers, or lifeguard stands are not required to be accessible or to be served by an accessible route.

1103.2.8 **Limited Access Spaces**

Nonoccupiable spaces accessed only by ladders, catwalks, crawl spaces, freight elevators, or very narrow passageways are not required to be accessible.

1103.2.9 **Equipment Spaces**

Spaces frequented only by personnel for maintenance, repair, or monitoring of equipment are not required to be accessible.

Such spaces include, but are not limited to, elevator pits, elevator penthouses, mechanical, electrical, or communications equipment rooms, piping or equipment catwalks, water or sewage treatment pump rooms and stations, electric substations and transformer vaults, and highway and tunnel utility facilities.

Chapter 3: IBC - WAC - Scoping Requirements (continued)

1103.2.10 **Single Occupant Structures**

Single occupant structures accessed only by passageways below grade or elevated above grade including, but not limited to, toll booths that are accessed only by underground tunnels, are not required to be accessible.

1103.2.11 **Residential Group R-1**

Buildings of Group R-1 containing not more than five sleeping units for rent or hire that are also occupied as the residence of the proprietor are not required to be accessible

1103.2.12 **Day Care Facilities**

Where a day care facility (Groups A-3, E, I-4 and R-3) is part of a dwelling unit, only the portion of the structure utilized for the day care facility is required to be accessible.

1103.2.13 **Detention and Correctional Facilities**

In detention and correctional facilities, common use areas that are used only by inmates or detainees and security personnel, and that do not serve holding cells or housing cells required to be accessible, are not required to be accessible or to be served by an accessible route.

1103.2.14 **Fuel-Dispensing Systems**

The operable parts on fuel-dispensing devices shall comply with *Chapter 54: Reach Ranges - 308.2.1 or 308.3.1 - pp. 206 & 207.*

1103.2.15 <u>**WAC - 7/01/05**</u>

<u>**Modifications**</u>

<u>Where full compliance with the 2003 International Building Code - Chapter 11 is impractical due to unique characteristics of the terrain, the building official is permitted to grant modifications in accordance with Section 104.10 of the 2003 International Building Code, provided that any portion of the building or structure that can be made accessible shall be made accessible to the greatest extent possible.</u>

Chapter 4:

IBC - ICC/ANSI A117.1 - WAC
ACCESSIBLE ROUTE

IBC - Chapter 11   **Accessibility**

1104   **Accessible Route**

1104.1   **Site Arrival Points**

Accessible routes within the site shall be provided from public transportation stops, accessible parking and accessible passenger loading zones and public streets or sidewalks to the accessible building entrance served.

> EXCEPTION:
>
> > An accessible route shall not be required between site arrival points and the building or facility entrance if the only means of access between them is a vehicular way not providing for pedestrian access.

1104.2   **Within a Site**

At least one accessible route shall connect accessible buildings, accessible facilities, accessible elements and accessible spaces that are on the same site.

> EXCEPTION:
>
> > An accessible route is not required between accessible buildings, accessible facilities, accessible elements and accessible spaces that have, as the only means of access between them, a vehicular way not providing for pedestrian access.

1104.3   **Connected Spaces**

When a building, or portion of a building, is required to be accessible, an accessible route shall be provided to each portion of the building, to accessible building entrances connecting accessible pedestrian walkways and the public way.

Where only one accessible route is provided, the accessible route shall not pass through kitchens, storage rooms, restrooms, closets or similar spaces.

Chapter 4: IBC - ICC/ANSI A117.1 - WAC - Accessible Route (continued)

EXCEPTIONS:

1. In assembly areas with fixed seating required to be accessible, an accessible route shall not be required to serve fixed seating where wheelchair spaces or designated aisle seats required to be on an accessible route are not provided.

2. Accessible routes shall not be required to mezzanines provided that the building or facility has no more than one story, or where multiple stories are not connected by an accessible route as permitted by *1104.4 - (following page).*

3. A single accessible route is permitted to pass through a kitchen or storage room in an accessible dwelling unit.

1104.3.1 **Employee Work Areas**

Common use circulation paths within employee work areas shall be accessible routes.

EXCEPTIONS:

1. Common use circulation paths, located within employee work areas that are less than 300 square feet (27.9 m²) in size and defined by permanently installed partitions, counters, casework or furnishings, shall not be required to be accessible routes.

2. Common use circulation paths, located within employee work areas, that are an integral component of equipment, shall not be required to be accessible routes.

3. Common use circulation paths, located within exterior employee work areas that are fully exposed to the weather, shall not be required to be accessible.

1104.3.2 **Press Boxes**

Press boxes in assembly areas shall be on an accessible route.

EXCEPTIONS:

1. An accessible route shall not be required to press boxes in bleachers that have points of entry at only one level, provided that the aggregate area of all press boxes is 500 square feet (46 m²) maximum.

2. An accessible route shall not be required to free-standing press boxes that are elevated above grade 12 feet (3658mm) minimum provided that the aggregate area of all press boxes is 500 square feet (46 m²) maximum.

Chapter 4: IBC - ICC/ANSI A117.1 - WAC - Accessible Route (continued)

1104.4   **WAC - 7/01/05**

Multilevel Buildings and Facilities

At least one accessible route shall connect each accessible level, including mezzanines, in multilevel buildings and facilities.

EXCEPTIONS:

1. An accessible route is not required to stories and mezzanines above and below accessible levels that have an aggregate area of not more than 3,000 square feet (278.7 m²).

    This exception shall not apply to:

    1.1 Multiple tenant facilities of Group M Occupancies containing five or more tenant spaces;

    1.2 Levels containing offices of health care providers (Group B or I);

    1.3 Passenger transportation facilities and airports (Group A-3 or B);

    or

    1.4 Buildings owned or leased by government agencies.

2. In Group A, I, R, and S Occupancies, levels that do not contain accessible elements or other spaces required by *Chapters 8-11 - 1107 - pp. 27-38 or Chapters 19-23 - 1108 - pp. 84-102* are not required to be served by an accessible route from an accessible level.

3. In air traffic control towers, an accessible route is not required to serve the cab and the floor immediately below the cab.

4. Where a two-story building or facility has one story with an occupant load of five or fewer persons that does not contain public use spacc, that story shall not be required to be connected by an accessible route to the story above or below.

1104.5   **Location**

Accessible routes shall coincide with or be located in the same area as a general circulation path.

Where the circulation path is interior, the accessible route shall also be interior.

Chapter 4: IBC - ICC/ANSI A117.1 - WAC - Accessible Route (continued)

EXCEPTION:

Accessible routes from parking garages contained within and serving Type B dwelling units are not required to be interior.

1104.6 **Security Barriers**

Security barriers, including, but not limited to, security bollards and security check points shall not obstruct a required accessible route or accessible means of egress.

EXCEPTION:

Where security barriers incorporate elements that cannot comply with these requirements, such as certain metal detectors, fluoroscopes or other similar devices, the accessible route shall be permitted to be provided adjacent to security screening devices.

The accessible route shall permit persons with disabilities passing around security barriers to maintain visual contact with their personal items to the same extent provided others passing through the security barrier.

ICC/ANSI - Chapter 4   ***Accessible Routes***

401   ***General***

401.1   ***Scope***

*Accessible routes required by the scoping provisions adopted by the administrative authority shall comply with the applicable provisions of this **Chapter - 402**.*

ICC/ANSI - 402   ***Accessible Routes***

402.1   ***General***

*Accessible routes shall comply with this **Chapter - 402**.*

402.2   ***Components***

Accessible routes shall consist of one or more of the following components:

Walking surfaces with a slope not steeper than 1:20, doors and doorways, ramps, curb ramps excluding the flared sides, elevators, and platform lifts.

All components of an accessible route shall comply with the applicable portions of ICC/ANSI A117.1.

Chapter 4: IBC - ICC/ANSI A117.1 - WAC - Accessible Route (continued)

402.3   *Revolving Doors - Revolving Gates - Turnstiles*

Revolving doors, revolving gates, and turnstiles shall not be part of an accessible route.

ICC/ANSI - Chapter 4   *Accessible Routes*

401   *General*

401.1   *Scope*

*Accessible routes required by the scoping provisions adopted by the administrative authority shall comply with the applicable provisions of this **Chapter - 403**.*

ICC/ANSI - 403   *Walking Surfaces*

403.1   *General*

*Walking surfaces that are part of an accessible route shall comply with this **Chapter - 403**.*

403.2   *Floor Surface*

*Floor surfaces shall comply with **Chapter 48: Floor Surfaces - 302 - pp. 195 & 196**.*

403.3   *Slope*

The running slope of walking surfaces shall not be steeper than 1:20.

The cross slope of a walking surface shall not be steeper than 1:48.

403.4   *Changes in Level*

*Changes in level shall comply with **Chapter 49: Changes in Level - 303 - p. 197**.*

<u>1101.2.2</u>   <u>**WAC - 7/01/06**</u>
<u>**ICC/ANSI A117.1 - Section 403.5**</u>

<u>**Clear Width of Accessible Route**</u>

Clear width of an accessible route shall comply with *Table A - (following page).*

For exterior routes of travel, the minimum clear width shall be 44 inches (1118mm).

Chapter 4: IBC - ICC/ANSI A117.1 - WAC - Accessible Route (continued)

Table A
Clear Width of an Accessible Route

Segment Length	Minimum Segment Width
≤ 24 inches (610mm)	32 inches (813mm)[1]
> 24 inches (610mm)	36 inches (914mm)

[1] *Consecutive segments of 32 inches (813mm) in width must be separated by a route segment 48 inches (1219mm) minimum in length and 36 inches (914mm) minimum in width.*

See Diagram 1 - p. 306.

403.5.1 **Clear Width at Turn**

Where an accessible route makes a 180 degree turn around an object which is less than 48 inches (1219mm) in width, clear widths shall be 42 inches (1067mm) minimum approaching the turn, 48 inches (1219mm) minimum during the turn, and 42 inches (1067mm) minimum leaving the turn.

See Diagram 2 - p. 307.

EXCEPTION:

403.5.1 - (above) *shall not apply where the clear width at the turn is 60 inches (1524mm) minimum.*

403.5.2 **Passing Space**

An accessible route with a clear width less than 60 inches (1524mm) shall provide passing spaces at intervals of 200 feet (60 960mm) maximum.

Passing spaces shall be either a 60-inch (1524mm) minimum by 60-inch (1524mm) minimum space, or an intersection of two walking surfaces that provide a T-shaped turning space complying with **Chapter 50: Turning Space - 304.3.2 - pp. 198 & 199,** *provided the base and arms of the T-shaped space extend 48 inches (1219mm) minimum beyond the intersection.*

See Diagrams 3(a),(b) - p. 308.

403.6 **Handrails**

Where handrails are required at the side of a corridor they shall comply with **Chapter 17: Means of Egress - Handrails - pp. 77-80.**

Chapter 4: IBC - ICC/ANSI A117.1 - WAC - Accessible Route (continued)

1101.2.1
WAC - 7/01/06
ICC/ANSI A117.1 - Section 403

Landings for Walking Surfaces

The maximum rise for any run is 30 inches (762mm).

Landings shall be provided at the top and bottom of any run.

Landings shall be level and have a minimum dimension measured in the direction of travel of not less than 60 inches (1524mm).

Chapter 5:

IBC - WAC
ACCESSIBLE ENTRANCES

IBC - Chapter 11   **Accessibility**

1105   **Accessible Entrances**

1105.1   **WAC - 7/01/05**

Public Entrances

In addition to accessible entrances required by *1105.1.1 through 1105.1.6 - (below & following page),* at least 50 percent of all public entrances shall be accessible.

All exterior exits which are located adjacent to accessible areas and within 6 inches (152mm) of grade shall be accessible

EXCEPTIONS:

1. An accessible entrance is not required in areas not required to be accessible.

2. Loading and service entrances that are not the only entrance to a tenant space.

1105.1.1   **Parking Garage Entrances**

Where provided, direct access for pedestrians from parking structures to buildings or facility entrances shall be accessible.

1105.1.2   **Entrances from Tunnels or Elevated Walkways**

Where direct access is provided for pedestrians from a pedestrian tunnel or elevated walkway to a building or facility, at least one entrance to the building or facility from each tunnel or walkway shall be accessible.

1105.1.3   **Restricted Entrances**

Where restricted entrances are provided to a building or facility, at least one restricted entrance to the building or facility shall be accessible.

Chapter 5: IBC - WAC - Accessible Entrances (continued)

1105.1.4 **Entrances for Inmates or Detainees**

Where entrances used only by inmates or detainees and security personnel are provided at judicial facilities, detention facilities or correctional facilities, at least one such entrance shall be accessible.

1105.1.5 **Service Entrances**

If a service entrance is the only entrance to a building or a tenant space in a facility, that entrance shall be accessible.

1105.1.6 **Tenant Spaces - Dwelling Units - Sleeping Units**

At least one accessible entrance shall be provided to each tenant, dwelling unit and sleeping unit in a facility.

EXCEPTIONS:

1. An accessible entrance is not required to tenants that are not required to be accessible.

2. An accessible entrance is not required to dwelling units and sleeping units that are not required to be accessible units, Type A units or Type B units.

Chapter 6:

IBC - ICC/ANSI A117.1 - WAC
PARKING

IBC - Chapter 11   **Accessibility**

1106   **Parking and Passenger Loading Facilities**

1106.1   **Required**

Where parking is provided, accessible parking spaces shall be provided in compliance with *Table B - (following page),* except as required by *1106.2 through 1106.4 - (following pages).*

The number of accessible parking spaces shall be determined based on the total number of parking spaces provided for the facility.

    EXCEPTION:

        This *chapter and Chapter 7: Passenger Loading Zones - pp. 24-26* does not apply to parking spaces used exclusively for buses, trucks, other delivery vehicles, law enforcement vehicles or vehicular impound and motor pools where lots accessed by the public are provided with an accessible passenger loading zone.

Chapter 6: IBC - ICC/ANSI A117.1 - WAC - Parking (continued)

Table B
Accessible Parking Spaces

Total Parking Spaces Provided	Required Minimum Number of Accessible Spaces
1 to 25	1
26 to 50	2
51 to 75	3
76 to 100	4
101 to 150	5
151 to 200	6
201 to 300	7
301 to 400	8
401 to 500	9
501 to 1,000	2% of total
More than 1,000	20, plus one for each 100 over 1,000

1106.2 **Groups R-2 and R-3**

Two percent, but not less than one, of each type of parking space provided for occupancies in Groups R-2 and R-3, which are required to have accessible, Type A or Type B dwelling or sleeping units, shall be accessible.

Where parking is provided within or beneath a building, accessible parking spaces shall also be provided within or beneath the building.

1106.3 <u>**WAC - 7/01/05**</u>

<u>**Outpatient Medical Care Facilities**</u>

<u>For Group I-1 and I-2 occupancies providing outpatient medical care facilities, 10 percent, but not less than one, of the parking spaces provided accessory to such occupancies shall be accessible.</u>

Chapter 6: IBC - ICC/ANSI A117.1 - WAC - Parking (continued)

1106.4   **WAC - 7/01/05**

Inpatient and Outpatient Medical Care Facilities

For Group I-1 and I-2 units and facilities specializing in the treatment of persons with mobility impairments on either an inpatient or outpatient basis, 20 percent, but not less than one, of the parking spaces provided accessory to such units and facilities shall be accessible.

1106.5   **Van Spaces**

For every six or fraction of six accessible parking spaces, at least one shall be a van-accessible parking space.

IBC - 406.2.2   **Clear Height**

The clear height of each floor level in vehicle and pedestrian traffic areas shall not be less than 7 feet (2134mm).

Vehicle and pedestrian areas accommodating van accessible parking required by *1106.5 - (above)* shall conform to this *chapter and Chapter 7: Passenger Loading Zones - pp. 24-26.*

1106.6   **WAC - 7/01/05**

Location

Accessible parking spaces shall be located on the shortest accessible route of travel from adjacent parking to an accessible building entrance.

Accessible parking spaces shall be dispersed among the various types of parking facilities provided.

In parking facilities that do not serve a particular building, accessible parking spaces shall be located on the shortest route to an accessible pedestrian entrance to the parking facility.

Where buildings have multiple accessible entrances with adjacent parking, accessible parking spaces shall be dispersed and located near the accessible entrances.

Wherever practical, the accessible route of travel shall not cross lanes of vehicular traffic.

Where crossing traffic lanes is necessary, the route of travel shall be designated and marked as a crosswalk.

Chapter 6: IBC - ICC/ANSI A117.1 - WAC - Parking (continued)

EXCEPTION:

>In multilevel parking structures, van-accessible parking spaces are permitted on one level.

ICC/ANSI - Chapter 5   ***General Site and Building Elements***

501   ***General***

501.1   ***Scope***

General site and building elements required to be accessible by the scoping provisions adopted by the administrative authority shall comply with the applicable provisions of this **Chapter - 502.**

ICC/ANSI - 502   ***Parking Spaces***

502.1   ***General***

Accessible car and van parking spaces shall comply with this **Chapter - 502.**

502.2   ***Vehicle Space Size***

Car parking spaces shall be 96 inches (2438mm) minimum in width.

Van parking spaces shall be 132 inches (3353mm) minimum in width.

>EXCEPTION:
>
>>*Van parking spaces shall be permitted to be 96 inches (2438mm) minimum in width where the adjacent access aisle is 96 inches (2438mm) minimum in width.*

See Diagram 4 - p. 309.

502.3   ***Vehicle Space Marking***

Car and van parking spaces shall be marked to define the width.

Where parking spaces are marked with lines, the width measurements of parking spaces and adjacent access aisles shall be made from the centerline of the markings.

>EXCEPTION:
>
>>*Where parking spaces or access aisles are not adjacent to another parking space or access aisle, measurements shall be permitted to include the full width of the line defining the parking space or access aisle.*

Chapter 6: IBC - ICC/ANSI A117.1 - WAC - Parking (continued)

502.4   *Access Aisle*

*Car and van parking spaces shall have an adjacent access aisle complying with **502.4 - (below)**.*

502.4.1   *Location*

Access aisles shall adjoin an accessible route.

Two parking spaces shall be permitted to share a common access aisle.

Access aisles shall not overlap with the vehicular way.

Parking spaces shall be permitted to have access aisles placed on either side of the car or van parking space.

Van parking spaces that are angled shall have access aisles located on the passenger side of the parking space.

502.4.2   *Width*

Access aisles serving car and van parking spaces shall be 60 inches (1524mm) minimum in width.

502.4.3   *Length*

Access aisles shall extend the full length of the parking spaces they serve.

502.4.4   *Marking*

Access aisles shall be marked so as to discourage parking in them.

Where access aisles are marked with lines, the width measurements of access aisles and adjacent parking spaces shall be made from the centerline of the markings.

    EXCEPTION:

        Where access aisles or parking spaces are not adjacent to another access aisle or parking space, measurements shall be permitted to include the full width of the line defining the access aisle or parking space.

*See **Diagram 5** - p. 310.*

502.5   *Floor Surfaces*

*Parking spaces and access aisles shall comply with **Chapter 48: Floor Surfaces - 302 - pp. 195 & 196** and have surface slopes not steeper than 1:48.*

Access aisles shall be at the same level as the parking spaces they serve.

502.6   ***Vertical Clearance***

Parking spaces for vans, access aisles serving them, and vehicular routes from an entrance to the van parking spaces, and from the van parking spaces to a vehicular exit serving them shall provide a vertical clearance of 98 inches (2489mm) minimum.

502.7   ***Identification***

Where accessible parking spaces are required to be identified by signs, the signs shall include the International Symbol of Accessibility complying with **Chapter 44: Signage - 703.6.3.1 - p. 181.**

Signs identifying van parking spaces shall contain the designation "van accessible."

Such signs shall be 60 inches (1524mm) minimum above the floor of the parking space, measured to the bottom of the sign.

502.8   ***Relationship to Accessible Routes***

Parking spaces and access aisles shall be designed so that cars and vans, when parked, cannot obstruct the required clear width of adjacent accessible routes.

Chapter 7:

IBC - ICC/ANSI A117.1 - WAC
PASSENGER LOADING ZONES

IBC - Chapter 11   **Accessibility**

1106   **Parking and Passenger Loading Facilities**

1106.7   **Passenger Loading Zones**

Passenger loading zones shall be designed and constructed in accordance with ICC/ANSI A117.1.

1106.7.1   **Continuous Loading Zones**

Where passenger loading zones are provided, one passenger loading zone in every continuous 100 linear feet (30.4m) maximum of loading zone space shall be accessible.

1106.7.2   **Medical Facilities**

A passenger loading zone shall be provided at an accessible entrance to licensed medical and long-term care facilities where people receive physical or medical treatment or care and where the period of stay exceeds 24 hours.

1106.7.3   **Valet Parking**

A passenger loading zone shall be provided at valet parking services.

<u>1106.7.4</u>   <u>**WAC - 7/01/05**</u>

<u>Sheltered Entrance</u>

<u>In Group I-2 occupancies, at least one accessible entrance that complies with *Chapter 5: Accessible Entrances - 1105 - pp. 16 & 17* shall be under shelter.</u>

<u>Every such entrance shall include a passenger loading zone which complies with *1106.7 - (above)*.</u>

ICC/ANSI - Chapter 5   *General Site and Building Elements*

501   *General*

501.1   *Scope*

*General site and building elements required to be accessible by the scoping provisions adopted by the administrative authority shall comply with the applicable provisions of this **Chapter - 503**.*

Chapter 7: IBC - ICC/ANSI A117.1 - WAC - Passenger Loading Zones (continued)

ICC/ANSI - 503   ***Passenger Loading Zones***

503.1   ***General***

*Accessible passenger loading zones shall comply with this **Chapter - 503**.*

503.2   ***Vehicle Pull-up Space Size***

Passenger loading zones shall provide a vehicular pull-up space 96 inches (2438mm) minimum in width and 20 feet (6096mm) minimum in length.

503.3   ***Access Aisle***

*Passenger loading zones shall have an adjacent access aisle complying with **503.3 - (below)**.*

503.3.1   ***Location***

Access aisles shall adjoin an accessible route.

Access aisles shall not overlap the vehicular way.

503.3.2   ***Width***

Access aisles serving vehicle pull-up spaces shall be 60 inches (1524mm) minimum in width.

503.3.3   ***Length***

Access aisles shall be 20 feet (6096mm) minimum in length.

503.3.4   ***Marking***

Access aisles shall be marked so as to discourage parking in them.

See Diagram 6 - p. 311.

503.4   ***Floor Surfaces***

*Vehicle pull-up spaces and access aisles serving them shall comply with **Chapter 48: Floor Surfaces - 302 - pp. 195 & 196** and shall have slopes not steeper than 1:48.*

Access aisles shall be at the same level as the vehicle pull-up space they serve.

503.5 *Vertical Clearance*

Vehicle pull-up spaces, access aisles serving them, and a vehicular route from an entrance to the passenger loading zone, and from the passenger loading zone to a vehicular exit serving them, shall provide a vertical clearance of 114 inches (2896mm) minimum.

Chapter 8:

INTERNATIONAL BUILDING CODE DWELLING UNITS AND SLEEPING UNITS

IBC - Chapter 11   **Accessibility**

1107   **Dwelling Units and Sleeping Units**

1107.1   **General**

In addition to the other requirements of the 2003 International Building Code - Chapter 11, occupancies having dwelling units or sleeping units shall be provided with accessible features in accordance with *1107.2, 1107.3, 1107.4 - (below & following page) and Chapters 9-11 - 1107.5 - 1107.7.5 - pp. 29-38.*

1107.2   **Design**

Dwelling units and sleeping units which are required to be accessible units shall comply with the 2003 International Building Code and the applicable portions of Chapters 1 through 9 of ICC/ANSI A117.1.

Type A and Type B units shall comply with the applicable portions of Chapter 10 of ICC/ANSI A117.1.

Units required to be Type A units are permitted to be designed and constructed as accessible units.

Units required to be Type B units are permitted to be designed and constructed as accessible units or as Type A units.

1107.3   **Accessible Spaces**

Rooms and spaces available to the general public or available for use by residents and serving accessible units, Type A units or Type B units shall be accessible.

Accessible spaces shall include toilet and bathing rooms, kitchen, living and dining areas and any exterior spaces, including patios, terraces and balconies.

    EXCEPTION:

        Recreational facilities in accordance with *Chapter 42: Recreational Facilities - 1109.14 - p. 166.*

Chapter 8: IBC - Dwelling Units and Sleeping Units (continued)

1107.4 **Accessible Route**

At least one accessible route shall connect accessible building or facility entrances with the primary entrance of each accessible unit, Type A unit and Type B unit within the building or facility and with those exterior and interior spaces and facilities that serve the units.

EXCEPTIONS:

1. If the slope of the finished ground level between accessible facilities and buildings exceeds one unit vertical in 12 units horizontal (1:12), or where physical barriers prevent the installation of an accessible route, a vehicular route with parking that complies with *Chapter 6: Parking - 1106 - pp. 18-20 and Chapter 7: Passenger Loading Zones - 1106.7 - p. 24* at each public or common use facility or building is permitted in place of the accessible route.

2. Exterior decks, patios, or balconies that are part of Type B units and have impervious surfaces, and that are not more than 4 inches (102mm) below the finished floor level of the adjacent interior space of the unit.

Chapter 9:

INTERNATIONAL BUILDING CODE DWELLING UNITS AND SLEEPING UNITS GROUP I OCCUPANCIES

IBC - Chapter 11	**Accessibility**
1107	**Dwelling Units and Sleeping Units**

See Chapter 8: Dwelling Units and Sleeping Units - 1107.1 through 1107.4 - pp. 27 & 28.

1107.5	**Group I**

Occupancies in Group I shall be provided with accessible features in accordance with *1107.5.1 through 1107.5.5 - (below & following pages).*

1107.5.1	**Group I-1**

Group I-1 occupancies shall be provided with accessible features in accordance with *1107.5.1.1 and 1107.5.1.2 - (below).*

1107.5.1.1	**Accessible Units**

At least 4 percent, but not less than one, of the dwelling units and sleeping units shall be accessible units.

1107.5.1.2	**Type B Units**

In structures with four or more dwelling or sleeping units intended to be occupied as a residence, every dwelling and sleeping unit intended to be occupied as a residence shall be a Type B unit.

> EXCEPTION:
>
> The number of Type B units is permitted to be reduced in accordance with *Chapter 11: General Exceptions - 1107.7 - pp. 36-38.*

1107.5.2	**Group I-2 Nursing Homes**

Nursing homes of Group I-2 shall be provided with accessible features in accordance with *1107.5.2.1 and 1107.5.2.2 - (following page).*

Chapter 9: IBC - Group I Occupancies (continued)

1107.5.2.1 **Accessible Units**

At least 50 percent, but not less than one, of the dwelling units and sleeping units shall be accessible units.

1107.5.2.2 **Type B Units**

In structures with four or more dwelling or sleeping units intended to be occupied as a residence, every dwelling and sleeping unit intended to be occupied as a residence shall be a Type B unit.

EXCEPTION:

> The number of Type B units is permitted to be reduced in accordance with *Chapter 11: General Exceptions - 1107.7 - pp. 36-38.*

1107.5.3 **Group I-2 Hospitals**

General purpose hospitals, psychiatric facilities, detoxification facilities and residential care/assisted living facilities of Group I-2 shall be provided with accessible features in accordance with *1107.5.3.1 and 1107.5.3.2 - (below).*

1107.5.3.1 **Accessible Units**

At least 10 percent, but not less than one, of the dwelling units and sleeping units shall be accessible units.

1107.5.3.2 **Type B Units**

In structures with four or more dwelling or sleeping units intended to be occupied as a residence, every dwelling and sleeping unit intended to be occupied as a residence shall be a Type B unit.

EXCEPTION:

> The number of Type B units is permitted to be reduced in accordance with *Chapter 11: General Exceptions - 1107.7 - pp. 36-38.*

1107.5.4 **Group I-2 Rehabilitation Facilities**

In hospitals and rehabilitation facilities of Group I-2 which specialize in treating conditions that affect mobility, or in units within either facility which specialize in treating conditions that affect mobility, 100 percent of the dwelling units and sleeping units shall be accessible units.

1107.5.5 Group I-3

Buildings, facilities or portions thereof with Group I-3 Occupancies shall comply with *1107.5.5.1 through 1107.5.5.3 - (below)*.

1107.5.5.1 Group I-3 Sleeping Units

In occupancies in Group I-3, at least 2 percent, but not less than one, of the dwelling units and sleeping units shall be accessible units.

1107.5.5.2 Special Holding Cells and Special Housing Cells or Rooms

In addition to the units required to be accessible by *1107.5.5.1 - (above)*, where special holding cells or special housing cells or rooms are provided, at least one serving each purpose shall be accessible.

Cells or rooms subject to this requirement include, but are not limited to, those used for purposes of orientation, protective custody, administrative or disciplinary detention or segregation, detoxification and medical isolation.

EXCEPTION:

> Cells or rooms specially designed without protrusions and that are used solely for purposes of suicide prevention shall not be required to include grab bars.

1107.5.5.3 Medical Care Facilities

Patient sleeping units or cells required to be accessible in medical care facilities shall be provided in addition to any medical isolation cells required to comply with *1107.5.5.2 - (above)*.

Chapter 10:

IBC - WAC
DWELLING UNITS AND SLEEPING UNITS
GROUP R OCCUPANCIES

IBC - Chapter 11	**Accessibility**
1107	**Dwelling Units and Sleeping Units**

See Chapter 8: Dwelling Units and Sleeping Units - 1107.1 through 1107.4 - pp. 27 & 28.

1107.6	**WAC - 7/01/05**

Group R

Occupancies in Group R shall be provided with accessible features in accordance with *1107.6.1 through 1107.6.4 - (below & following pages).*

Accessible and Type A units shall be apportioned among efficiency dwelling units, single bedroom units and multiple bedroom units, in proportion to the numbers of such units in the building.

Accessible hotel guest rooms shall be apportioned among the various classes of sleeping accommodations.

1107.6.1	**Group R-1**

Group R-1 occupancies shall be provided with accessible features in accordance with *1107.6.1.1 and 1107.6.1.2 - (below & following page).*

1107.6.1.1	**Accessible Units**

In occupancies in Group R-1, accessible dwelling units and sleeping units shall be provided in accordance with *Table C - (following page).*

All facilities on a site shall be considered to determine the total number of accessible units.

Accessible units shall be dispersed among the various classes of units.

Roll-in showers provided in accessible units shall include a permanently mounted folding shower seat.

Chapter 10: IBC - WAC - Group R Occupancies (continued)

Table C
Accessible Dwelling and Sleeping Units

Total Number of Units Provided	Minimum Required Number of Accessible Units Associated with Roll-in Showers	Total Number of Required Accessible Units
1 to 25	0	1
26 to 50	0	2
51 to 75	1	4
76 to 100	1	5
101 to 150	2	7
151 to 200	2	8
201 to 300	3	10
301 to 400	4	12
401 to 500	4	13
501 to 1,000	1% of total	3% of total
Over 1,000	10, plus 1 for each 100 over 1,000	30, plus 2 for each 100 over 1,000

1107.6.1.2 **Type B Units**

In structures with four or more dwelling or sleeping units intended to be occupied as a residence, every dwelling and sleeping unit intended to be occupied as a residence shall be a Type B unit.

EXCEPTION:

The number of Type B units is permitted to be reduced in accordance with *Chapter 11: General Exceptions - 1107.7 - pp. 36-38.*

1107.6.2 **Group R-2**

Accessible units, Type A and Type B units shall be provided in occupancies in Group R-2 in accordance with *1107.6.2.1 and 1107.6.2.2 - (following pages).*

Chapter 10: IBC - WAC - Group R Occupancies (continued)

1107.6.2.1 **Apartment Houses - Monasteries - Convents**

Type A and Type B units shall be provided in apartment houses, monasteries and convents in accordance with *1107.6.2.1.1 and 1107.6.2.1.2 - (below)*.

1107.6.2.1.1 **WAC - 7/01/05**

Type A Units

In occupancies in Group R-2 containing more than 10 dwelling units or sleeping units, at least 5 percent, but not less than one, of the units shall be a Type A unit.

All units on a site shall be considered to determine the total number of units and the required number of Type A units.

Type A units shall be dispersed among the various classes of units.

EXCEPTIONS:

1. The number of Type A units is permitted to be reduced in accordance with *Chapter 11: General Exceptions - 1107.7 - pp. 36-38.*

2. Existing structures on a site shall not contribute to the total number of units on a site.

1107.6.2.1.2 **Type B Units**

Where there are four or more dwelling units or sleeping units intended to be occupied as a residence in a single structure, every dwelling unit and sleeping unit intended to be occupied as a residence shall be a Type B unit.

EXCEPTION:

The number of Type B units is permitted to be reduced in accordance with *Chapter 11: General Exceptions - 1107.7 - pp. 36-38.*

1107.6.2.2 **Boarding Houses - Dormitories - Fraternity Houses
Sorority Houses**

Accessible units and Type B dwelling units shall be provided in boarding houses, dormitories, fraternity houses and sorority houses in accordance with *1107.6.2.2.1 and 1107.6.2.2.2 - (following page)*.

Chapter 10: IBC - WAC - Group R Occupancies (continued)

1107.6.2.2.1   **Accessible Units**

Accessible dwelling units and sleeping units shall be provided in accordance with this *Chapter - Table C - p. 33*.

1107.6.2.2.2   **Type B Units**

Where there are four or more dwelling units or sleeping units intended to be occupied as a residence in a single structure, every dwelling unit and every sleeping unit intended to be occupied as a residence shall be a Type B unit.

> EXCEPTION:
>
> > The number of Type B units is permitted to be reduced in accordance with *Chapter 11: General Exceptions - 1107.7 - pp. 36-38*.

1107.6.3   **Group R-3**

In occupancies in Group R-3 where there are four or more dwelling units or sleeping units intended to be occupied as a residence in a single structure, every dwelling and sleeping unit intended to be occupied as a residence shall be a Type B unit.

> EXCEPTION:
>
> > The number of Type B units is permitted to be reduced in accordance with *Chapter 11: General Exceptions - 1107.7 - pp. 36-38*.

1107.6.4   **Group R-4**

Group R-4 occupancies shall be provided with accessible features in accordance with *1107.6.4.1 and 1107.6.4.2 - (below)*.

1107.6.4.1   **Accessible Units**

At least one of the dwelling or sleeping units shall be an accessible unit.

1107.6.4.2   **Type B Units**

In structures with four or more dwelling or sleeping units intended to be occupied as a residence, every dwelling and sleeping unit intended to be occupied as a residence shall be a Type B unit.

> EXCEPTION:
>
> > The number of Type B units is permitted to be reduced in accordance with *Chapter 11: General Exceptions - 1107.7 - pp. 36-38*.

Chapter 11:

INTERNATIONAL BUILDING CODE DWELLING UNITS AND SLEEPING UNITS GENERAL EXCEPTIONS

IBC - Chapter 11   **Accessibility**

1107   **Dwelling Units and Sleeping Units**

See Chapter 8: Dwelling Units and Sleeping Units - 1107.1 through 1107.4 - pp. 27 & 28.

1107.7   **General Exceptions**

Where specifically permitted by *Chapter 9: Group I Occupancies - 1107.5 - pp. 29-31 or Chapter 10: Group R Occupancies - 1107.6 - pp. 32-35* the required number of Type A and Type B units is permitted to be reduced in accordance with *1107.7.1 through 1107.7.5 - (below & following pages).*

1107.7.1   **Buildings without Elevator Service**

Where no elevator service is provided in a building, only the dwelling and sleeping units that are located on stories indicated in *1107.7.1.1 and 1107.7.1.2 - (below & following page)* are required to be Type A and Type B units.

The number of Type A units shall be determined in accordance with *Chapter 10: Group R Occupancies - 1107.6.2.1.1 - p. 34.*

1107.7.1.1   **One Story with Type B Units Required**

At least one story containing dwelling units or sleeping units intended to be occupied as a residence shall be provided with an accessible entrance from the exterior of the building and all units intended to be occupied as a residence on that story shall be Type B units.

1107.7.1.2   **Additional Stories with Type B Units**

On all other stories that have a building entrance in proximity to arrival points intended to serve units on that story, as indicated in *Items 1 and 2 - (below & following page),* all dwelling units and sleeping units intended to be occupied as a residence served by that entrance on that story shall be Type B units.

1. Where the slopes of the undisturbed site measured between the planned entrance and all vehicular or pedestrian arrival points within 50 feet (15 240mm) of the planned entrance are 10 percent or less

Chapter 11: IBC - General Exceptions (continued)

and

2. Where the slopes of the planned, finished grade measured between the entrance and all vehicular or pedestrian arrival points within 50 feet (15 240mm) of the planned entrance are 10 percent or less.

Where no such arrival points are within 50 feet (15 240mm) of the entrance, the closest arrival point shall be used unless that arrival point serves the story required by *1107.7.1.1 - (preceding page)*.

1107.7.2   Multistory Units

A multistory dwelling or sleeping unit which is not provided with elevator service is not required to be a Type B unit.

Where a multistory unit is provided with external elevator service to only one floor, the floor provided with elevator service shall be the primary entry to the unit, shall comply with the requirements for a Type B unit and a toilet facility shall be provided on that floor.

1107.7.3   Elevator Service to the Lowest Story with Units

Where elevator service in the building provides an accessible route only to the lowest story containing dwelling or sleeping units intended to be occupied as a residence, only the units on that story which are intended to be occupied as a residence are required to be Type B units.

1107.7.4   Site Impracticality

On a site with multiple non-elevator buildings, the number of units required by *1107.7.1 - (preceding page & above)* to be Type B units is permitted to be reduced to a percentage which is equal to the percentage of the entire site having grades, prior to development, which are less than 10 percent, provided that all of the following conditions are met:

1. Not less than 20 percent of the units required by *1107.7.1 - (preceding page & above)* on the site are Type B units;

2. Units required by *1107.7.1 - (preceding page & above),* where the slope between the building entrance serving the units on that story and a pedestrian or vehicular arrival point is no greater than 8.33 percent, are Type B units;

3. Units required by *1107.7.1 - (preceding page & above),* where an elevated walkway is planned between a building entrance serving the units on that story and a pedestrian or vehicular arrival point and the slope between them is 10 percent or less are Type B units;

and

Chapter 11: IBC - General Exceptions (continued)

    4.   Units served by an elevator in accordance with *1107.7.3 - (preceding page)* are Type B units.

1107.7.5   **Design Flood Elevation**

The required number of Type A and Type B units shall not apply to a site where the lowest floor or the lowest structural building members of non-elevator buildings are required to be at or above the design flood elevation resulting in:

    1.   A difference in elevation between the minimum required floor elevation at the primary entrances and vehicular and pedestrian arrival points within 50 feet (15 240mm) exceeding 30 inches (762mm),

         and

    2.   A slope exceeding 10 percent between the minimum required floor elevation at the primary entrances and vehicular and pedestrian arrival points within 50 feet (15 240mm).

Where no such arrival points are within 50 feet (15 240mm) of the primary entrances, the closest arrival point shall be used.

Chapter 12:
ICC/ANSI A117.1
DWELLING UNITS AND SLEEPING UNITS
ACCESSIBLE UNITS

ICC/ANSI - Chapter 10 *Dwelling Units and Sleeping Units*

1001 *General*

1001.1 *Scoping*

*Dwelling units and sleeping units required to be Accessible units, Type A units, Type B units, or units with accessible communication features by the scoping provisions adopted by the administrative authority shall comply with the applicable provisions of this **Chapter - 1002.***

ICC/ANSI - 1002 *Accessible Units*

1002.1 *General*

*Accessible units shall comply with this **Chapter - 1002.***

1002.2 *Primary Entrance*

The accessible primary entrance shall be on an accessible route from public and common areas.

The primary entrance shall not be to a bedroom.

1002.3 *Accessible Route*

*Accessible routes within Accessible units shall comply with **1002.3 - (below & following page)**.*

*Exterior spaces less than 30 inches (762mm) in depth or width shall comply with **1002.3.1, 1002.3.3 - (below & following page), Chapter 48: Floor Surfaces - 302 - pp. 195 & 196, and Chapter 49: Changes in Level - 303 - p. 197.***

1002.3.1 *Location*

At least one accessible route shall connect all spaces and elements that are a part of the unit.

Where only one accessible route is provided, it shall not pass through bathrooms and toilet rooms, closets, or similar spaces.

Chapter 12: ICC/ANSI A117.1 - Accessible Units (continued)

EXCEPTION:

> *An accessible route is not required to unfinished attics and unfinished basements that are part of the unit.*

1002.3.2 **Turning Space**

All rooms served by an accessible route shall provide a turning space complying with **Chapter 50: Turning Space - 304 - pp. 198 & 199.**

1002.3.3 **Components**

Accessible routes shall consist of one or more of the following elements: walking surfaces with a slope not steeper than 1:20, ramps, elevators, and platform lifts.

1002.4 **Walking Surfaces**

Walking surfaces that are part of an accessible route shall comply with **Chapter 4: Accessible Route - 403 - pp. 13-15.**

1002.5 **Doors and Doorways**

The primary entrance door to the unit, and all other doorways intended for user passage, shall comply with **Chapter 56: Doors and Doorways - 404 - pp. 209-216.**

EXCEPTION:

> *Existing doors to hospital patient sleeping rooms shall be exempt from the requirement for space at the latch side provided the door is 44 inches (1118mm) minimum in width.*

1002.6 **Ramps**

Ramps shall comply with **Chapter 16: Means of Egress - Ramps - 405 - pp. 73-76.**

1002.7 **Elevators**

Elevators within the unit shall comply with **Chapter 31: Elevators - 407 - pp. 128-141, Chapter 32: Limited-Use/Limited-Application Elevators - 408 - pp. 142-144, or Chapter 33: Private Residence Elevators - 409 - pp. 145-148.**

1002.8 **Platform Lifts**

Platform) lifts within the unit shall comply with **Chapter 34: Lifts - 410 - pp. 150 & 151.**

Chapter 12: ICC/ANSI A117.1 - Accessible Units (continued)

1002.9   ***Operable Parts***

*Lighting controls, electrical switches and receptacle outlets, environmental controls, appliance controls, operating hardware for operable windows, plumbing fixture controls, and user controls for security or intercom systems shall comply with **Chapter 55: Operable Parts - 309 - p. 208**.*

EXCEPTIONS:

1. *Receptacle outlets serving a dedicated use.*

2. *One receptacle outlet shall not be required to comply with **Chapter 55: Operable Parts - 309 - p. 208** where all of the following conditions are met:*

    (a) *the receptacle outlet is above a length of countertop that is uninterrupted by a sink or appliance;*

    and

    (b) *at least one receptacle outlet complying with **1002.9 - (above & below)** is provided for that length of countertop;*

    and

    (c) *all other receptacle outlets provided for that length of countertop comply with **1002.9 - (above & below)**.*

3. *Floor receptacle outlets.*

4. *HVAC diffusers.*

5. *Controls mounted on ceiling fans.*

6. *Where redundant controls other than light switches are provided for a single element, one control in each space shall not be required to be accessible.*

1002.10   ***Laundry Equipment***

*Washing machines and clothes dryers shall comply with **Chapter 64: Washing Machines and Clothes Dryers - 611 - p. 239**.*

1002.11   ***Toilet and Bathing Facilities***

*Toilet and bathing facilities shall comply with **Chapter 25 - 603 - pp. 105 & 106, Chapter 27 - 604 - pp. 109-117 and Chapters 58 through 63 - 604.10 through 610 - pp. 221-238**.*

Chapter 12: ICC/ANSI A117.1 - Accessible Units (continued)

1002.11.1   *Vanity Counter Top Space*

If vanity counter top space is provided in nonaccessible dwelling or sleeping units within the same facility, equivalent vanity counter top space, in terms of size and proximity to the lavatory, shall also be provided in Accessible units.

1002.12   *Kitchens*

*Kitchens shall comply with **Chapter 29: Kitchens and Kitchenettes - 804 - pp. 121-124**.*

*At least one work surface, 30-inches (762mm) minimum in length, shall comply with **Chapter 21: Dining Areas - 902 - pp. 96 & 97**.*

1002.13   *Windows*

*Where operable windows are provided, at least one window in each sleeping, living, or dining space shall have operable parts complying with **1002.9** - (preceding page).*

*Each required operable window shall have operable parts complying with **1002.9** - (preceding page).*

1002.14   *Storage Facilities*

*Where storage facilities are provided, they shall comply with **Chapter 35: Storage - 905 - p. 153**.*

*Kitchen cabinets shall comply with **Chapter 29: Kitchens and Kitchenettes - 804.5 - p. 122**.*

Chapter 13:
ICC/ANSI A117.1
DWELLING UNITS AND SLEEPING UNITS
TYPE A UNITS

ICC/ANSI - Chapter 10   ***Dwelling Units and Sleeping Units***

1001   ***General***

1001.1   ***Scoping***

Dwelling units and sleeping units required to be Accessible units, Type A units, Type B units, or units with accessible communication features by the scoping provisions adopted by the administrative authority shall comply with the applicable provisions of this **Chapter - 1003.**

ICC/ANSI - 1003   ***Type A Units***

1003.1   ***General***

Type A units shall comply with this **Chapter - 1003.**

1003.2   ***Primary Entrance***

The accessible primary entrance shall be on an accessible route from public and common areas.

The primary entrance shall not be to a bedroom.

1003.3   ***Accessible Route***

Accessible routes within Type A units shall comply with **1003.3 - (below & following page).**

Exterior spaces less than 30 inches (762mm) in depth or width shall comply with **1003.3.1, 1003.3.3 - (below & following page), Chapter 48: Floor Surfaces - 302 - pp. 195 & 196, and Chapter 49: Changes in Level - 303 - p. 197.**

1003.3.1   ***Location***

At least one accessible route shall connect all spaces and elements that are a part of the unit.

Where only one accessible route is provided, it shall not pass through bathrooms, closets, or similar spaces.

Chapter 13: ICC/ANSI A117.1 - Type A Units (continued)

EXCEPTION:

> *An accessible route is not required to unfinished attics and unfinished basements that are part of the unit.*

1003.3.2 **Turning Space**

All rooms served by an accessible route shall provide a turning space complying with **Chapter 50: Turning Space - 304 - pp. 198 & 199.**

EXCEPTION:

> *Toilet rooms and bathrooms that are not required to comply with this* **Chapter - 1003.11 - pp. 46-49.**

1003.3.3 **Components**

Accessible routes shall consist of one or more of the following elements: walking surfaces with a slope not steeper than 1:20, ramps, elevators, and platform lifts.

1003.4 **Walking Surfaces**

Walking surfaces that are part of an accessible route shall comply with **Chapter 4: Accessible Route - 403 - pp. 13-15.**

1003.5 **Doors and Doorways**

The primary entrance door to the unit, and all other doorways intended for user passage, shall comply with **Chapter 56: Doors and Doorways - 404 - pp. 209-216.**

EXCEPTIONS:

> *1. Thresholds at exterior sliding doors shall be permitted to be 3/4-inch (19.1mm) maximum in height, provided they are beveled with a slope not greater than 1:2.*
>
> *2. In toilet rooms and bathrooms not required to comply with this* **Chapter - 1003.11 - pp. 46-49,** *maneuvering clearances required by* **Chapter 56: Doors and Doorways - 404.2.3 - pp. 210-212** *are not required on the toilet room or bathroom side of the door.*

1003.6 **Ramps**

Ramps shall comply with **Chapter 16: Means of Egress - Ramps - 405 - pp. 73-76.**

Chapter 13: ICC/ANSI A117.1 - Type A Units (continued)

1003.7 *Elevators*

*Elevators within the unit shall comply with **Chapter 31: Elevators - 407 - pp. 128-141**, **Chapter 32: Limited-Use/Limited-Application Elevators - 408 - pp. 142-144**, or **Chapter 33: Private Residence Elevators - 409 - pp. 145-148**.*

1003.8 *Platform Lifts*

*Platform) lifts within the unit shall comply with **Chapter 34: Lifts - 410 - pp. 150 & 151**.*

1003.9 *Operable Parts*

*Lighting controls, electrical switches and receptacle outlets, environmental controls, appliance controls, operating hardware for operable windows, plumbing fixture controls, and user controls for security or intercom systems shall comply with **Chapter 55: Operable Parts - 309 - p. 208**.*

EXCEPTIONS:

1. *Receptacle outlets serving a dedicated use.*

2. *One receptacle outlet is not required to comply with **Chapter 55: Operable Parts - 309 - p. 208** where all of the following conditions are met:*

    (a) *the receptacle outlet is above a length of countertop that is uninterrupted by a sink or appliance;*

    and

    (b) *at least one receptacle complying with **1003.9 - (above & below)** is provided for that length of countertop;*

    and

    (c) *all other receptacle outlets provided for that length of countertop comply with **1003.9 - (above & below)**.*

3. *Floor receptacle outlets.*

4. *HVAC diffusers.*

5. *Controls mounted on ceiling fans.*

6. *Where redundant controls other than light switches are provided for a single element, one control in each space shall not be required to be accessible.*

Chapter 13: ICC/ANSI A117.1 - Type A Units (continued)

1003.10   ***Laundry Equipment***

Washing machines and clothes dryers shall comply with ***Chapter 64: Washing Machines and Clothes Dryers - 611 - p. 239.***

1003.11   ***Toilet and Bathing Facilities***

1003.11.1   ***General***

*All toilet and bathing areas shall comply with this **Chapter - 1003.11**.*

*At least one toilet and bathing facility shall comply with this **Chapter - 1003.11**.*

*At least one lavatory, one water closet and either a bathtub or shower within the unit shall comply with this **Chapter - 1003.11**.*

The accessible toilet and bathing fixtures shall be in a single toilet/bathing area, such that travel between fixtures does not require travel through other parts of the unit.

1003.11.2   ***Doors***

Doors shall not swing into the clear floor space or clearance for any fixture.

> *EXCEPTION:*
>
> > *Where a clear floor space complying with **Chapter 51: Clear Floor Space - 305.3 - p. 200** is provided within the room beyond the arc of the door swing.*

1003.11.3   ***Overlap***

Clear floor spaces, clearances at fixtures and turning spaces are permitted to overlap.

1003.11.4   ***Reinforcement***

Reinforcement shall be provided for the future installation of grab bars and shower seats at water closets, bathtubs, and shower compartments.

*Where walls are located to permit the installation of grab bars and seats complying with **Chapter 27: Water Closet Compartment - 604.5 - pp. 111-113, Chapter 60: Bathtubs - 607.4 - pp. 224-226, Chapter 61: Shower Compartments - 608.3 and 608.4 - pp. 229-231**, reinforcement shall be provided for the future installation of grab bars and seats meeting those requirements.*

Chapter 13: ICC/ANSI A117.1 - Type A Units (continued)

EXCEPTION:

Reinforcement is not required in a room containing only a lavatory and a water closet, provided the room does not contain the only lavatory or water closet on the accessible level of the dwelling unit.

1003.11.5 **Lavatory**

Lavatories shall comply with **Chapter 28: Sinks - 606 - pp. 118-120.**

EXCEPTION:

Cabinetry shall be permitted under the lavatory, provided:

(a) the cabinetry can be removed without removal or replacement of the lavatory;

(b) the floor finish extends under such cabinetry;

and

(c) the walls behind and surrounding cabinetry are finished.

1003.11.6 **Mirrors**

Mirrors above lavatories shall have the bottom edge of the reflecting surface 40 inches (1016mm) maximum above the floor.

1003.11.7 **Water Closet**

Water closets shall comply with **1003.11.7 - (below & following page).**

See Diagrams 7(a),(b),(c),(d) - p. 312.

1003.11.7.1 **Location**

The water closet shall be positioned with a wall to the rear and to one side.

The centerline of the water closet shall be 16 inches (406mm) minimum and 18 inches (457mm) maximum from the side wall.

Chapter 13: ICC/ANSI A117.1 - Type A Units (continued)

1003.11.7.2   *Clearance*

A clearance around the water closet of 60 inches (1524mm) minimum, measured perpendicular from the side wall, and 56 inches (1422mm) minimum, measured perpendicular from the rear wall, shall be provided.

1003.11.7.3   *Overlap*

The required clearance around the water closet shall be permitted to overlap the water closet, associated grab bars, paper dispensers, coat hooks, shelves, accessible routes, clear floor space required at other fixtures, and the wheelchair turning space.

No other fixtures or obstructions shall be located within the required water closet clearance.

    EXCEPTION:

        *A lavatory complying with **1003.11.5 - (preceding page)** shall be permitted on the rear wall 18 inches (457mm) minimum from the centerline of the water closet where the clearance at the water closet is 66 inches (1676mm) minimum measured perpendicular from the rear wall.*

1003.11.7.4   *Height*

The top of the water closet seat shall be 15 inches (381mm) minimum and 19 inches (483mm) maximum above the floor, measured to the top of the seat.

1003.11.7.5   *Flush Controls*

*Hand-operated flush controls shall comply with this **Chapter - 1003.9 - p. 45**.*

Flush controls shall be located on the open side of the water closet.

1003.11.8   *Bathtub*

*Bathtubs shall comply with **Chapter 60: Bathtubs - 607 - pp. 224-227**.*

*See **Diagrams 8(a),(b) - p. 313**.*

    EXCEPTIONS:

    1.   *The removable in-tub seat required by **Chapter 60: Bathtubs - 607.3 - p. 224** is not required.*

Chapter 13: ICC/ANSI A117.1 - Type A Units (continued)

> 2. *Countertops and cabinetry shall be permitted at the control end of the clearance, provided such countertops and cabinetry can be removed and the floor finish extends under such cabinetry.*

1003.11.9 **Showers**

Showers shall comply with **Chapter 61: Shower Compartments - 608 - pp. 228-233.**

See Diagram 9 - p. 314.

> EXCEPTION:
>
> *Countertops and cabinetry shall be permitted at the control end of the clearance, provided such countertops and cabinetry can be removed and the floor finish extends under such cabinetry.*

1003.12 **Kitchens**

Kitchens shall comply with **1003.12 - (below & following pages).**

1003.12.1 **Clearance**

Clearance complying with **1003.12.1 - (below)** shall be provided.

1003.12.1.1 **Minimum Clearance**

Clearance between all opposing base cabinets, countertops, appliances, or walls within kitchen work areas shall be 40 inches (1016mm) minimum.

See Diagrams 10(a),(b) - p. 315.

1003.12.1.2 **U-Shaped Kitchens**

In kitchens with counters, appliances, or cabinets on three contiguous sides, clearance between all opposing base cabinets, countertops, appliances, or walls within kitchen work areas shall be 60 inches (1524mm) minimum.

See Diagram 11 - p. 316.

1003.12.2 **Clear Floor Space**

Clear floor spaces required by **1003.12.3 through 1003.12.6 - (following pages)** shall comply with **Chapter 51: Clear Floor Space - 305 - pp. 200 & 201.**

Chapter 13: ICC/ANSI A117.1 - Type A Units (continued)

1003.12.3   *Work Surface*

*At least one section of counter shall provide a work surface 30-inch (762mm) minimum in length complying with **1003.12.3 - (below)**.*

See Diagram 12(a) - p. 317.

1003.12.3.1   *Clear Floor Space*

A clear floor space, positioned for a forward approach to the work surface, shall be provided.

*Knee and toe clearance complying with **Chapter 52: Knee and Toe Clearance - 306 - pp. 202 & 203** shall be provided.*

The clear floor space shall be centered on the work surface.

EXCEPTION:

Cabinetry shall be permitted under the work surface, provided:

(a)   *the cabinetry can be removed without removal or replacement of the work surface,*

(b)   *the floor finish extends under such cabinetry,*

and

(c)   *the walls behind and surrounding cabinetry are finished.*

1003.12.3.2   *Height*

The work surface shall be 34 inches (864mm) maximum above the floor.

EXCEPTION:

A counter that is adjustable to provide a work surface at variable heights 29 inches (737mm) minimum and 36 inches (914mm) maximum above the floor, or that can be relocated within that range without cutting the counter or damaging adjacent cabinets, walls, doors, and structural elements, shall be permitted.

1003.12.3.3   *Exposed Surfaces*

There shall be no sharp or abrasive surfaces under the exposed portions of work surface counters.

Chapter 13: ICC/ANSI A117.1 - Type A Units (continued)

1003.12.4 **Sink**

*Sinks shall comply with **1003.12.4** - (below & following page).*

See Diagram 12(b) - p. 317.

1003.12.4.1 **Clear Floor Space**

A clear floor space, positioned for a forward approach to the sink, shall be provided.

*Knee and toe clearance complying with **Chapter 52: Knee and Toe Clearance - 306 - pp. 202 & 203** shall be provided.*

The clear floor space shall be centered on the sink bowl.

> EXCEPTIONS:
>
> 1. *The requirement for knee and toe clearance shall not apply to more than one bowl of a multi-bowl sink.*
>
> 2. *Cabinetry shall be permitted to be added under the sink, provided:*
>
>   (a) *the cabinetry can be removed without removal or replacement of the sink,*
>
>   (b) *the floor finish extends under such cabinetry,*
>
>   and
>
>   (c) *the walls behind and surrounding cabinetry are finished.*

1003.12.4.2 **Height**

The front of the sink shall be 34 inches (864mm) maximum above the floor, measured to the higher of the rim or the counter surface.

> EXCEPTION:
>
> *A sink and counter that is adjustable to variable heights 29 inches (737mm) minimum and 36 inches (914mm) maximum above the floor or that can be relocated within that range without cutting the counter or damaging adjacent cabinets, walls, doors and structural elements, provided rough-in plumbing permits connections of supply and drain pipes for sinks mounted at the height of 29 inches (737mm), shall be permitted.*

Chapter 13: ICC/ANSI A117.1 - Type A Units (continued)

1003.12.4.3　　　　　　　　　　　　*Faucets*

*Faucets shall comply with **Chapter 55: Operable Parts - 309 - p. 208**.*

1003.12.4.4　　　　　　　*Exposed Pipes and Surfaces*

Water supply and drain pipes under sinks shall be insulated or otherwise configured to protect against contact.

There shall be no sharp or abrasive surfaces under sinks.

1003.12.5　　　　　　　　　　　　*Kitchen Storage*

A clear floor space, positioned for a parallel or forward approach to the kitchen cabinets, shall be provided.

1003.12.6　　　　　　　　　　　　　*Appliances*

*Where provided, kitchen appliances shall comply with **1003.12.6 - (below & following page)**.*

1003.12.6.1　　　　　　　　　　　*Operable Parts*

*All appliance controls shall comply with this **Chapter - 1003.9 - p. 45**.*

EXCEPTIONS:

1. *Appliance doors and door latching devices shall not be required to comply with **Chapter 55: Operable Parts - 309.4 - p. 208**.*

2. *Bottom-hinged appliance doors, when in the open position, shall not be required to comply with **Chapter 55: Operable Parts - 309.3 - p. 208**.*

1003.12.6.2　　　　　　　　　　　*Clear Floor Space*

A clear floor space, positioned for a parallel or forward approach, shall be provided at each kitchen appliance.

Clear floor spaces shall be permitted to overlap.

1003.12.6.3　　　　　　　　　　　　*Dishwasher*

A clear floor space, positioned adjacent to the dishwasher door, shall be provided.

The dishwasher door in the open position shall not obstruct the clear floor space for the dishwasher or an adjacent sink.

Chapter 13: ICC/ANSI A117.1 - Type A Units (continued)

1003.12.6.4   ***Range or Cooktop***

A clear floor space, positioned for a parallel or forward approach to the space for a range or cooktop, shall be provided.

Where the clear floor space is positioned for a forward approach, knee and toe clearance complying with **Chapter 52: Knee and Toe Clearance - 306 - pp. 202 & 203** *shall be provided.*

Where knee and toe space is provided, the underside of the range or cooktop shall be insulated or otherwise configured to protect from burns, abrasions, or electrical shock.

The location of controls shall not require reaching across burners.

1003.12.6.5   ***Oven***

Ovens shall comply with **1003.12.6.5 - (below).**

Ovens shall have controls on front panels, on either side of the door.

1003.12.6.5.1   ***Side-Hinged Door Ovens***

Side-hinged door ovens shall have a countertop positioned adjacent to the latch side of the oven door.

1003.12.6.5.2   ***Bottom-Hinged Door Ovens***

Bottom-hinged door ovens shall have a countertop positioned adjacent to one side of the door.

1003.12.6.6   ***Refrigerator/Freezer***

Combination refrigerators and freezers shall have at least 50 percent of the freezer compartment shelves, including the bottom of the freezer, 54 inches (1372mm) maximum above the floor when the shelves are installed at the maximum heights possible in the compartment.

The clear floor space, positioned for a parallel approach to the space dedicated to a refrigerator/freezer, shall be provided.

The centerline of the clear floor space shall be offset 24 inches (610mm) maximum from the centerline of the dedicated space.

1003.12.6.7   ***Trash Compactor***

A clear floor space, positioned for a parallel or forward approach to the trash compactor, shall be provided.

Chapter 13: ICC/ANSI A117.1 - Type A Units (continued)

1003.13 **Windows**

*Where operable windows are provided, at least one window in each sleeping, living, or dining space shall have operable parts complying with this **Chapter - 1003.9 - p. 45**.*

*Each required operable window shall have operable parts complying with this **Chapter - 1003.9 - p. 45**.*

1003.14 **Storage Facilities**

*Where storage facilities are provided, they shall comply with **1003.14 - (below)**.*

*Kitchen cabinets shall comply with this **Chapter - 1003.12.5 - p. 52**.*

1003.14.1 **Clear Floor Space**

*A clear floor space complying with **Chapter 51: Clear Floor Space - 305.3 - p. 200**, positioned for a parallel or forward approach, shall be provided at each storage facility.*

1003.14.2 **Height**

*A portion of the storage area of each storage facility shall comply with at least one of the reach ranges specified in **Chapter 54: Reach Ranges - 308 - pp. 206 & 207**.*

1003.14.3 **Operable Parts**

*Operable parts on storage facilities shall comply with **Chapter 55: Operable Parts - 309 - p. 208**.*

Chapter 14:
ICC/ANSI A117.1
DWELLING UNITS AND SLEEPING UNITS
TYPE B UNITS

ICC/ANSI - Chapter 10   *Dwelling Units and Sleeping Units*

1001   *General*

1001.1   *Scoping*

*Dwelling units and sleeping units required to be Accessible units, Type A units, Type B units, or units with accessible communication features by the scoping provisions adopted by the administrative authority shall comply with the applicable provisions of this **Chapter - 1004**.*

1004   ***Type B Units***

1004.1   *General*

*Type B dwelling units shall comply with this **Chapter - 1004**.*

1004.2   *Primary Entrance*

The accessible primary entrance shall be on an accessible route from public and common use areas.

The primary entrance shall not be to a bedroom.

1004.3   *Accessible Route*

*Accessible routes within Type B units shall comply with **1004.3** - (below & following page).*

1004.3.1   *Location*

At least one accessible route shall connect all spaces and elements that are a part of the unit.

Where only one accessible route is provided, it shall not pass through bathrooms and toilet rooms, closets or similar spaces.

   EXCEPTION:

      One of the following is not required to be on an accessible route:

      1.   A raised floor area in a portion of a living, dining, or sleeping room;

Chapter 14: ICC/ANSI A117.1 - Type B Units (continued)

or

2. *A sunken floor area in a portion of a living, dining, or sleeping room;*

or

3. *A mezzanine that does not have plumbing fixtures or an enclosed habitable space.*

1004.3.2 **Components**

Accessible routes shall consist of one or more of the following elements: walking surfaces with a slope not steeper than 1:20, doorways, ramps, elevators, and platform lifts.

1004.4 **Walking Surfaces**

*Walking surfaces that are part of an accessible route shall comply with **1004.4 - (below)**.*

1004.4.1 **Width**

*Clear width of an accessible route shall comply with **Chapter 4: Accessible Route - 403.5 - pp. 13 & 14**.*

1004.4.2 **Changes in Level**

*Changes in level shall comply with **Chapter 49: Changes in Level - 303 - p. 197**.*

EXCEPTION:

Where exterior deck, patio or balcony surface materials are impervious, the finished exterior impervious surface shall be 4 inches (102mm) maximum below the floor level of the adjacent interior spaces of the unit.

1004.5 **Doors and Doorways**

*Doors and doorways shall comply with **1004.5 - (below & following page)**.*

1004.5.1 **Primary Entrance Door**

*The primary entrance door to the unit shall comply with **Chapter 56: Doors and Doorways - 404 - pp. 209-216**.*

Chapter 14: ICC/ANSI A117.1 - Type B Units (continued)

EXCEPTION:

> *Maneuvering clearances required by **Chapter 56: Doors and Doorways - 404.2.3 - pp. 210-212** shall not be required on the unit side of the primary entrance door.*

1004.5.2   **User Passage Doorways**

*Doorways intended for user passage shall comply with **1004.5.2 - (below)**.*

1004.5.2.1   **Clear Width**

Doorways shall have a clear opening of 31-3/4 inches (806mm) minimum.

Clear opening of swinging doors shall be measured between the face of the door and stop, with the door open 90 degrees.

1004.5.2.2   **Thresholds**

*Thresholds shall comply with **Chapter 49: Changes in Level - 303 - p. 197**.*

EXCEPTION:

> *Thresholds at exterior sliding doors shall be permitted to be 3/4-inch (19.1mm) maximum in height, provided they are beveled with a slope not steeper than 1:2.*

1004.5.2.3   **Automatic Doors**

*Automatic doors shall comply with **Chapter 56: Doors and Doorways - 404.3 - pp. 215 & 216**.*

1004.5.2.4   **Double Leaf Doorways**

*Where an inactive leaf with operable parts higher than 48 inches (1219mm) or lower than 15 inches (381mm) above the floor is provided, the active leaf shall provide the clearance required by **1004.5.2.1 - (above)**.*

1004.6   **Ramps**

*Ramps shall comply with **Chapter 16: Means of Egress - Ramps - 405 - pp. 73-76**.*

1004.7   **Elevators**

*Elevators within the unit shall comply with **Chapter 31: Elevators - 407 - pp. 128-141, Chapter 32: Limited-Use/Limited-Application Elevators - 408 - pp. 142-144, or Chapter 33: Private Residence Elevators - 409 - pp. 145-148**.*

Chapter 14: ICC/ANSI A117.1 - Type B Units (continued)

1004.8   ***Platform Lifts***

*Platform lifts within the unit shall comply with **Chapter 34: Lifts - 410 - pp. 150 & 151.***

1004.9   ***Operable Parts***

*Lighting controls, electrical switches and receptacle outlets, environmental controls, and user controls for security or intercom systems shall comply with **Chapter 55: Operable Parts - 309.2 and 309.3 - p. 208.***

       EXCEPTIONS:

       1.   *Receptacle outlets serving a dedicated use.*

       2.   *One receptacle outlet is not required to comply with **Chapter 55: Operable Parts - 309.2 and 309.3 - p. 208** where all of the following conditions are met:*

            (a)   *the receptacle outlet is above a length of countertop that is uninterrupted by a sink or appliance;*

                  and

            (b)   *at least one receptacle outlet complying with **1004.9 - (above & below)** is provided for that length of countertop;*

                  and

            (c)   *all other receptacle outlets provided for that length of countertop comply with **1004.9 - (above & below)**.*

       3.   *Floor receptacle outlets.*

       4.   *HVAC diffusers.*

       5.   *Controls mounted on ceiling fans.*

       6.   *Controls or switches mounted on appliances.*

       7.   *Plumbing fixture controls.*

1004.10   ***Laundry Equipment***

*Washing machines and clothes dryers shall comply with **1004.10 - (following page)**.*

Chapter 14: ICC/ANSI A117.1 - Type B Units (continued)

1004.10.1   ***Clear Floor Space***

*A clear floor space complying with **Chapter 51: Clear Floor Space - 305.3 - p. 200**, positioned for parallel approach, shall be provided.*

The clear floor space shall be centered on the appliance.

1004.11   ***Toilet and Bathing Facilities***

*Toilet and bathing fixtures shall comply with **1004.11** - (below & following pages).*

    EXCEPTION:

        Fixtures on levels not required to be accessible.

1004.11.1   ***Clear Floor Space***

*Clear floor space required by **1004.11.3.1** or **1004.11.3.2** - (following pages) shall comply with **1004.11.1** - (below) and **Chapter 57: Clear Floor Space - 305.3 - p. 200**.*

1004.11.1.1   ***Doors***

Doors shall not swing into the clear floor space for any fixture.

    EXCEPTION:

        *Where a clear floor space complying with **Chapter 51: Clear Floor Space - 305.3 - p. 200**, excluding knee and toe clearances under elements, is provided within the room beyond the arc of the door swing.*

1004.11.1.2   ***Knee and Toe Clearance***

*Clear floor space shall be permitted to include knee and toe clearances complying with **Chapter 52: Knee and Toe Clearance - 306 - pp. 202 & 203**.*

1004.11.1.3   ***Overlap***

Clear floor spaces shall be permitted to overlap.

1004.11.2   ***Reinforcement***

Reinforcement shall be provided for future installation of grab bars and shower seats at water closets, bathtubs, and shower compartments.

Chapter 14: ICC/ANSI A117.1 - Type B Units (continued)

*Where walls are located to permit installation of grab bars and seats complying with **Chapter 27: Water Closet Compartment - 604.5 - pp. 111-113, Chapter 60: Bathtubs - 607.4 - pp. 224-226, and Chapter 61: Shower Compartments - 608.3 and 608.4 - pp. 229-231**, reinforcement shall be provided for future installation of grab bars and seats meeting those requirements.*

EXCEPTION:

Reinforcement is not required in a room containing only a lavatory and a water closet, provided the room does not contain the only lavatory or water closet on the accessible level of the unit.

1004.11.3 **Toilet and Bathing Rooms**

*Either all toilet and bathing rooms provided shall comply with **1004.11.3.1 (Option A) - (below & following pages)**, or one toilet and bathing room shall comply with this **Chapter - 1004.11.3.2 (Option B) - pp. 62-64**.*

1004.11.3.1 **Option A**

*Each fixture provided shall comply with **1004.11.3.1 - (below & following pages)**.*

EXCEPTION:

A lavatory and a water closet in a room containing only a lavatory and water closet, provided the room does not contain the only lavatory or water closet on the accessible level of the unit.

1004.11.3.1.1 **Lavatory**

*A clear floor space complying with **Chapter 51: Clear Floor Space - 305.3 - p. 200**, positioned for a parallel approach, shall be provided.*

The clear floor space shall be centered on the lavatory.

See Diagram 13 - p. 318.

EXCEPTIONS:

1. *A lavatory complying with **Chapter 28: Sinks - 606 - pp. 118-120**.*

2. *Cabinetry shall be permitted under the lavatory, provided such cabinetry can be removed without removal or replacement of the lavatory, and floor finish extends under such cabinetry.*

Chapter 14: ICC/ANSI A117.1 - Type B Units (continued)

1004.11.3.1.2   ***Water Closet***

The lateral distance from the centerline of the water closet to a bathtub or lavatory shall be 18 inches (457mm) minimum on the side opposite the direction of approach and 15 inches (381mm) minimum on the other side.

The lateral distance from the centerline of the water closet to an adjacent wall shall be 18 inches (457mm).

The lateral distance from the centerline of the water closet to a lavatory or bathtub shall be 15 inches (381mm) minimum.

The water closet shall be positioned to allow for future installation of a grab bar on the side with 18 inches (457mm) clearance.

Clearance around the water closet shall comply with **1004.11.3.1.2.1, 1004.11.3.1.2.2, or 1004.11.3.1.2.3 - (below).**

See Diagrams 14(a),(b),(c),(d) - p. 319.

1004.11.3.1.2.1   ***Parallel Approach***

A clearance 56 inches (1422mm) minimum measured from the wall behind the water closet, and 48 inches (1219mm) minimum measured from a point 18 inches (457mm) from the centerline of the water closet on the side designated for future installation of grab bars shall be provided.

Vanities or lavatories on the wall behind the water closet are permitted to overlap the clearance.

1004.11.3.1.2.2   ***Forward Approach***

A clearance 66 inches (1676mm) minimum measured from the wall behind the water closet, and 48 inches (1219mm) minimum measured from a point 18 inches (457mm) from the centerline of the water closet on the side designated for future installation of grab bars shall be provided.

Vanities or lavatories on the wall behind the water closet are permitted to overlap the clearance.

1004.11.3.1.2.3   ***Parallel or Forward Approach***

A clearance 56 inches (1422mm) minimum measured from the wall behind the water closet, and 42 inches (1067mm) minimum measured from the centerline of the water closet shall be provided.

1004.11.3.1.3   ***Bathing Facilities***

Where a bathtub or shower compartment is provided, it shall conform with **1004.11.3.1.3.1, 1004.11.3.1.3.2, or 1004.11.3.1.3.3 - *(following page).***

Chapter 14: ICC/ANSI A117.1 - Type B Units (continued)

1004.11.3.1.3.1   ***Parallel Approach Bathtubs***

A clearance 60 inches (1524mm) minimum in length and 30 inches (762mm) minimum in width shall be provided in front of bathtubs with a parallel approach.

*Lavatories complying with **Chapter 28: Sinks - 606 - pp. 118-120** shall be permitted in the clearance.*

*A lavatory complying with this **Chapter - 1004.11.3.1.1 - p. 60** shall be permitted at the control end of the bathtub if a clearance 48 inches (1219mm) minimum in length and 30 inches (762mm) minimum in width for a parallel approach is provided in front of the bathtub.*

See Diagrams 15(a),(b) - p. 320.

1004.11.3.1.3.2   ***Forward Approach Bathtubs***

A clearance 60 inches (1524mm) minimum in length and 48 inches (1219mm) minimum in width shall be provided in front of bathtubs with a forward approach.

A water closet shall be permitted in the clearance at the control end of the bathtub.

See Diagram 16 - p. 321.

1004.11.3.1.3.3   ***Shower Compartment***

If a shower compartment is the only bathing facility, the shower compartment shall have dimensions of 36 inches (914mm) minimum in width and 36 inches (914mm) minimum in depth.

A clearance of 48 inches (1219mm) minimum in length, measured perpendicular from the shower head wall, and 30 inches (762mm) minimum in depth, measured from the face of the shower compartment, shall be provided.

Reinforcing for shower seat is not required in shower compartments larger than 36 inches (914mm) in width and 36 inches (914mm) in depth.

See Diagram 17 - p. 322.

1004.11.3.2   ***Option B***

*One of each type of fixture provided shall comply with **1004.11.3.2 - (below & following pages)**.*

The accessible fixtures shall be in a single toilet/bathing area, such that travel between fixtures does not require travel through other parts of the unit.

Chapter 14: ICC/ANSI A117.1 - Type B Units (continued)

1004.11.3.2.1   *Lavatory*

Lavatories shall comply with **1004.11.3.2.1** *- (below).*

See Diagrams 18(a),(b) - p. 323.

1004.11.3.2.1.1   *Clear Floor Space*

A clear floor space complying with **Chapter 51: Clear Floor Space - 305.3 - p. 200,** *positioned for a parallel approach, shall be provided.*

    EXCEPTIONS:

        1.   *A lavatory complying with* **Chapter 28: Sinks - 606 - pp. 118-120.**

        2.   *Cabinetry shall be permitted under the lavatory, provided such cabinetry can be removed without removal or replacement of the lavatory, and floor finish extends under such cabinetry.*

1004.11.3.2.1.2   *Position*

The clear floor space shall be centered on the lavatory.

1004.11.3.2.1.3   *Height*

The front of the lavatory shall be 34 inches (864mm) maximum above the floor, measured to the higher of the fixture rim or counter surface.

1004.11.3.2.2   *Water Closet*

The water closet shall comply with this **Chapter - 1004.11.3.1.2 - p. 61.**

1004.11.3.2.3   **Bathing Facilities**

Where either a bathtub or shower compartment is provided, it shall conform with **1004.11.3.2.3.1** *or 1004.11.3.2.3.2 - (below & following page).*

1004.11.3.2.3.1   **Bathtub**

A clearance 48 inches (1219mm) minimum in length measured perpendicular from the control end of the bathtub, and 30 inches (762mm) minimum in width shall be provided in front of bathtubs.

See Diagram 19 - p. 324.

Chapter 14: ICC/ANSI A117.1 - Type B Units (continued)

1004.11.3.2.3.2   *Shower Compartment*

*A shower compartment shall comply with this **Chapter - 1004.11.3.1.3.3 - p. 62**.*

1004.12   *Kitchens*

*Kitchens shall comply with **1004.12 - (below & following page)**.*

1004.12.1   *Clearance*

*Clearance complying with **1004.12.1 - (below)** shall be provided.*

1004.12.1.1   *Minimum Clearance*

Clearance between all opposing base cabinets, countertops, appliances, or walls within kitchen work areas shall be 40 inches (1016mm) minimum.

See Diagrams 20(a),(b) - p. 325.

1004.12.1.2   *U-Shaped Kitchens*

In kitchens with counters, appliances, or cabinets on three contiguous sides, clearance between all opposing base cabinets, countertops, appliances, or walls within kitchen work areas shall be 60 inches (1524mm) minimum.

See Diagram 21 - p. 326.

1004.12.2   *Clear Floor Space*

*Clear floor space at appliances shall comply with **1004.12.2 - (below & following page)** and **Chapter 51: Clear Floor Space - 305.3 - p. 200**.*

1004.12.2.1   *Sink*

A clear floor space, positioned for a parallel approach to the sink, shall be provided.

The clear floor space shall be centered on the sink bowl.

 EXCEPTION:

  *Sinks complying with **Chapter 28: Sinks - 606 - pp. 118-120** shall be permitted to have a clear floor space positioned for a parallel or forward approach.*

Chapter 14: ICC/ANSI A117.1 - Type B Units (continued)

1004.12.2.2 *Dishwasher*

A clear floor space, positioned for a parallel or forward approach to the dishwasher, shall be provided.

The clear floor space shall be positioned beyond the swing of the dishwasher door.

1004.12.2.3 *Cooktop*

A clear floor space, positioned for a parallel or forward approach to the cooktop, shall be provided.

The centerline of the clear floor space shall align with the centerline of the cooktop.

Where the clear floor space is positioned for a forward approach, knee and toe clearance complying with **Chapter 52: Knee and Toe Clearance - 306 - pp. 202 & 203** *shall be provided.*

Where knee and toe space is provided, the underside of the range or cooktop shall be insulated or otherwise configured to prevent burns, abrasions, or electrical shock.

1004.12.2.4 *Oven*

A clear floor space, positioned for a parallel or forward approach to the oven, shall be provided.

1004.12.2.5 *Refrigerator/Freezer*

A clear floor space, positioned for a parallel or forward approach to the refrigerator/freezer, shall be provided.

1004.12.2.6 *Trash Compactor*

A clear floor space, positioned for a parallel or forward approach to the trash compactor, shall be provided.

Chapter 15:
ICC/ANSI A117.1
DWELLING UNITS AND SLEEPING UNITS UNITS WITH ACCESSIBLE COMMUNICATION FEATURES

ICC/ANSI - Chapter 10 *Dwelling Units and Sleeping Units*

1001 *General*

1001.1 *Scoping*

*Dwelling units and sleeping units required to be Accessible units, Type A units, Type B units, or units with accessible communication features by the scoping provisions adopted by the administrative authority shall comply with the applicable provisions of this **Chapter - 1005.***

1005 *Units with Accessible Communication Features*

1005.1 *General*

*Units required to have accessible communication features shall comply with this **Chapter - 1005.***

1005.2 *Unit Smoke Detection*

Where provided, unit smoke detection shall include audible notification complying with NFPA 72 listed in ICC/ANSI A117.1-2003 - Section 105.2.2.

1005.3 *Building Fire Alarm System*

Where a building fire alarm system is provided, the system wiring shall be extended to a point within the unit in the vicinity of the unit smoke detection system.

1005.4 *Visible Notification Appliances*

*Visible notification appliances, where provided within the unit as part of the unit smoke detection system or the building fire alarm system, shall comply with **1005.4** - (below & following page).*

1005.4.1 *Appliance*

*Visible notification appliance shall comply with **Chapter 18: Fire Protection Systems - Alarms - 702 - p. 83.***

Chapter 15: ICC/ANSI A117.1 - Accessible Communication Features (continued)

1005.4.2 *Activation*

All visible notification appliances provided within the unit for smoke detection notification shall be activated upon smoke detection.

All visible notification appliances provided within the unit for building fire alarm notification shall be activated upon activation of the building fire alarm in the portion of the building containing the unit.

1005.4.3 *Interconnection*

The same visible notification appliances shall be permitted to provide notification of unit smoke detection and building fire alarm activation.

1005.4.4 *Prohibited Use*

Visible notification appliances used to indicate unit smoke detection or building fire alarm activation shall not be used for any other purpose within the unit.

1005.5 *Unit Primary Entrance*

*Communication features shall be provided at the unit primary entrance complying with **1005.5 - (below)**.*

1005.5.1 *Notification*

A hard-wired electric doorbell shall be provided.

A button or switch shall be provided on the public side of the unit primary entrance.

Activation of the button or switch shall initiate an audible tone within the unit.

1005.5.2 *Identification*

A means for visually identifying a visitor without opening the unit entry door shall be provided.

Peepholes, where used, shall provide a minimum 180-degree range of view.

1005.6 *Site - Building - Floor Entrance*

*Where a system permitting voice communication between a visitor and the occupant of the unit is provided at a location other than the unit entry door, the system shall comply with **1005.6 - (following page)**.*

Chapter 15: ICC/ANSI A117.1 - Accessible Communication Features (continued)

1005.6.1   *Public or Common-Use Interface*

The public or common-use system interface shall include the capability of supporting voice and TTY communication with the unit interface.

1005.6.2   *Unit Interface*

The unit system interface shall include a telephone jack capable of supporting voice and TTY communication with the public or common-use system interface.

1005.7   *Closed-Circuit Communication Systems*

*Where a closed-circuit communication system is provided, the public or common-use system interface shall comply with **1005.6.1 - (above)**, and the unit system interface in units required to have accessible communication features shall comply with **1005.6.2 - (above)**.*

Chapter 16:
IBC - WAC - ICC/ANSI A117.1
MEANS OF EGRESS
RAMPS

IBC - 1010   **Ramps**

1010.1   **Scope**

The provisions of chapter shall apply to ramps used as a component of a means of egress.

EXCEPTIONS:

1. Other than ramps that are part of the accessible routes providing access in accordance with *Chapter 20: Assembly Area Seating - 1108.2.2 through 1108.2.4.1 - pp. 85-87,* ramped aisles within assembly rooms or spaces shall conform with the provisions in this *Chapter - 1024.11 - p. 73, Chapter 17: Means of Egress - Handrails - 1024.13 - pp. 79 & 80* and in the 2003 International Building Code - Section 1024.11.

2. Curb ramps shall comply with *Chapter 57: Curb Ramps - pp. 217-220.*

3. Vehicle ramps in parking garages for pedestrian exit access shall not be required to comply with *1010.3 through 1010.9 - (below & following pages)* when they are not an accessible route serving accessible parking spaces, other required elements or part of an accessible means of egress.

1010.2   **Slope**

Ramps used as part of a means of egress shall have a running slope not steeper than one unit vertical in 12 units horizontal (8 percent slope).

The slope of other ramps shall not be steeper than one unit vertical in eight units horizontal (12.5 percent slope).

EXCEPTION:

Aisle ramp slope in occupancies of Group A shall comply with this *Chapter - 1024.11 - p. 73, Chapter 17: Means of Egress - Handrails - 1024.13 - pp. 79 & 80* and Section 1024.11 of the 2003 International Building Code.

1010.3   **Cross Slope**

The slope measured perpendicular to the direction of travel of a ramp shall not be steeper than one unit vertical in 48 units horizontal (2 percent slope).

Chapter 16: IBC - WAC - ICC/ANSI A117.1 - Ramps (continued)

1010.4 **Vertical Rise**

The rise for any ramp run shall be 30 inches (762mm) maximum.

1010.5 **Minimum Dimensions**

The minimum dimensions of means of egress ramps shall comply with *1010.5.1 through 1010.5.3 - (below)*.

1010.5.1 **Width**

The minimum width of a means of egress ramp shall not be less than that required for corridors by Section 1016.2 of the 2003 International Building Code.

The clear width of a ramp and the clear width between handrails, if provided, shall be 36 inches (914mm) minimum.

1010.5.2 **Headroom**

The minimum headroom in all parts of the means of egress ramp shall not be less than 80 inches (2032mm).

1010.5.3 **Restrictions**

Means of egress ramps shall not reduce in width in the direction of egress travel.

Projections into the required ramp and landing width are prohibited.

Doors opening onto a landing shall not reduce the clear width to less than 42 inches (1067mm).

1010.6 **Landings**

Ramps shall have landings at the bottom and top of each ramp, points of turning, entrance, exits and at doors.

See Diagram 22 - p. 327.

Landings shall comply with *1010.6.1 through 1010.6.5 - (below & following page)*.

1010.6.1 **Slope**

Landings shall have a slope not steeper than one unit vertical in 48 units horizontal (2 percent slope) in any direction.

Changes in level are not permitted.

Chapter 16: IBC - WAC - ICC/ANSI A117.1 - Ramps (continued)

1010.6.2 **Width**

The landing shall be at least as wide as the widest ramp run adjoining the landing.

See Diagram 22 - p. 327.

1010.6.3 **Length**

The landing length shall be 60 inches (1524mm) minimum.

See Diagram 22 - p. 327.

> EXCEPTION:
>
> Landings in nonaccessible Group R-2 and R-3 individual dwelling units, as applicable in Section 101.2 of the 2003 International Building Code, are permitted to be 36 inches (914mm) minimum.

1010.6.4 **Change in Direction**

Where changes in direction of travel occur at landings provided between ramp runs, the landing shall be 60 inches (1524mm) by 60 inches (1524mm) minimum.

See Diagram 22 - p. 327.

> EXCEPTION:
>
> Landings in nonaccessible Group R-2 and R-3 individual dwelling units, as applicable in Section 101.2 of the 2003 International Building Code, are permitted to be 36 inches (914mm) by 36 inches (914mm) minimum.

1010.6.5 **Doorways**

Where doorways are located adjacent to a ramp landing, maneuvering clearances required by *Chapter 56: Doors and Doorways - 404.2.3 - pp. 210-212* are permitted to overlap the required landing area.

1010.7 **Ramp Construction**

All ramps shall be built of materials consistent with the types permitted for the type of construction of the building; except that wood handrails shall be permitted for all types of construction.

Ramps used as an exit shall conform to the applicable requirements of Sections 1019.1 and 1019.1.1 through 1019.1.3 of the 2003 International Building Code for vertical exit enclosures.

Chapter 16: IBC - WAC - ICC/ANSI A117.1 - Ramps (continued)

1010.7.1 **Ramp Surface**

The surface of ramps shall be of slip-resistant materials that are securely attached.

1010.7.2 **Outdoor Conditions**

Outdoor ramps and outdoor approaches to ramps shall be designed so that water will not accumulate on walking surfaces.

In other than occupancies in Group R-3, and occupancies in Group U that are accessory to an occupancy in Group R-3, surfaces and landings which are part of exterior ramps in climates subject to snow or ice shall be designed to minimize the accumulation of same.

WAC - 7/01/05

1010.8 **Handrails**

Ramps with a rise greater than 6 inches (152mm) shall have handrails on both sides complying with *Chapter 17: Means of Egress - Handrails - 1009.11 - pp. 77-79.*

At least one handrail shall extend in the direction of ramp run not less than 12 inches (305mm) horizontally beyond the top and bottom of the ramp run.

1010.9 **Edge Protection**

Edge protection complying with *1010.9.1 or 1010.9.2 - (below & following page)* shall be provided on each side of ramp runs and at each side of ramp landings.

EXCEPTIONS:

1. Edge protection is not required on ramps not required to have handrails, provided they have flared sides that comply with *Chapter 57: Curb Ramps - pp. 217-220* curb ramp provisions.

2. Edge protection is not required on the sides of ramp landings serving an adjoining ramp run or stairway.

3. Edge protection is not required on the sides of ramp landings having a vertical drop off of not more than 0.5 inches (12.7mm) within 10 inches (254mm) horizontally of the required landing area.

1010.9.1 **Railings**

A rail shall be mounted below the handrail 17 to 19 inches (432mm to 483mm) above the ramp or landing surface.

Chapter 16: IBC - WAC - ICC/ANSI A117.1 - Ramps (continued)

1010.9.2 **Curb or Barrier**

A curb or barrier shall be provided that prevents the passage of a 4-inch (102mm) diameter sphere, where any portion of the sphere is within 4 inches (102mm) of the floor or ground surface.

See Diagram 23(b) - p. 328.

1010.10 **Guards**

Guards shall be provided where required by Section 1012 of the 2003 International Building Code and shall be constructed in accordance with Section 1012 of the 2003 International Building Code.

WAC - 7/01/05

1024.11 **Assembly Aisle Walking Surface**

Aisles with a slope not exceeding one unit vertical in eight units horizontal (12.5-percent slope) shall consist of a ramp having a slip-resistant walking surface.

Aisles with a slope exceeding one unit vertical in eight units horizontal (12.5-percent slope) shall consist of a series of risers and treads that extends across the full width of aisles and complies with Sections 1024.11.1 through 1024.11.3 of the 2003 International Building Code.

EXCEPTION:

> When provided with fixed seating, aisles in Group A-1 occupancies shall be permitted to have a slope not steeper than one unit vertical in five units horizontal (20-percent slope).

ICC/ANSI - Chapter 4 *Accessible Routes*

401 *General*

401.1 *Scope*

*Accessible routes required by the scoping provisions adopted by the administrative authority shall comply with the applicable provisions of this **Chapter - 405.***

ICC/ANSI - 405 *Ramps*

405.1 *General*

*Ramps along accessible routes shall comply with this **Chapter - 405.***

Chapter 16: IBC - WAC - ICC/ANSI A117.1 - Ramps (continued)

405.2   ***Slope***

Ramp runs shall have a running slope not steeper than 1:12.

> *EXCEPTION:*
>
> *In existing buildings or facilities, ramps shall be permitted to have slopes steeper than 1:12 complying with **Table D - (below)** where such slopes are necessary due to space limitations.*

Table D
Allowable Ramp Dimensions for Construction in Existing Sites Buildings and Facilities

Slope[1]	*Maximum Rise*
Steeper than 1:10 but not steeper than 1:8	*3 inches (76mm)*
Steeper than 1:12 but not steeper than 1:10	*6 inches (152mm)*

[1] *A slope steeper than 1:8 shall not be permitted.*

405.3   ***Cross Slope***

Cross slope of ramp runs shall not be steeper than 1:48.

405.4   ***Floor Surfaces***

*Floor surfaces of ramp runs shall comply with **Chapter 48: Floor Surfaces - 302 - pp. 195 & 196.***

405.5   ***Clear Width***

The clear width of a ramp run shall be 36 inches (914mm) minimum.

Where handrails are provided on the ramp run, the clear width shall be measured between the handrails.

405.6   ***Rise***

The rise for any ramp run shall be 30 inches (762mm) maximum.

405.7   ***Landings***

Ramps shall have landings at bottom and top of each ramp run.

*Landings shall comply with **405.7 - (above & following page).***

Chapter 16: IBC - WAC - ICC/ANSI A117.1 - Ramps (continued)

See Diagram 22 - p. 327.

405.7.1   ***Slope***

Landings shall have a slope not steeper than 1:48 and shall comply with **Chapter 48: Floor Surfaces - 302 - pp. 195 & 196.**

405.7.2   ***Width***

Clear width of landings shall be at least as wide as the widest ramp run leading to the landing.

See Diagram 22 - p. 327.

405.7.3   ***Length***

Landings shall have a clear length of 60 inches (1524mm) minimum.

See Diagram 22 - p. 327.

405.7.4   ***Change in Direction***

Ramps that change direction at ramp landings shall be sized to provide a turning space complying with **Chapter 50: Turning Space - 304.3 - pp. 198 & 199.**

405.7.2   ***Doorways***

Where doorways are adjacent to a ramp landing, maneuvering clearances required by **Chapter 56: Doors and Doorways - 404.2.3 - pp. 210-212 and 404.3.2 - p. 215** *shall be permitted to overlap the landing area.*

Where doors that are subject to locking are adjacent to a ramp landing, landings shall be sized to provide a turning space complying with **Chapter 50: Turning Space - 304.3 - pp. 198 & 199.**

405.8   ***Handrails***

Ramp runs with a rise greater than 6 inches (152mm) shall have handrails complying with **Chapter 17: Means of Egress - Handrails - 505 - pp. 77-80.**

405.9   ***Edge Protection***

Edge protection complying with **405.9.1 or 405.9.2 - (following page)** *shall be provided on each side of ramp runs and at each side of ramp landings.*

Chapter 16: IBC - WAC - ICC/ANSI A117.1 - Ramps (continued)

EXCEPTIONS:

1. *Ramps not required to have handrails where curb ramp flares complying with **Chapter 57: Curb Ramps - 406.3 - p. 217** are provided.*

2. *Sides of ramp landings serving an adjoining ramp run or stairway.*

3. *Sides of ramp landings having a vertical drop-off of 1/2-inch (13mm) maximum within 10 inches (254mm) horizontally of the minimum landing area.*

405.9.1 **Extended Floor Surface**

*The floor surface of the ramp run or ramp landing shall extend 12 inches (305mm) minimum beyond the inside face of a railing complying with **Chapter 17: Means of Egress - Handrails - 505 - pp. 77-80**.*

See Diagram 23(a) - p. 328.

405.9.2 **Curb or Barrier**

A curb or barrier shall be provided that prevents the passage of a 4-inch (102mm) diameter sphere where any portion of the sphere is within 4 inches (102mm) of the floor.

See Diagram 21(b) - p. 289.

405.10 **Wet Conditions**

Landings subject to wet conditions shall be designed to prevent the accumulation of water.

Chapter 17:

IBC - WAC
MEANS OF EGRESS
HANDRAILS

IBC - Chapter 10 - 1009.11 **Handrails**

Stairways shall have handrails on each side.

Handrails shall be adequate in strength and attachment in accordance with *1607.7 - (below)*.

Handrails for ramps, where required by *Chapter 16: Means of Egress - Ramps - 1010.8 - p. 72*, shall comply with this chapter and Sections 1009.12 and 1009.12.1 of the 2003 International Building Code.

EXCEPTIONS:

1. Aisle stairs complying with *Chapter 16: Means of Egress - Ramps - 1024.11 - p. 73, this Chapter - 1024.13 - pp. 79-80* and Section 1024 of the 2003 International Building Code provided with a center handrail need not have additional handrails.

2. Stairways within dwelling units, spiral stairways and aisle stairs serving seating only on one side are permitted to have a handrail on one side only.

3. Decks, patios and walkways that have a single change in elevation where the landing depth on each side of the change in elevation is greater than what is required for a landing do not require handrails.

4. In Group R-3 occupancies, a change in elevation consisting of a single riser at an entrance or egress door does not require handrails.

5. Changes in room elevations of only one riser within dwelling units and sleeping units in Group R-2 and R-3 occupancies do not require handrails.

1607.7 **Loads on Handrails - Guards - Grab Bars - Vehicle Barriers**

Handrails, guards, grab bars as designed in ICC/ANSI A117.1, and vehicle barriers shall be designed and constructed to the structural loading conditions set forth in section 1607.7 of the 2003 International Building Code.

1009.11.1 **Height**

Handrail height, measured above stair tread nosings, or finish surface of ramp slope, shall be uniform, not less than 34 inches (864mm) and not more than 38 inches (965mm).

Chapter 17: IBC - WAC - Handrails (continued)

See Diagram 24(a) - p. 329.

1009.11.2 **Intermediate Handrails**

Intermediate handrails are required so that all portions of the stairway width required for egress capacity are within 30 inches (762mm) of a handrail.

On monumental stairs, handrails shall be located along the most direct path of egress travel.

1009.11.3 **Handrail Graspability**

Handrails with a circular cross section shall have an outside diameter of at least 1.25 inches (32mm) and not greater than 2 inches (51mm) or shall provide equivalent graspability.

If the handrail is not circular, it shall have a perimeter dimension of at least 4 inches (102mm) and not greater than 6.25 inches (159mm) with a maximum cross-section dimension of 2.25 inches (57mm).

Edges shall have a minimum radius of 0.01-inch (0.25mm).

See Diagram 24(d) - p. 329.

1009.11.4 **Continuity**

Handrail-gripping surfaces shall be continuous, without interruption by newel posts or other obstructions.

EXCEPTIONS:

1. Handrails within dwelling units are permitted to be interrupted by a newel post at a stair landing.

2. Within a dwelling unit, the use of a volute, turnout or starting easing is allowed on the lowest tread.

3. Handrail brackets or balusters attached to the bottom surface of the handrail that do not project horizontally beyond the sides of the handrail within 1.5 inches (38mm) of the bottom of the handrail shall not be considered to be obstructions and provided further that for each 0.5 inches (12.7mm) of additional handrail perimeter dimension above 4 inches (102mm), the vertical clearance dimension of 1.5 inches (38mm) shall be permitted to be reduced by 0.125 inches (3mm).

Chapter 17: IBC - WAC - Handrails (continued)

1009.11.5 **Handrail Extensions**

Handrails shall return to a wall, guard or the walking surface or shall be continuous to the handrail of an adjacent stair flight.

Where handrails are not continuous between flights, the handrails shall extend horizontally at least 12 inches (305mm) beyond the top riser and continue to slope for the depth of one tread beyond the bottom riser.

See Diagram 25 - p. 330.

EXCEPTIONS:

1. Handrails within a dwelling unit that is not required to be accessible need extend only from the top riser to the bottom riser.

2. Aisle handrails in Group A Occupancies in accordance with *1024.13 - (below & following page)* and Sections 1024.13.1 and 1024.13.2 of the 2003 International Building Code.

1009.11.6 **Clearance**

Clear space between a handrail and a wall or other surface shall be a minimum of 1.5 inches (38mm).

See Diagram 24(b) - p. 329.

A handrail and a wall or other surface adjacent to the handrail shall be free of any sharp or abrasive elements.

1009.11.7 **Stairway Projections**

Projections into the required width at each handrail shall not exceed 4.5 inches (114mm) at or below the handrail height.

Projections into the required width shall not be limited above the minimum headroom height required in Section 1009.2 of the 2003 International Building Code.

WAC - 7/01/05

1024.13 **Handrails**

Ramped aisles having a slope exceeding one unit vertical in 15 units horizontal (6.7-percent slope) and aisle stairs shall be provided with handrails located either at the side or within the aisle width.

Chapter 17: IBC - WAC - Handrails (continued)

EXCEPTIONS:

1. Handrails are not required for ramped aisles having a gradient no greater than one unit vertical in five units horizontal (20-percent slope) and seating on both sides.

2. Handrails are not required if, at the side of the aisle, there is a guard that complies with the graspability requirements of handrails.

Chapter 18:
IBC - ICC/ANSI A117.1
FIRE PROTECTION SYSTEMS
ALARMS

IBC - 907.9   **Fire Protection Systems**

907.9   **Alarm Notification Appliances**

Alarm notification appliances shall be provided and shall be listed for their purpose.

907.9.1   **Visible Alarms**

Visible alarm notification appliances shall be provided in accordance with *907.9.1.1 through 907.9.1.3 - (below & following page).*

EXCEPTIONS:

1. Visible alarm notification appliances are not required in alterations, except where an existing fire alarm system is upgraded or replaced, or a new fire alarm system is installed.

2. Visible alarm notification appliances shall not be required in exits as defined in Section 1002.1 of the 2003 International Building Code.

907.9.1.1   **Public and Common Areas**

Visible alarm notification appliances shall be provided in public and common areas.

907.9.1.2   **Employee Work Areas**

Where employee work areas have audible alarm coverage, the wiring systems shall be designed so that visible alarm notification appliances can be integrated into the alarm system.

907.9.1.3   **Groups I-1 and R-1**

Group I-1 and Group R-1 sleeping units in accordance with *Table E - (following page)* shall be provided with a visible alarm notification appliance, activated by both the in-room smoke alarm and the building fire alarm system.

Chapter 18: IBC - ICC/ANSI A117.1 - Alarms (continued)

Table E
Visible and Audible Alarms

Number of Sleeping Units	Sleeping Units with Visible and Audible Alarms
6 to 25	2
26 to 50	4
51 to 75	7
76 to 100	9
101 to 150	12
151 to 200	14
201 to 300	17
301 to 400	20
401 to 500	22
501 to 1,000	5% of total
1,001 and over	50 plus 3 for each 100 over 1,000

907.9.1.4 **Group R-2**

In Group R-2 Occupancies required by the 2003 International Building Code - Section 907, and *907 - (preceding page, below & following page)* to have a fire alarm system, all dwelling units and sleeping units shall be provided with the capability to support visible alarm notification appliances in accordance with *702 - (following page)*.

907.9.2 **Audible Alarms**

Audible alarm notification appliances shall be provided and shall sound a distinctive sound that is not to be used for any purpose other than that of a fire alarm.

The audible alarm notification appliances shall provide a sound pressure level of 15 decibels (dBA) above the average ambient sound level or 5 dBA above the maximum sound level having a duration of at least 60 seconds, whichever is greater, in every occupied space within the building.

The minimum sound pressure levels shall be: 70 dBA in occupancies in Group R and Group I-1; 90 dBA in mechanical equipment rooms; and 60 dBA in other occupancies.

Chapter 18: IBC - ICC/ANSI A117.1 - Alarms (continued)

The maximum sound pressure level for audible alarm notification appliances shall be 120 dBA at the minimum hearing distance from the audible appliance.

Where the average ambient noise is greater than 105 dBA, visible alarm notification appliances shall be provided in accordance with NFPA 72 and audible alarm notification appliances shall not be required.

EXCEPTION:

Visible alarm notification appliances shall be allowed in lieu of audible alarm notification appliances in critical care areas of Group I-2 occupancies.

ICC/ANSI - Chapter 7   ***Communication Elements and Features***

701   ***General***

701.1   ***Scope***

*Communications elements and features required to be accessible by the scoping provisions adopted by the administrative authority shall comply with the applicable provisions of this **Chapter - 702**.*

ICC/ANSI - 702   ***Alarms***

702.1   ***General***

Accessible audible and visual alarms and notification appliances shall be installed in accordance with NFPA 72 listed in ICC/ANSI A117.1-2003 - Section 105.2.2, be powered by a commercial light and power source, be permanently connected to the wiring of the premises electric system, and be permanently installed.

Chapter 19:

INTERNATIONAL BUILDING CODE
SPECIAL OCCUPANCIES

IBC - Chapter 11	**Accessibility**
1108	**Special Occupancies**
1108.1	**General**

In addition to the other requirements of the 2003 International Building Code - Chapter 11, the requirements of *Chapter 20: Assembly Area Seating - 1108.2 - pp. 85-89, Chapter 21: Dining Areas - 1108.2.9 - p. 95, Chapter 22: Self-Service Storage Facilities - 1108.3 - p. 98 and Chapter 23: Judicial Facilities - 1108.4 - pp. 99 & 100* shall apply to specific occupancies.

Chapter 20:

IBC - ICC/ANSI A117.1
SPECIAL OCCUPANCIES
ASSEMBLY AREA SEATING

IBC - Chapter 11   **Accessibility**

1108   **Special Occupancies**

1108.1   **General**

See Chapter 19: Special Occupancies - 1108.1 - p. 84.

1108.2   **Assembly Area Seating**

Assembly areas with fixed seating shall comply with *1108.2.1 through 1108.2.8 - (below & following pages).*

Dining areas shall comply with *Chapter 21: Dining Areas - 1108.2.9 - p. 95.*

1108.2.1   **Services**

Services and facilities provided in areas not required to be accessible shall be provided on an accessible level and shall be accessible.

1108.2.2   **Wheelchair Spaces**

In theaters, bleachers, grandstands, stadiums, arenas and other fixed seating assembly areas, accessible wheelchair spaces complying with ICC/ANSI A117.1 shall be provided in accordance with *1108.2.2.1 through 1108.2.2.3 - (below & following page).*

1108.2.2.1   **General Seating**

Wheelchair spaces shall be provided in accordance with *Table F - (following page).*

Chapter 20: IBC - ICC/ANSI A117.1 - Assembly Area Seating (continued)

Table F
Accessible Wheelchair Spaces

Capacity of Seating in Assembly Areas	Minimum Required Number of Wheelchair Spaces
4 to 25	1
26 to 50	2
51 to 100	4
101 to 300	5
301 to 500	6
501 to 5,000	6, plus 1 for each 150, or fraction thereof, between 501 through 5,000
5,001 and over	36, plus 1 for each 200, or fraction thereof, over 5,000

1108.2.2.2 **Luxury Boxes - Club Boxes - Suites**

In each luxury box, club box, and suite within arenas, stadiums and grandstands, wheelchair spaces shall be provided in accordance with *Table F - (above)*.

1108.2.2.3 **Other Boxes**

In boxes other than those required to comply with *1108.2.2.2 - (above)*, the total number of wheelchair spaces provided shall be determined in accordance with *Table F - (above)*.

Wheelchair spaces shall be located in not less than 20 percent of all boxes provided.

1108.2.3 **Integration**

Wheelchair spaces shall be an integral part of the seating plan.

1108.2.4 **Dispersion of Wheelchair Spaces**

Dispersion of wheelchair spaces shall be based on the availability of accessible routes to various seating areas including seating at various levels in multilevel facilities.

1108.2.4.1 **Multilevel Assembly Seating Areas**

In multilevel assembly seating areas, wheelchair spaces shall be provided on the main floor level and on one of each two additional floor or mezzanine levels.

Chapter 20: IBC - ICC/ANSI A117.1 - Assembly Area Seating (continued)

Wheelchair spaces shall be provided in each luxury box, club box and suite within assembly facilities.

EXCEPTIONS:

1. In multilevel assembly spaces utilized for worship services, where the second floor or mezzanine level contains 25 percent or less of the total seating capacity, wheelchair spaces shall be permitted to all be located on the main level.

2. In multilevel assembly seating where the second floor or mezzanine level provides 25 percent or less of the total seating capacity and 300 or fewer seats, wheelchair spaces shall be permitted to all be located on the main level.

1108.2.5 **Companion Seats**

At least one companion seat complying with ICC/ANSI A117.1 shall be provided for each wheelchair space required by *1108.2.2 - (preceding pages)*.

1108.2.6 **Designated Aisle Seats**

At least five percent, but not less than one, of the total number of aisle seats provided shall be designated aisle seats.

1108.2.7 **Assistive Listening Systems**

Each assembly area where audible communications are integral to the use of the space shall have an assistive listening system.

EXCEPTION:

Other than in courtrooms, an assistive listening system is not required where there is no audio amplification system.

1108.2.7.1 **Receivers**

Receivers shall be provided for assistive listening systems in accordance with *Table G - (following page)*.

EXCEPTION:

Where a building contains more than one assembly area, the total number of required receivers shall be permitted to be calculated according to the total number of seats in the assembly areas in the building provided that all receivers are usable with all systems, and if assembly areas required to provide assistive listening are under one management.

Chapter 20: IBC - ICC/ANSI A117.1 - Assembly Area Seating (continued)

Table G
Receivers for Assistive Listening Systems

Capacity of Seating in Assembly Areas	Minimum Required Number of Receivers	Minimum Number of Receivers to be Hearing-Aid Compatible
50 or less	2	2
51 to 200	2, plus 1 per 25 seats over 50 seats*	2
201 to 500	2, plus 1 per 25 seats over 50 seats*	1 per 4 receivers*
501 to 1,000	20, plus 1 per 33 seats over 500 seats*	1 per 4 receivers*
1,001 to 2,000	35, plus 1 per 50 seats over 1,000 seats*	1 per 4 receivers*
Over 2,000	55, plus 1 per 100 seats over 2,000 seats*	1 per 4 receivers*

NOTE: * = or fraction thereof

1108.2.7.2 **Public Address Systems**

Where stadiums, arenas and grandstands provide audible public announcements, they shall also provide equivalent text information regarding events and facilities in compliance with *1108.2.7.2.1 and 1108.2.7.2.2 - (below).*

1108.2.7.2.1 **Prerecorded Text Messages**

Where electronic signs are provided and have the capability to display prerecorded text messages containing information that is the same, or substantially equivalent, to information that is provided audibly, signs shall display text that is equivalent to audible announcements.

EXCEPTION:

Announcements that cannot be prerecorded in advance of the event shall not be required to be displayed.

1108.2.7.2.2 **Real-Time Messages**

Where electronic signs are provided and have the capability to display real-time messages containing information that is the same, or substantially equivalent, to information that is provided audibly, signs shall display text that is equivalent to audible announcements.

Chapter 20: IBC - ICC/ANSI A117.1 - Assembly Area Seating (continued)

1108.2.8 **Performance Areas**

An accessible route shall directly connect the performance area to the assembly seating area where a circulation path directly connects a performance area to an assembly seating area.

An accessible route shall be provided from performance areas to ancillary areas or facilities used by performers.

ICC/ANSI - Chapter 8   ***Special Rooms and Spaces***

801   ***General***

801.1   ***Scope***

*Special rooms and spaces required to be accessible by the scoping provisions adopted by the administrative authority shall comply with the applicable provisions of this **Chapter - 802.***

ICC/ANSI - 802   ***Assembly Areas***

802.1   ***General***

*Wheelchair spaces and wheelchair space locations in assembly areas with spectator seating shall comply with this **Chapter - 802.***

802.2   ***Floor Surfaces***

*The floor surface of wheelchair space locations shall have a slope not steeper than 1:48 and shall comply with **Chapter 48: Floor Surfaces - 302 - pp. 195 & 196.***

802.3   ***Width***

A single wheelchair space shall be 36 inches (914mm) minimum in width.

Where two adjacent wheelchair spaces are provided, each wheelchair space shall be 33 inches (838mm) minimum in width.

*See **Diagram 26(a) - p. 331.***

802.4   ***Depth***

Where a wheelchair space location can be entered from the front or rear, the wheelchair space shall be 48 inches (1219mm) minimum in depth.

Where a wheelchair space location can only be entered from the side, the wheelchair space shall be 60 inches (1524mm) minimum in depth.

Chapter 20: IBC - ICC/ANSI A117.1 - Assembly Area Seating (continued)

See Diagram 26(b) - p. 331.

802.5   ***Approach***

The wheelchair space location shall adjoin an accessible route.

The accessible route shall not overlap the wheelchair space location.

802.5.1   ***Overlap***

A wheelchair space location shall not overlap the required width of an aisle.

802.6   ***Integration of Wheelchair Space Locations***

Wheelchair space locations shall be an integral part of any seating area.

802.7   ***Companion Seat***

*A companion seat, complying with **802.7 - (below)**, shall be provided beside each wheelchair space.*

802.7.1   ***Companion Seat Type***

The companion seat shall be comparable in size and quality to assure equivalent comfort to the seats within the seating area adjacent to the wheelchair space location.

Companion seats shall be permitted to be movable.

802.7.2   ***Companion Seat Alignment***

In row seating, the companion seat shall be located to provide shoulder alignment with the wheelchair space occupant.

The shoulder of the wheelchair space occupant is considered to be 36 inches (914mm) from the front of the wheelchair space.

The floor surface for the companion seat shall be at the same elevation as the wheelchair space floor surface.

802.8   ***Designated Aisle Seats***

*Designated aisle seats shall comply with **802.8 - (following page)**.*

Chapter 20: IBC - ICC/ANSI A117.1 - Assembly Area Seating (continued)

802.8.1   ***Armrests***

Where armrests are provided on seating in the immediate area of designated aisle seats, folding or retractable armrests shall be provided on the aisle side of the designated aisle seat.

802.8.2   ***Identification***

Each designated aisle seat shall be identified by a sign or marker.

802.9   ***Lines of Sight***

*Where spectators are expected to remain seated for purposes of viewing events, spectators in wheelchair space locations shall be provided with a line of sight in accordance with **802.9.1** - **(below & following page)**.*

*Where spectators in front of wheelchair space locations will be expected to stand at their seats for purposes of viewing events, spectators in wheelchair space locations shall be provided with a line of sight in accordance with **802.9.2** - **(following pages)**.*

802.9.1   ***Line of Sight Over Seated Spectators***

Where spectators are expected to remain seated during events, spectators seated in wheelchair space locations shall be provided with lines of sight to the performance area or playing field comparable to that provided to spectators in closest proximity to the wheelchair space location.

*Where seating provides lines of sight over heads, spectators in wheelchair space locations shall be afforded lines of sight complying with **802.9.1.1** - **(below)**.*

*Where wheelchair space locations provide lines of sight over the shoulder and between heads, spectators in wheelchair space locations shall be afforded lines of sight complying with **802.9.1.2** - **(below & following page)**.*

802.9.1.1   ***Lines of Sight Over Heads***

Spectators seated in wheelchair space locations shall be afforded lines of sight over the heads of seated individuals in the first row in front of the wheelchair space location.

See Diagram 27(a) - p. 332.

802.9.1.2   ***Lines of Sight Between Heads***

Spectators seated in wheelchair space locations shall be afforded lines of sight over the shoulders and between the heads of seated individuals in the first row in front of the wheelchair space location.

Chapter 20: IBC - ICC/ANSI A117.1 - Assembly Area Seating (continued)

See Diagram 27(b) - p. 332.

802.9.2   *Line of Sight over Standing Spectators*

*Wheelchair space locations required to provide a line of sight over standing spectators shall comply with **802.9.2** - (below & following pages).*

See Diagram 28 - p. 333.

802.9.2.1   *Distance from Adjacent Seating*

The front of the wheelchair space location shall be 12 inches (305mm) maximum from the back of the chair or bench in front.

802.9.2.2   *Elevation*

*The elevation of the tread on which a wheelchair space location is located shall comply with **Table H** - (following page).*

For riser heights other than those provided, interpolations shall be permitted.

Chapter 20: IBC - ICC/ANSI A117.1 - Assembly Area Seating (continued)

Table H
Required Wheelchair Space Location Elevation over Standing Spectators

Minimum Height of the Wheelchair Space Location
Based on Row Spacing[1]

Riser Height	Rows less than 33 inches (838mm)[2]	Rows 33 inches (838mm) to 44 inches (1118mm)[2]	Rows over 44 inches (1118mm)[2]
0" - (0mm)	16" - (406mm)	16" - (406mm)	16" - (406mm)
4" - (102mm)	22" - (559mm)	21" - (533mm)	21" - (533mm)
8" - (203mm)	31" - (787mm)	30" - 762mm)	28" - (711mm)
12"- (305mm)	40" - (1016mm)	37" - (940mm)	35" - (889mm)
16" - (406mm)	49" - (1245mm)	45" - (1143mm)	42" - (1067mm)
20" - (508mm)[3]	58" - (1473mm)	53" - (1346mm)	49" - (1245mm)
24" - (610mm)	N/A	61" - (1549mm)	56" - (1422mm)
28" - (711mm)[4]	N/A	69" - (1753mm)	63" - (1600mm)
32" - (813mm)	N/A	N/A	70" - (1778mm)
36" - (914mm) and higher	N/A	N/A	77" - (1956mm)

[1] The height of the wheelchair space location is the vertical distance from the tread of the row of seats directly in front of the wheelchair space location to the tread of the wheelchair space location.

[2] The row spacing is the back-to-back horizontal distance between the rows of seats in front of the wheelchair space location.

[3] Seating treads less than 33 inches (838mm) in depth are not permitted with risers greater than 18 inches (457mm) in height.

[4] Seating treads less than 44 inches (1118mm) in depth are not permitted with risers greater than 27 inches (686mm) in height.

NOTE:

Table H - (above) *is based on providing a spectator in a wheelchair a line of sight over the head of a spectator two rows in front of the wheelchair space location using average anthropometrical data.*

Chapter 20: IBC - ICC/ANSI A117.1 - Assembly Area Seating (continued)

Table H - (preceding page) is based on the following calculation:

$[(2X+34)(Y-2.25)/X]+(20.2-Y)$ where "Y" is the riser height of the rows in front of the wheelchair space location and "X" is the tread depth of the rows in front of the wheelchair space location.

The calculation is based on the front of the wheelchair space location being located 12 inches (305mm) from the back of the seating tread directly in front and the eye of the standing spectator being set back 8 inches (203mm) from the riser.

Chapter 21:

IBC - ICC/ANSI A117.1
SPECIAL OCCUPANCIES
DINING AREAS

IBC - Chapter 11		Accessibility
1108		**Special Occupancies**
1108.1		**General**

See Chapter 19: Special Occupancies - 1108.1 - p. 84.

1108.2.9 **Dining Areas**

In dining areas, the total floor area allotted for seating and tables shall be accessible.

EXCEPTIONS:

1. In buildings or facilities not required to provide an accessible route between levels, an accessible route to a mezzanine seating area is not required, provided that the mezzanine contains less than 25 percent of the total area and the same services are provided in the accessible area.

2. In sports facilities, tiered dining areas providing seating required to be accessible shall be required to have accessible routes serving at least 25 percent of the dining area, provided that accessible routes serve accessible seating and where each tier is provided with the same services.

1108.2.9.1 **Dining Surfaces**

Where dining surfaces for the consumption of food or drink are provided, at least 5 percent, but not less than one, of the seating and standing spaces at the dining surfaces shall be accessible and be distributed throughout the facility.

ICC/ANSI - Chapter 9   ***Built-in Furnishings and Equipment***

901   ***General***

901.1   ***Scope***

*Built-in furnishings and equipment required to be accessible by the scoping provisions adopted by the administrative authority shall comply with the applicable provisions of this **Chapter - 902**.*

Chapter 21: IBC - ICC/ANSI A117.1 - Dining Areas (continued)

ICC/ANSI - 902   ***Dining Surfaces and Work Surfaces***

902.1   ***General***

*Accessible dining surfaces and work surfaces shall comply with this **Chapter - 902**.*

     EXCEPTION:

         *Dining surfaces and work surfaces primarily for children's use shall be permitted to comply with **902.4 - (below & following page)**.*

902.2   ***Clear Floor Space***

*Clear floor space complying with **Chapter 51: Clear Floor Space - 305 - pp. 200 & 201**, positioned for a forward approach, shall be provided.*

*Knee and toe clearance complying with **Chapter 52: Knee and Toe Clearance - 306 - pp. 202 & 203** shall be provided.*

902.3   ***Height***

The tops of dining surfaces and work surfaces shall be 28 inches (711mm) minimum and 34 inches (864mm) maximum in height above the floor.

902.4   ***Dining Surfaces and Work Surfaces for Children's Use***

*Accessible dining surfaces and work surfaces primarily for children's use shall comply with **902.4 - (below & following page)**.*

     EXCEPTION:

         *Dining surfaces and work surfaces used primarily by children ages 5 and younger shall not be required to comply with **902.4 - (below & following page)** where a clear floor space complying with **Chapter 51: Clear Floor Space - 305 - pp. 200 & 201**, positioned for a parallel approach, is provided.*

902.4.1   ***Clear Floor Space***

*A clear floor space complying with **Chapter 51: Clear Floor Space - 305 - pp. 200 & 201**, positioned for forward approach, shall be provided.*

*Knee and toe clearance complying with **Chapter 52: Knee and Toe Clearance - 306 - pp. 202 & 203** shall be provided.*

Chapter 21: IBC - ICC/ANSI A117.1 - Dining Areas (continued)

EXCEPTION:

Knee clearance 24 inches (610mm) minimum above the floor shall be permitted.

902.4.2   ***Height***

The tops of tables and counters shall be 26 inches (660mm) minimum and 30 inches (762mm) maximum above the floor.

Chapter 22:

INTERNATIONAL BUILDING CODE
SPECIAL OCCUPANCIES
SELF-SERVICE STORAGE FACILITIES

IBC - Chapter 11   **Accessibility**

1108   **Special Occupancies**

1108.1   **General**

See Chapter 19: Special Occupancies - 1108.1 - p. 84.

1108.3   **Self-Service Storage Facilities**

Self-service storage facilities shall provide accessible individual self-storage spaces in accordance with *Table I - (below)*.

Table I
Accessible Self-Service Storage Facilities

Total Spaces in Facility	Minimum Number of Required Accessible Spaces
1 to 200	5%, but not less than 1
Over 200	10, plus 2% of total number of units over 200

1108.3.1   **Dispersion**

Accessible individual self-service storage spaces shall be dispersed throughout the various classes of spaces provided.

Where more classes of spaces are provided than the number of required accessible spaces, the number of accessible spaces shall not be required to exceed that required by *Table I - (above)*.

Accessible spaces are permitted to be dispersed in a single building of a multibuilding facility.

Chapter 23:
IBC - ICC/ANSI A117.1
SPECIAL OCCUPANCIES
JUDICIAL FACILITIES

IBC - Chapter 11   **Accessibility**

1108   **Special Occupancies**

1108.1   **General**

See Chapter 19: Special Occupancies - 1108.1 - p. 84.

1108.4   **Judicial Facilities**

Judicial facilities shall comply with *1108.4.1 through 1108.4.3 - (below & following page).*

1108.4.1   **Courtrooms**

Each courtroom shall be accessible.

1108.4.2   **Holding Cells**

Where provided, central holding cells and court-floor holding cells shall comply with *1108.4.2.1 and 1108.4.2.2 - (below).*

1108.4.2.1   **Central Holding Cells**

Where separate central holding cells are provided for adult males, juvenile males, adult females or juvenile females, one of each type shall be accessible.

Where central holding cells are provided and are not separated by age or sex, at least one accessible cell shall be provided.

1108.4.2.2   **Court-Floor Holding Cells**

Where separate court-floor holding cells are provided for adult males, juvenile males, adult females or juvenile females, each courtroom shall be served by one accessible cell of each type.

Where court-floor holding cells are provided and are not separated by age or sex, courtrooms shall be served by at least one accessible cell.

Accessible cells shall be permitted to serve more than one courtroom.

Chapter 23: IBC - ICC/ANSI A117.1 - Judicial Facilities (continued)

1108.4.3 **Visiting Areas**

Visiting areas shall comply with *1108.4.3.1 and 1108.4.3.2 - (below)*.

1108.4.3.1 **Cubicles and Counters**

At least 5 percent, but no fewer than one, of cubicles shall be accessible on both the visitor and detainee sides.

Where counters are provided, at least one shall be accessible on both the visitor and detainee sides.

EXCEPTION:

This requirement shall not apply to the detainee side of cubicles or counters at noncontact visiting areas not serving holding cells.

1108.4.3.2 **Partitions**

Where solid partitions or security glazing separate visitors from detainees, at least one of each type of cubicle or counter partition shall be accessible.

ICC/ANSI - Chapter 8 *Special Rooms and Spaces*

801 *General*

801.1 *Scope*

*Special rooms and spaces required to be accessible by the scoping provisions adopted by the administrative authority shall comply with the applicable provisions of this **Chapter - 806**.*

ICC/ANSI - 806 *Holding Cells and Housing Cells*

806.1 *General*

*Holding cells and housing cells shall comply with this **Chapter - 806**.*

806.2 *Features for People Using Wheelchairs or Other Mobility Aids*

*Cells required to have features for people using wheelchairs or other mobility aids shall comply with **806.2** - (following page).*

Chapter 23: IBC - ICC/ANSI A117.1 - Judicial Facilities (continued)

806.2.1 *Turning Space*

Turning space complying with **Chapter 50: Turning Space - 304 - pp. 198 & 199** shall be provided within the cell.

806.2.2 *Benches*

Where benches are provided, at least one bench shall comply with **Chapter 39: Service Facilities - 903 - pp. 160 & 161.**

806.2.3 *Beds*

Where beds are provided, clear floor space complying with **Chapter 51: Clear Floor Space - 305 - pp. 200 & 201** shall be provided on at least one side of the bed.

The clear floor space shall be positioned for parallel approach to the side of the bed.

806.2.4 *Toilet and Bathing Facilities*

Toilet facilities or bathing facilities provided as part of a cell shall comply with **Chapter 25: Toilet and Bathing Facilities - 603 - pp. 105 & 106.**

806.3 *Communication Features*

Cells required to have communication features shall comply with **806.3 - (below).**

806.3.1 *Alarms*

Where audible emergency alarm systems are provided to serve the occupant of cells, visual alarms complying with **Chapter 18: Fire Protection Systems - Alarms - 702 - p. 83** shall be provided.

> EXCEPTION:
>
> > In cells where inmates or detainees are not allowed independent means of egress, visual alarms shall not be required.

806.3.2 *Telephones*

Where provided, telephones within cells shall have volume controls complying with **Chapter 65: Telephones - 704.3 - p. 241.**

Chapter 23: IBC - ICC/ANSI A117.1 - Judicial Facilities (continued)

ICC/ANSI - Chapter 8   ***Special Rooms and Spaces***

801   ***General***

801.1   ***Scope***

*Special rooms and spaces required to be accessible by the scoping provisions adopted by the administrative authority shall comply with the applicable provisions of this **Chapter - 807**.*

ICC/ANSI - 807   ***Courtrooms***

807.1   ***General***

*Courtrooms shall comply with this **Chapter - 807**.*

807.2   ***Turning Space***

*Where provided, each area that is raised or depressed and accessed by ramps or platform lifts with entry ramps shall provide an unobstructed turning space complying with **Chapter 50: Turning Space - 304 - pp. 198 & 199**.*

807.3   ***Clear Floor Space***

*Within the defined area of each jury box and witness stand, a clear floor space complying with **Chapter 51: Clear Floor Space - 305 - pp. 200 & 201** shall be provided.*

> *EXCEPTION:*
>
> > *In alterations, wheelchair spaces are not required to be located within the defined area of raised jury boxes or witness stands and shall be permitted to be located outside these spaces where ramps or platform lifts restrict or project into the means of egress required by the administrative authority.*

807.4   ***Judges' Benches and Courtroom Stations***

*Judges' benches, clerks' stations, bailiffs' stations, deputy clerks' stations, court reporters' stations and litigants' and counsel stations shall comply with **Chapter 21: Dining Areas - 902 - pp. 96 & 97**.*

Chapter 24:

INTERNATIONAL BUILDING CODE
OTHER FEATURES AND FACILITIES

IBC - Chapter 11		**Accessibility**
1109		**Other Features and Facilities**
1109.1		**General**

Accessible building features and facilities shall be provided in accordance with *Chapters 25-47 - 1109.2 through 1109.15 - pp. 104-169.*

> EXCEPTION:
>
> Type A and Type B dwelling and sleeping units shall comply with ICC/ANSI A117.1.

Chapter 25:
IBC - ICC/ANSI A117.1 - WAC
OTHER FEATURES AND FACILITIES
TOILET AND BATHING FACILITIES

IBC - Chapter 11   **Accessibility**

1109   **Other Features and Facilities**

1109.1   **General**

See Chapter 24: Other Features and Facilities - 1109.1 - p. 103.

1109.2   **Toilet and Bathing Facilities**

Toilet rooms and bathing facilities shall be accessible.

Where a floor level is not required to be connected by an accessible route, the only toilet rooms or bathing facilities provided within the facility shall not be located on the inaccessible floor.

At least one of each type of fixture, element, control or dispenser in each accessible toilet room and bathing facility shall be accessible.

    EXCEPTIONS:

    1.   In toilet rooms or bathing facilities accessed only through a private office, not for common or public use, and intended for use by a single occupant, any of the following alternatives are allowed:

        1.1   Doors are permitted to swing into the clear floor space provided the door swing can be reversed to meet the requirements of ***Chapter 56: Doors and Doorways - pp. 209-216.***

        1.2   The height requirements for the water closet in ***Chapter 27: Water Closet Compartment - pp. 109-117*** are not applicable.

        1.3   Grab bars are not required to be installed in a toilet room, provided that the reinforcement has been installed in the walls and located so as to permit the installation of such grab bars,

                and

        1.4   The requirement for height, knee and toe clearance shall not apply to a lavatory.

Chapter 25: IBC - ICC/ANSI A117.1 - WAC - Toilet and Bathing Facilities (continued)

2. This chapter is not applicable to toilet and bathing facilities that serve dwelling units or sleeping units that are not required to be accessible by *Chapters 8-11 - 1107 - pp. 27-38.*

3. Where multiple single-user toilet rooms or bathing facilities are clustered at a single location and contain fixtures in excess of the minimum required number of plumbing fixtures, at least 5 percent, but not less than one room for each use at each cluster, shall be accessible.

4. Toilet room fixtures that are in excess of those required by the International Plumbing Code and that are designated for use by children in day care and primary school occupancies.

5. Where no more than one urinal is provided in a toilet room or bathing facility, the urinal is not required to be accessible.

6. Toilet rooms that are part of critical-care or intensive-care patient sleeping rooms are not required to be accessible.

ICC/ANSI - Chapter 6   ***Plumbing Elements and Facilities***

601   *General*

601.1   *Scope*

*Plumbing elements and facilities required to be accessible by scoping provisions adopted by the administrative authority shall comply with the applicable provisions of this **Chapter - 603**.*

ICC/ANSI - 603   ***Toilet and Bathing Rooms***

603.1   *General*

*Accessible toilet and bathing rooms shall comply with this **Chapter - 603**.*

603.2   *Clearances*

603.2.1   *Turning Space*

*A turning space complying with **Chapter 50: Turning Space - 304 - pp. 198 & 199** shall be provided within the room.*

603.2.2   *Overlap*

Clear floor spaces, clearances at fixtures, and turning spaces shall be permitted to overlap.

Chapter 25: IBC - ICC/ANSI A117.1 - WAC - Toilet and Bathing Facilities (continued)

603.2.3 *Door Swing*

Doors shall not swing into the clear floor space or clearance for any fixture.

EXCEPTIONS:

1. *Doors to a toilet and bathing room for a single occupant, accessed only through a private office and not for common use or public use shall be permitted to swing into the clear floor space, provided the swing of the door can be reversed to meet **603.2.3 - (above).***

2. *Where the room is for individual use and a clear floor space complying with **Chapter 51: Clear Floor Space - 305.3 - p. 200** is provided within the room beyond the arc of the door swing.*

603.3 *Mirrors*

Mirrors located above lavatories, sinks or counters shall be mounted with the bottom edge of the reflecting surface 40 inches (1016mm) maximum above the floor.

1101.2.5 **WAC - 7/01/06**
ICC/ANSI A117.1 - Section 603.4

Coat Hooks - Shelves - Dispensers - Other Fixtures

Coat hooks provided shall accommodate a forward reach or side reach complying with **Chapter 54: Reach Ranges - 308 - pp. 206 & 207.**

Where provided, shelves shall be installed so that the top of the shelf is 40 inches (1016mm) maximum above the floor or ground.

Drying equipment, towel or other dispensers, and disposal fixtures shall be located 40 inches (1016mm) maximum above the floor or ground to any rack, operating controls, receptacle or dispenser.

Chapter 26:

INTERNATIONAL BUILDING CODE
OTHER FEATURES AND FACILITIES
UNISEX TOILET AND BATHING ROOMS

IBC - Chapter 11   **Accessibility**

1109   **Other Features and Facilities**

1109.1   **General**

See Chapter 24: Other Features and Facilities - 1109.1 - p. 103.

1109.2.1   **Unisex Toilet and Bathing Rooms**

In assembly and mercantile occupancies, an accessible unisex toilet room shall be provided where an aggregate of six or more male and female water closets is required.

In buildings of mixed occupancy, only those water closets required for the assembly or mercantile occupancy shall be used to determine the unisex toilet room requirement.

In recreational facilities where separate-sex bathing rooms are provided, an accessible unisex bathing room shall be provided.

Fixtures located within required unisex toilet and bathing rooms shall be included in determining the number of fixtures provided in an occupancy.

    EXCEPTION:

        Where each separate-sex bathing room has only one shower or bathtub fixture, a unisex bathing room is not required.

1109.2.1.1   **Standard**

Unisex toilet and bathing rooms shall comply with *1109.2.1.2 through 1109.2.1.7 - (below & following page)* and ICC/ANSI A117.1.

1109.2.1.2   **Unisex Toilet Rooms**

Unisex toilet rooms shall include only one water closet and only one lavatory.

A unisex bathing room in accordance with *1109.2.1.3 - (following page)* shall be considered a unisex toilet room.

Chapter 26: IBC - Unisex Toilet and Bathing Rooms (continued)

EXCEPTION:

> A urinal is permitted to be provided in addition to the water closet in a unisex toilet room.

1109.2.1.3 Unisex Bathing Rooms

Unisex bathing rooms shall include only one shower or bathtub fixture.

Unisex bathing rooms shall also include one water closet and one lavatory.

Where storage facilities are provided for separate-sex bathing rooms, accessible storage facilities shall be provided for unisex bathing rooms.

1109.2.1.4 Location

Unisex toilet and bathing rooms shall be located on an accessible route.

Unisex toilet rooms shall be located not more than one story above or below separate-sex toilet rooms.

The accessible route from any separate-sex toilet room to a unisex toilet room shall not exceed 500 feet (152 400mm).

1109.2.1.5 Prohibited Location

In passenger transportation facilities and airports, the accessible route from separate-sex toilet rooms to a unisex toilet room shall not pass through security checkpoints.

1109.2.1.6 Clear Floor Space

Where doors swing into a unisex toilet or bathing room, a clear floor space not less than 30 inches by 48 inches (762mm by 1219mm) shall be provided, within the room, beyond the area of the door swing.

1109.2.1.7 Privacy

Doors to unisex toilet and bathing rooms shall be securable from within the room.

Chapter 27:
IBC - ICC/ANSI A117.1 - WAC
OTHER FEATURES AND FACILITIES
WATER CLOSET COMPARTMENT

IBC - Chapter 11		Accessibility

1109   **Other Features and Facilities**

1109.1   **General**

See Chapter 24: Other Features and Facilities - 1109.1 - p. 103.

1109.2.2   **Water Closet Compartment**

Where water closet compartments are provided in a toilet room or bathing facility, at least one wheelchair-accessible compartment shall be provided.

Where the combined total water closet compartments and urinals provided in a toilet room or bathing facility is six or more, at least one ambulatory-accessible water closet compartment shall be provided in addition to the wheelchair-accessible compartment.

Wheelchair-accessible and ambulatory-accessible compartments shall comply with ICC/ANSI A117.1.

ICC/ANSI - Chapter 6   *Plumbing Elements and Facilities*

601   *General*

601.1   *Scope*

*Plumbing elements and facilities required to be accessible by scoping provisions adopted by the administrative authority shall comply with the applicable provisions of this **Chapter - 604**.*

ICC/ANSI - 604   *Water Closets and Toilet Compartments*

604.1   *General*

*Accessible water closets and toilet compartments shall comply with this **Chapter - 604**.*

*Compartments containing more than one plumbing fixture shall comply with **Chapter 25: Toilet and Bathing Facilities - 603 - pp. 105 & 106**.*

*Wheelchair accessible compartments shall comply with this **Chapter - Wheelchair Accessible Compartments - 604.8 - pp. 114-116**.*

Chapter 27: IBC - ICC/ANSI A117.1 - WAC - Water Closet Compartment (continued)

*Ambulatory accessible compartments shall comply with this **Chapter - Ambulatory Accessible Compartments - 604.9 - pp. 116 & 117**.*

EXCEPTION:

*Water closets and toilet compartments primarily for children's use shall be permitted to comply with **Chapter 58: Water Closets and Toilet Compartments for Children's Use - 604.10 - pp. 221 & 222** as applicable.*

604.2   *Location*

The water closet shall be located with a wall or partition to the rear and to one side.

The centerline of the water closet shall be 16 inches (406mm) minimum to 18 inches (457mm) maximum from the side wall or partition.

*Water closets located in ambulatory accessible compartments specified in this **Chapter - Ambulatory Accessible Compartments - 604.9 - pp. 116 & 117** shall have the centerline of the water closet 17 inches (432mm) minimum to 19 inches (483mm) maximum from the side wall or partition.*

*See **Diagrams 29(a),(b) - p. 334**.*

604.3   *Clearance*

604.3.1   *Size*

A clearance around a water closet 60 inches (1524mm) minimum, measured perpendicular from the side wall, and 56 inches (1422mm) minimum, measured perpendicular from the rear wall, shall be provided.

604.3.2   *Overlap*

The required clearance around the water closet shall be permitted to overlap the water closet, associated grab bars, paper dispensers, sanitary napkin receptacles, coat hooks, shelves, accessible routes, clear floor space at other fixtures and the turning space.

No other fixtures or obstructions shall be within the required water closet clearance.

*See **Diagram 30(a) - p. 335**.*

604.4   *Height*

The height of water closet seats shall be 17 inches (432mm) minimum and 19 inches (483mm) maximum above the floor, measured to the top of the seat.

Chapter 27: IBC - ICC/ANSI A117.1 - WAC - Water Closet Compartment (continued)

Seats shall not be sprung to return to a lifted position.

EXCEPTION:

> *A water closet in a toilet room for a single occupant, accessed only through a private office and not for common use or public use, shall not be required to comply with **604.4 - (preceding page & above)**.*

See Diagram 30(b) - p. 335.

604.5   *Grab Bars*

*Grab bars for water closets shall comply with **Chapter 62: Grab Bars - 609 - pp. 234-236** and shall be provided in accordance with **604.5.1 and 604.5.2 - (following pages)**.*

Grab bars shall be provided on the rear wall and on the side wall closest to the water closet.

EXCEPTIONS:

1. *Grab bars are not required to be installed in a toilet room for a single occupant, accessed only through a private office and not for common use or public use, provided reinforcement has been installed in walls and located so as to permit the installation of grab bars complying with **604.5 - (above, below & following pages)**.*

2. *In detention or correction facilities, grab bars are not required to be installed in housing or holding cells or rooms that are specially designed without protrusions for purposes of suicide prevention.*

3. *In Type A units, grab bars are not required to be installed where reinforcement complying with **Chapter 13: Type A Units - 1003.11.4 - pp. 46 & 47** is installed for the future installation of grab bars.*

4. *In Type B units located in institutional facilities and assisted living facilities, two swing-up grab bars shall be permitted to be installed in lieu of the rear wall and side wall grab bars.*

    *Swing-up grab bars shall comply with this **Chapter - 604.5.3 - p. 113** and **Chapter 62: Grab Bars - 609 - pp. 234-236**.*

5. *In a Type B unit, where fixtures are located on both sides of the water closet, a swing-up grab bar complying with this **Chapter - 604.5.3 - p. 113** and **Chapter 62: Grab Bars - 609 - pp. 234-236** shall be permitted.*

Chapter 27: IBC - ICC/ANSI A117.1 - WAC - Water Closet Compartment (continued)

*The swing-up grab bar shall be installed on the side of the water closet with the 18-inch (457mm) clearance required by **Chapter 14: Type B Units - 1004.11.3.1.2 - p. 61**.*

604.5.1   ***Fixed Side Wall Grab Bars***

Fixed side wall grab bars shall be 42 inches (1067mm) minimum in length, located 12 inches (305mm) maximum from the rear wall and extending 54 inches (1372mm) minimum from the rear wall.

In addition, a vertical grab bar 18 inches (457mm) minimum in length shall be mounted with the bottom of the bar located between 39 inches (991mm) and 41 inches (1041mm) above the floor, and with the centerline of the bar located between 39 inches (991mm) and 41 inches (1041mm) from the rear wall.

EXCEPTIONS:

1. *In Type A and Type B units, the vertical grab bar component is not required.*

2. *In a Type B unit, when a side wall is not available for a 42-inch (1067mm) grab bar, the side wall grab bar shall be permitted to be 18 inches (457mm) minimum in length, located 12 inches (305mm) maximum from the rear wall and extending 30 inches (762mm) minimum from the rear wall.*

*See **Diagram 31(a) - p. 336**.*

604.5.2   ***Rear Wall Grab Bars***

The rear wall grab bar shall be 36 inches (914mm) minimum in length, and extend from the centerline of the water closet 12 inches (305mm) minimum on the side closest to the wall, and 24 inches (610mm) minimum on the transfer side.

EXCEPTIONS:

1. *The rear grab bar shall be permitted to be 24 inches (610mm) minimum in length, centered on the water closet, where wall space does not permit a grab bar 36 inches (914mm) minimum in length due to the location of a recessed fixture adjacent to the water closet.*

2. *In a Type A or Type B unit, the rear grab bar shall be permitted to be 24 inches (610mm) minimum in length, centered on the water closet, where wall space does not permit a grab bar 36 inches (914mm) minimum in length.*

Chapter 27: IBC - ICC/ANSI A117.1 - WAC - Water Closet Compartment (continued)

> 3. *Where an administrative authority requires flush controls for flush valves to be located in a position that conflicts with the location of the rear grab bar, that grab bar shall be permitted to be split or shifted to the open side of the toilet area.*

See Diagram 31(b) - p. 336.

604.5.3   *Swing-Up Grab Bars*

Where swing-up grab bars are installed, a clearance of 18 inches (457mm) minimum from the centerline of the water closet to any side wall or obstruction shall be provided.

A swing-up grab bar shall be installed with the centerline of the grab bar 15-3/4 inches (400mm) from the centerline of the water closet.

Swing-up grab bars shall be 28 inches (711mm) minimum in length, measured from the wall to the end of the horizontal portion of the grab bar.

See Diagram 32 - p. 337.

604.6   *Flush Controls*

Flush controls shall be hand-operated or automatic.

Hand-operated flush controls shall comply with **Chapter 55: Operable Parts - 309 - p. 208.**

Flush controls shall be located on the open side of the water closet.

> EXCEPTION:
>
> *In ambulatory accessible compartments complying with this* **Chapter - Ambulatory Accessible Compartments - 604.9 - pp. 116 & 117,** *flush controls shall be permitted to be located on either side of the water closet.*

1101.2.6   **WAC - 7/01/06**
                         ICC/ANSI A117.1 - Section 604.6

                                 Flush Controls

<u>Hand-operated flush controls for water closets shall be mounted not more than 44 inches (1118mm) above the floor.</u>

Chapter 27: IBC - ICC/ANSI A117.1 - WAC - Water Closet Compartment (continued)

604.7   *Dispensers*

*Toilet paper dispensers shall comply with **Chapter 55: Operable Parts - 309.4 - p. 208** and shall be 7 inches (178mm) minimum and 9 inches (229mm) maximum in front of the water closet measured to the centerline of the dispenser.*

The outlet of the dispenser shall be 15 inches (381mm) minimum and 48 inches (1219mm) maximum above the floor, and shall not be located behind the grab bars.

Dispensers shall not be of a type that control delivery, or do not allow continuous paper flow.

See Diagrams 33(a),(b) - p. 338.

604.8   **Wheelchair Accessible Compartments**

604.8.1   **General**

*Wheelchair accessible compartments shall comply with this **Chapter - 604.8.***

604.8.2   *Size*

The minimum area of a wheelchair accessible compartment shall be 60 inches (1524mm) minimum in width measured perpendicular to the side wall, and 56 inches (1422mm) minimum in depth for wall-hung water closets, and 59 inches (1499mm) minimum in depth for floor-mounted water closets measured perpendicular to the rear wall.

See Diagrams 34(a),(b) - p. 339.

The minimum area of a wheelchair accessible compartment for primarily children's use shall be 60 inches (1524mm) minimum in width measured perpendicular to the side wall, and 59 inches (1499mm) minimum in depth for wall-hung and floor-mounted water closets measured perpendicular to the rear wall.

See Diagram 34(b) - p. 339.

604.8.3   *Doors*

*Toilet compartment doors, including door hardware, shall comply with **Chapter 56: Doors and Doorways - 404 - pp. 209-216**, except that if the approach is to the latch side of the compartment door, clearance between the door side of the stall and any obstruction shall be 42 inches (1067mm) minimum.*

Doors shall be located in the front partition or in the side wall or partition farthest from the water closet.

Chapter 27: IBC - ICC/ANSI A117.1 - WAC - Water Closet Compartment (continued)

Where located in the front partition, the door opening shall be 4 inches (102mm) maximum from the side wall or partition farthest from the water closet.

Where located in the side wall or partition, the door opening shall be 4 inches (102mm) maximum from the front partition.

The door shall be self-closing.

*A door pull complying with **Chapter 56: Doors and Doorways - 404.2.6 - p. 213** shall be placed on both sides of the door near the latch.*

Toilet compartment doors shall not swing into the required minimum area of the compartment.

See Diagram 35 - p. 340.

604.8.4   *Approach*

Wheelchair accessible compartments shall be arranged for left-hand or right-hand approach to the water closet.

604.8.5   *Toe Clearance*

The front partition and at least one side partition shall provide a toe clearance of 9 inches (229mm) minimum above the floor and extending 6 inches (152mm) beyond the compartment-side face of the partition, exclusive of partition support members.

See Diagrams 36(a),(c) - p. 341.

Compartments primarily for children's use shall provide a toe clearance of 12 inches (305mm) minimum above the floor and extending 6 inches (152mm) beyond the compartment side face of the partition, exclusive of partition support members.

See Diagram 36(b) - p. 341.

    EXCEPTIONS:

    1.   *Toe clearance at the front partition is not required in a compartment greater than 62 inches (1575mm) in depth with a wall-hung water closet, or 65 inches (1651mm) in depth with a floor-mounted water closet.*

          In a compartment primarily for children's use, greater than 65 inches (1651mm) in depth, toe clearance at the front partition is not required.

    2.   *Toe clearance at the side partition is not required in a compartment greater than 66 inches (1676mm) in width.*

Chapter 27: IBC - ICC/ANSI A117.1 - WAC - Water Closet Compartment (continued)

604.8.6   *Grab Bars*

*Grab bars shall comply with **Chapter 62: Grab Bars - 609 - pp. 234-236**.*

*Side wall grab bars complying with this **Chapter - 604.5.1 - p. 112** located on the wall closest to the water closet, and a rear wall grab bar complying with this **Chapter - 604.5.2 - pp. 112 & 113**, shall be provided.*

604.9   *Ambulatory Accessible Compartments*

604.9.1   *General*

*Ambulatory accessible compartments shall comply with this **Chapter - 604.9**.*

604.9.2   *Size*

The minimum area of an ambulatory accessible compartment shall be 60 inches (1524mm) minimum in depth and 36 inches (914mm) in width.

604.9.3   *Doors*

*Toilet compartment doors, including door hardware, shall comply with **Chapter 56: Doors and Doorways - 404 - pp. 209-216**, except if the approach is to the latch side of the compartment door the clearance between the door side of the compartment and any obstruction shall be 42 inches (1067mm) minimum.*

The door shall be self-closing.

*A door pull complying with **Chapter 56: Doors and Doorways - 404.2.6 - p. 213** shall be placed on both sides of the door near the latch.*

Compartment doors shall not swing into the required minimum area of the compartment.

604.9.4   *Grab Bars*

*Grab bars shall comply with **Chapter 62: Grab Bars - 609 - pp. 234-236**.*

*Side wall grab bars complying with this **Chapter - 604.5.1 - p. 112** shall be provided on both sides of the compartment.*

See Diagram 37 - p. 342.

Chapter 27: IBC - ICC/ANSI A117.1 - WAC - Water Closet Compartment (continued)

604.10   *Water Closets and Toilet Compartments for Children's Use*

See Chapter 58: Water Closets and Toilet Compartments for Children's Use - 604.10 - pp. 221 & 222.

1101.2.5
WAC - 7/01/06
ICC/ANSI A117.1 - Section 604.11

Coat Hooks - Shelves - Dispensers - Other Fixtures

Coat hooks provided shall accommodate a forward reach or side reach complying with ***Chapter 54: Reach Ranges - 308 - pp. 206 & 207.***

Where provided, shelves shall be installed so that the top of the shelf is 40 inches (1016mm) maximum above the floor or ground.

Drying equipment, towel or other dispensers, and disposal fixtures shall be located 40 inches (1016mm) maximum above the floor or ground to any rack, operating controls, receptacle or dispenser.

Chapter 28:
IBC - ICC/ANSI A117.1
OTHER FEATURES AND FACILITIES
SINKS

IBC - Chapter 11	**Accessibility**
1109	**Other Features and Facilities**
1109.1	*General*

See Chapter 24: Other Features and Facilities - 1109.1 - p. 103.

1109.3	**Sinks**

Where sinks are provided, at least 5 percent, but not less than one, provided in accessible spaces shall comply with ICC/ANSI A117.1.

EXCEPTIONS:

1. Mop or service sinks are not required to be accessible.

2. Sinks designated for use by children in day care and primary school occupancies.

ICC/ANSI - Chapter 6	*Plumbing Elements and Facilities*
601	*General*
601.1	*Scope*

*Plumbing elements and facilities required to be accessible by scoping provisions adopted by the administrative authority shall comply with the applicable provisions of this **Chapter - 606.***

ICC/ANSI - 606	*Lavatories and Sinks*
606.1	*General*

*Accessible lavatories and sinks shall comply with this **Chapter - 606.***

606.2	*Clear Floor Space*

*A clear floor space complying with **Chapter 51: Clear Floor Space - 305.3 - p. 200**, positioned for forward approach, shall be provided.*

Chapter 28: IBC - ICC/ANSI A117.1 - Sinks (continued)

*Knee and toe clearance complying with **Chapter 52: Knee and Toe Clearance - 306 - pp. 202 & 203** shall be provided.*

The dip of the overflow shall not be considered in determining knee and toe clearances.

EXCEPTIONS:

1. *A parallel approach complying with **Chapter 57: Clear Floor Space - 305.3 - p. 200** shall be permitted to a kitchen sink in a space where a cook top or conventional range is not provided.*

2. *The requirement for knee and toe clearance shall not apply to a lavatory in a toilet and bathing facility for a single occupant, accessed only through a private office and not for common use or public use.*

3. *A knee clearance of 24 inches (610mm) minimum above the floor shall be permitted at lavatories and sinks used primarily by children ages 6 through 12 where the rim or counter surface is 31 inches (787mm) maximum above the floor.*

4. *A parallel approach complying with **Chapter 51: Clear Floor Space - 305 - pp. 200 & 201** shall be permitted at lavatories and sinks used primarily by children ages 5 and younger.*

5. *The requirement for knee and toe clearance shall not apply to more than one bowl of a multibowl sink.*

6. *A parallel approach shall be permitted at wet bars.*

606.3   **Height**

The front of lavatories and sinks shall be 34 inches (864mm) maximum above the floor, measured to the higher of the rim or counter surface.

*See **Diagram 38 - p. 343**.*

EXCEPTION:

*A lavatory in a toilet and bathing facility for a single occupant, accessed only through a private office and not for common use or public use, shall not be required to comply with **606.3 - (above)**.*

606.4   **Faucets**

*Faucets shall comply with **Chapter 55: Operable Parts - 309 - p. 208**.*

Chapter 28: IBC - ICC/ANSI A117.1 - Sinks (continued)

Hand-operated, metering faucets shall remain open for 10 seconds minimum.

606.5   *Lavatories with Enhanced Reach Range*

Where enhanced reach range is required at lavatories, faucets and soap dispenser controls, they shall have a reach depth of 11 inches (279mm) maximum or, if automatic, shall be activated within a reach depth of 11 inches (279mm) maximum.

Water and soap flow shall be provided with a reach depth of 11 inches (279mm) maximum.

EXCEPTION:

In Type A and Type B units, reach range for lavatory faucets and soap dispensers is not required.

606.6   *Exposed Pipes and Surfaces*

Water supply and drain pipes under lavatories and sinks shall be insulated or otherwise configured to protect against contact.

There shall be no sharp or abrasive surfaces under lavatories and sinks.

606.7   *Operable Parts*

*Operable parts on towel dispensers and hand dryers shall comply with **Table J** - (below).*

Table J
Maximum Reach Depth and Height

Maximum Reach Depth	.5-inch (12.7mm)	2 inches (51mm)	5 inches (127mm)	6 inches (152mm)	9 inches (229mm)	11 inches (279mm)
Maximum Reach Height	48-inch (1219mm)	46-inch (1168mm)	42 inches (1067mm)	40 inches (1016mm)	36 inches (914mm)	34 inches (864mm)

Chapter 29:
IBC - ICC/ANSI A117.1
OTHER FEATURES AND FACILITIES
KITCHENS AND KITCHENETTES

IBC - Chapter 11	**Accessibility**
1109	**Other Features and Facilities**
1109.1	**General**

See Chapter 24: Other Features and Facilities - 1109.1 - p. 103.

1109.4	**Kitchens - Kitchenettes - Wet Bars**

Where kitchens and kitchenettes are provided in accessible spaces or rooms, they shall be accessible in accordance with ICC/ANSI A117.1.

ICC/ANSI - Chapter 8	***Special Rooms and Spaces***
801	***General***
801.1	***Scope***

*Special rooms and spaces required to be accessible by the scoping provisions adopted by the administrative authority shall comply with the applicable provisions of this **Chapter - 804**.*

ICC/ANSI - 804	***Kitchens and Kitchenettes***
804.1	***General***

*Accessible kitchens and kitchenettes shall comply with this **Chapter - 804**.*

804.2	***Clearance***

*Where a pass-through kitchen is provided, clearances shall comply with **804.2.1 - (following page)**.*

*Where a U-shaped kitchen is provided, clearances shall comply with **804.2.2 - (following page)**.*

> *EXCEPTION:*
>
> > *Spaces that do not provide a cooktop or conventional range shall not be required to comply with **804.2 - (above & following page)**.*

Chapter 29: IBC - ICC/ANSI A117.1 - Kitchens and Kitchenettes (continued)

804.2.1   *Pass-Through Kitchens*

In pass-through kitchens where counters, appliances or cabinets are on two opposing sides, or where counters, appliances or cabinets are opposite a parallel wall, clearances between all opposing base cabinets, countertops, appliances, or walls within kitchen work areas shall be 40 inches (1016mm) minimum.

Pass-through kitchens shall have two entries.

See Diagrams 39(a),(b) - p. 344.

804.2.2   *U-Shaped Areas*

In kitchens enclosed on three contiguous sides, clearance between all opposing base cabinets, countertops, appliances, or walls within kitchen work areas shall be 60 inches (1524mm) minimum.

See Diagrams 40(a),(b) - p. 341.

804.3   *Work Surface*

Work surfaces shall comply with **Chapter 21: Dining Areas - 902 - pp. 96 & 97.**

 EXCEPTION:

  Spaces that do not provide a cooktop or conventional range shall not be required to provide an accessible work surface.

804.4   *Sinks*

Sinks shall comply with **Chapter 28: Lavatories and Sinks - 606 - pp. 118-120.**

804.5   *Storage*

At least 50 percent of shelf space in cabinets shall comply with **Chapter 35: Storage - 905 - p. 153.**

804.6   *Appliances*

Where provided, kitchen appliances shall comply with **804.6 - (below & following pages).**

804.6.1   *Clear Floor Space*

A clear floor space complying with **Chapter 51: Clear Floor Space - 305 - pp. 200 & 201** shall be provided at each kitchen appliance.

Chapter 29: IBC - ICC/ANSI A117.1 - Kitchens and Kitchenettes (continued)

Clear floor spaces are permitted to overlap.

804.6.2   ***Operable Parts***

*All appliance controls shall comply with **Chapter 55: Operable Parts - 309 - p. 208.***

    EXCEPTIONS:

    *1.   Appliance doors and door latching devices shall not be required to comply with **Chapter 55: Operable Parts - 309.4 - p. 208.***

    *2.   Bottom-hinged appliance doors, when in the open position, shall not be required to comply with **Chapter 55: Operable Parts - 309.3 - p. 208.***

804.6.3   ***Dishwasher***

A clear floor space, positioned adjacent to the dishwasher door, shall be provided.

The dishwasher door in the open position shall not obstruct the clear floor space for the dishwasher or an adjacent sink.

804.6.4   ***Range or Cooktop***

A clear floor space, positioned for a parallel or forward approach to the space for a range or cooktop, shall be provided.

*Where the clear floor space is positioned for a forward approach, knee and toe clearance complying with **Chapter 52: Knee and Toe Clearance - 306 - pp. 202 & 203** shall be provided.*

Where knee and toe space is provided, the underside of the range or cooktop shall be insulated or otherwise configured to prevent burns, abrasions, or electrical shock.

The location of controls shall not require reaching across burners.

804.6.5   ***Oven***

*Ovens shall comply with **804.6.5 - (below & following page).***

804.6.5.1   ***Side-Hinged Door Ovens***

*Side-hinged door ovens shall have a work surface complying with **804.3 - (preceding page)** positioned adjacent to the latch side of the oven door.*

Chapter 29: IBC - ICC/ANSI A117.1 - Kitchens and Kitchenettes (continued)

804.6.5.2   ***Bottom-Hinged Door Ovens***

*Bottom-hinged door ovens shall have a work surface complying with this **Chapter - 804.3 - p. 122** positioned adjacent to one side of the door.*

804.6.5.3   ***Controls***

Ovens shall have controls on front panels.

804.6.6   ***Refrigerator/Freezer***

Combination refrigerators and freezers shall have at least 50 percent of the freezer compartment shelves, including the bottom of the freezer, 54 inches (1372mm) maximum above the floor when the shelves are installed at the maximum heights possible in the compartment.

A clear floor space, positioned for a parallel approach to the space dedicated to a refrigerator/freezer shall be provided.

The centerline of the clear floor space shall be offset 24 inches (610mm) maximum from the centerline of the dedicated space.

Chapter 30:
IBC - ICC/ANSI A117.1 - WAC
OTHER FEATURES AND FACILITIES
DRINKING FOUNTAINS

IBC - Chapter 11   **Accessibility**

1109   **Other Features and Facilities**

1109.1   **General**

See Chapter 24: Other Features and Facilities - 1109.1 - p. 103.

<u>1109.5</u>   <u>**WAC - 7/01/05**</u>

<u>**Drinking Fountains**</u>

<u>On floors where drinking fountains are provided, at least 50 percent, but not less than one fountain, shall be accessible.</u>

<u>At least one fountain shall be mounted at a standard height.</u>

ICC/ANSI - Chapter 6   ***Plumbing Elements and Facilities***

601   *General*

601.1   *Scope*

*Plumbing elements and facilities required to be accessible by scoping provisions adopted by the administrative authority shall comply with the applicable provisions of this **Chapter - 602**.*

ICC/ANSI - 602   ***Drinking Fountains and Water Coolers***

602.1   *General*

*Accessible drinking fountains shall comply with this **Chapter - 602** and **Chapter 53: Protruding Objects - 307 - pp. 204 & 205**.*

602.2   *Clear Floor Space*

*A clear floor space complying with **Chapter 51: Clear Floor Space - 305 - pp. 200 & 201**, positioned for a forward approach to the drinking fountain, shall be provided.*

*Knee and toe space complying with **Chapter 52: Knee and Toe Clearance - 306 - pp. 202 & 203** shall be provided.*

Chapter 30: IBC - ICC/ANSI A117.1 - WAC - Drinking Fountains (continued)

The clear floor space shall be centered on the drinking fountain.

EXCEPTIONS:

1. Drinking fountains for standing persons.

*2. Drinking fountains primarily for children's use shall be permitted where the spout is 30 inches (762mm) maximum above the floor, and a parallel approach complying with **Chapter 51: Clear Floor Space - 305 - pp. 200 & 201,** centered on the drinking fountain, is provided.*

*3. In existing buildings, existing drinking fountains providing a parallel approach complying with **Chapter 51: Clear Floor Space - 305 - pp. 200 & 201,** centered on the drinking fountain, shall be permitted.*

*4. Where specifically permitted by the administrative authority, a parallel approach complying with **Chapter 51: Clear Floor Space - 305 - pp. 200 & 201,** centered on the drinking fountain, shall be permitted for drinking fountains that replace existing drinking fountains with a parallel approach.*

602.3 **Operable Parts**

*Operable parts shall comply with **Chapter 55: Operable Parts - 309 - p. 208.***

602.4 **Spout Outlet Height**

Spout outlets of wheelchair accessible drinking fountains shall be 36 inches (914mm) maximum above the floor.

Spout outlets of drinking fountains for standing persons shall be 38 inches (965mm) minimum and 43 inches (1092mm) maximum above the floor.

602.5 **Spout Location**

The spout shall be located 15 inches (381mm) minimum from the vertical support and 5 inches (127mm) maximum from the front edge of the drinking fountain, including bumpers.

Where only a parallel approach is provided, the spout shall be located 3-1/2 inches (89mm) maximum from the front edge of the drinking fountain, including bumpers.

See Diagrams 41(a),(b) - p. 346.

602.6 **Water Flow**

The spout shall provide a flow of water 4 inches (102mm) minimum in height.

The angle of the water stream from spouts within 3 inches (76mm) of the front of the drinking fountain shall be 30 degrees maximum, and from spouts between 3 inches (76mm) and 5 inches (127mm) from the front of the drinking fountain shall be 15 degrees maximum, measured horizontally relative to the front face of the drinking fountain.

Chapter 31:
IBC - ICC/ANSI A117.1 - WAC
OTHER FEATURES AND FACILITIES
ELEVATORS

IBC - Chapter 11   **Accessibility**

1109   **Other Features and Facilities**

1109.1   **General**

See Chapter 24: Other Features and Facilities - 1109.1 - p. 103.

<u>1109.6</u>   <u>**WAC - 7/01/05**</u>

<u>**Elevators**</u>

<u>Passenger elevators on an accessible route shall be accessible and comply with ICC/ANSI A117.1.</u>

<u>Elevators required to be accessible shall be designed and constructed to comply with Chapter 296-96 of the Washington Administrative Code.</u>

ICC/ANSI - Chapter 4   ***Accessible Routes***

401   ***General***

401.1   ***Scope***

*Accessible routes required by the scoping provisions adopted by the administrative authority shall comply with the applicable provisions of this **Chapter - 407**.*

ICC/ANSI - 407   ***Elevators***

407.1   ***General***

*Elevators shall comply with this **Chapter - 407** and ASME A17.1 listed in ICC/ANSI A117.7-2003 - Section 105.2.5.*

Elevators shall be passenger elevators as classified by ASME A17.1.

Elevator operation shall be automatic.

407.2   ***Elevator Landing Requirements***

*Elevator landings shall comply with **407.2** - (following pages).*

Chapter 31: IBC - ICC/ANSI A117.1 - WAC - Elevators (continued)

407.2.1   *Call Controls*

*Where elevator call buttons or keypads are provided, they shall comply with **407.2.1 - (below & following pages) and Chapter 55: Operable Parts - 309.4 - p. 208.***

Call buttons shall be raised or flush.

Objects beneath hall call buttons shall protrude 1-inch (25.4mm) maximum.

> *EXCEPTIONS:*
>
> *1.   Existing elevators shall be permitted to have recessed call buttons.*
>
> *2.   The restriction on objects beneath call buttons shall not apply to existing call buttons.*

407.2.1.1   *Height*

*Call buttons and keypads shall be located within one of the reach ranges specified in **Chapter 54: Reach Ranges - 308 - pp. 206 & 207,** measured to the centerline of the highest operable part.*

> *EXCEPTION:*
>
> *Existing call buttons and existing keypads shall be permitted to be located 54 inches (1372mm) maximum above the floor, measured to the centerline of the highest operable part.*

See Diagram 42 - p. 347.

407.2.1.2   *Size*

Call buttons shall be 3/4-inch (19.1mm) minimum in the smallest dimension.

> *EXCEPTION:*
>
> *Existing elevator call buttons shall not be required to comply with **407.2.1.2 - (above).***

407.2.1.3   *Clear Floor Space*

*A clear floor space complying with **Chapter 51: Clear Floor Space - 305 - pp. 200 & 201** shall be provided at call controls.*

407.2.1.4 *Location*

The call button that designates the up direction shall be located above the call button that designates the down direction.

EXCEPTION:

*Destination-oriented elevators shall not be required to comply with **407.2.1.4 - (above)**.*

407.2.1.5 *Signals*

Call buttons shall have visible signals to indicate when each call is registered and when each call is answered.

EXCEPTIONS:

1. *Destination-oriented elevators shall not be required to comply with **407.2.1.5 - (above)**, provided visible and audible signals complying with **407.2.1.7 - (below & following page)** are provided.*

2. *Existing elevators shall not be required to comply with **407.2.1.5 - (above)**.*

407.2.1.6 *Keypads*

*Where keypads are provided, keypads shall be in a standard telephone keypad arrangement and shall comply with this **Chapter - 407.4.7.2 - p. 139**.*

407.2.1.7 *Destination-Oriented Elevator Signals*

Destination-oriented elevators shall be provided with visible and audible signals to indicate which car is responding to a call.

The audible signal shall be activated by pressing a function button.

The function button shall be identified by the International Symbol for Accessibility and tactile indication.

*The International Symbol for Accessibility, complying with **Chapter 44: Signage - 703.6.3.1 - p. 181**, shall be 5/8-inch (15.9mm) in height and be a visual character complying with **Chapter 44: Signage - 703.2 - pp. 173-176**.*

The tactile indication shall be three raised dots, spaces 1/4-inch (6.4mm) at base diameter, in the form of an equilateral triangle.

Chapter 31: IBC - ICC/ANSI A117.1 - WAC - Elevators (continued)

The function button shall be located immediately below the keypad arrangement or floor butoons.

See Diagram 43 - p. 348.

407.2.2 **Hall Signals**

*Hall signals, including in-car signals, shall comply with **407.2.2 - (below & following page)**.*

407.2.2.1 **Visible and Audible Signals**

A visible and audible signal shall be provided at each hoistway entrance to indicate which car is answering a call and the car's direction of travel.

Where in-car signals are provided, they shall be visible from the floor area adjacent to the hall call buttons.

   EXCEPTIONS:

   *1.   Destination-oriented elevators shall not be required to comply with **407.2.2.1 - (above)**, provided visible and audible signals complying with   **407.2.1.7 - (preceding page & above)** are provided.*

   2.   In existing elevators, a signal indicating the direction of car travel shall not be required.

407.2.2.2 **Visible Signals**

Visible signal fixtures shall be centered at 72 inches (1829mm) minimum above the floor.

The visible signal elements shall be 2-1/2 inches (64mm) minimum measured along the vertical centerline of the element.

Signals shall be visible from the floor area adjacent to the hall call button.

See Diagrams 44(a),(b) - p. 349.

   EXCEPTIONS:

   1.   Destination-oriented elevators shall be permitted to have signals visible from the floor area adjacent to the hoistway entrance.

   *2.   Existing elevators shall not be required to comply with **407.2.2.2 - (above)**.*

407.2.2.3 *Audible Signals*

Audible signals shall sound once for the up direction and twice for the down direction, or shall have verbal annunciators that indicate the direction of elevator car travel.

Audible signals shall have a frequency of 1500 Hz maximum.

Verbal annunciators shall have a frequency of 300 Hz minimum and 3,000 Hz maximum.

The audible signal or verbal annunciator shall be 10 dBA minimum above ambient, but shall not exceed 80 dBA, measured at the hall call button.

EXCEPTIONS:

1. *Destination-oriented elevators shall not be required to comply with **407.2.2.3 - (above)**, provided the audible tone and verbal announcement is the same as those given at the call button or call button keypad.*

2. *The requirement for the frequency and range of audible signals shall not apply in existing elevators.*

407.2.2.4 *Differentiation*

Each destination-oriented elevator in a bank of elevators shall have audible and visible means for differentiation.

407.2.3 *Hoistway Signs*

*Signs at elevator hoistways shall comply with **407.2.3 - (below & following page)**.*

407.2.3.1 *Floor Designation*

*Floor designations shall be provided in tactile characters complying with **Chapter 44: Signage - 703.3 - pp. 176-178** located on both jambs of elevator hoistway entrances.*

Tactile characters shall be 2 inches (51mm) minimum in height.

A tactile star shall be provided on both jambs at the main entry level.

See Diagram 45 - p. 350.

Chapter 31: IBC - ICC/ANSI A117.1 - WAC - Elevators (continued)

407.2.3.2 *Car Designations*

Destination-oriented elevators shall provide are identification in tactile characters complying with **Chapter 44: Signage - 703.3 - pp. 176-178** *located on both jambs of the hoistway immediately below the floor designation.*

Tactile characters shall be 2 inches (51mm) minimum in height.

See Diagram 46 - p. 351.

407.2.4 *Destination Signs*

Where signs indicate that elevators do not serve all landings, signs in tactile characters complying with **Chapter 44: Signage - 703.3 - pp. 176-178** *shall be provided above the hall call button fixture.*

> *EXCEPTION:*
>
> > *Destination-oriented elevator systems shall not be required to comply with* **407.2.4** *- (above).*

407.3 *Elevator Door Requirements*

Hoistway and elevator car doors shall comply with **407.3** *- (below & following pages).*

407.3.1 *Type*

Elevator doors shall be horizontal sliding type.

Car gates shall be prohibited.

407.3.2 *Operation*

Elevator hoistway and car doors shall open and close automatically.

> *EXCEPTION:*
>
> > *Existing manually operated hoistway swing doors shall be permitted, provided:*
> >
> > a) *they comply with* **Chapter 56: Doors and Doorways - 404.2.2 - pp. 209 & 210 and 404.2.8 - p. 214;**
> >
> > b) *the car closing is not initiated until the hoistway door is closed.*

Chapter 31: IBC - ICC/ANSI A117.1 - WAC - Elevators (continued)

407.3.3   ***Reopening Device***

*Elevator doors shall be provided with a reopening device complying with **407.3.3 - (below)** that shall stop and reopen a car door and hoistway door automatically if the door becomes obstructed by an object or person.*

    EXCEPTION:

        *In existing elevators, manually operated doors shall not be required to comply with **407.3.3 - (above & below)**.*

407.3.3.1   ***Height***

The reopening device shall be activated by sensing an obstruction passing through the opening at 5 inches (127mm) nominal and 29 inches (737mm) nominal above the floor.

407.3.3.2   ***Contact***

The reopening device shall not require physical contact to be activated, although contact shall be permitted before the door reverses.

407.3.3.3   ***Duration***

The reopening device shall remain effective for 20 seconds minimum.

407.3.4   ***Door and Signal Timing***

The minimum acceptable time from notification that a car is answering a call until the doors of that car starts to close shall be calculated from the following equation:

$T = D/(1.5 \text{ ft/s})$ or $T = (D/(445 \text{ mm/s}) = 5$ seconds minimum, where T equals the total time in seconds and D equals the distance (in feet or millimeters) from the point in the lobby or corridor 60 inches (1524mm) directly in front of the farthest call button controlling that car to the centerline of its hoistway door.

    EXCEPTIONS:

    1.   *For cars with in-car lanterns, T shall be permitted to begin when the signal is visible from the point 60 inches (1524mm) directly in front of the farthest hall call button and the audible signal is sounded.*

    2.   *Destination-oriented elevators shall not be required to comply with **407.3.4 - (above)**.*

Chapter 31: IBC - ICC/ANSI A117.1 - WAC - Elevators (continued)

407.3.5   ***Door Delay***

Elevator doors shall remain fully open in response to a car call for 3 seconds minimum.

407.3.6   ***Width***

*Elevator door clear opening width shall comply with **Table K** - (below).*

    EXCEPTION:

        *In existing elevators, a power-operated car door complying with **Chapter 56: Doors and Doorways - 404.2.2 - pp. 209 & 210** shall be permitted.*

Table K
Minimum Dimensions of Elevator Cars[1]

Door Location	Door Clear Opening Width	Inside Car Side to Side	Inside Car Back Wall to Front Return	Inside Car Back Wall to Inside Face of Door
Centered	42 inches (1067mm)	80 inches (2032mm)	51 inches (1295mm)	54 inches (1372mm)
Side (Off Center)	36 inches (914mm)[1]	68 inches (1727mm)	51 inches (1295mm)	54 inches (1372mm)
Any	36 inches (914mm)[1]	54 inches (1372mm)	80 inches (2032mm)	80 inches (2032mm)
Any	36 inches (914mm)[1]	60 inches (1524mm)[2]	60 inches (1524mm)[2]	60 inches (1524mm)[2]

[1]   A tolerance of minus 5/8-inch (16mm) is permitted.

[2]   Other car configurations that provide a 36-inch (914mm) clear door opening width and a turning space complying with **Chapter 50: Turning Space - 304 - pp. 198 & 199** with the door closed are permitted.

407.4   ***Elevator Car Requirements***

*Elevator cars shall comply with **407.4** - (below & following pages).*

407.4.1   ***Car Dimensions***

*Inside dimensions of elevator cars shall comply with **Table K** - (above).*

Chapter 31: IBC - ICC/ANSI A117.1 - WAC - Elevators (continued)

EXCEPTION:

> *Existing elevator car configurations that provide a clear floor area of 16 square feet (1.5m²) minimum, and provide a clear inside dimension of 36 inches (914mm) minimum in width and 54 inches (1372mm) minimum in depth, shall be permitted.*

See Diagrams 47(a),(b),(c),(d),(e) - p. 352.

407.4.2 *Floor Surfaces*

Floor surfaces in elevator cars shall comply with **Chapter 48: Floor Surfaces - 302 - pp. 195 & 196.**

407.4.3 *Platform to Hoistway Clearance*

The clearance between the car platform sill and the edge of any hoistway landing shall be in compliance with ASME/ANSI A17.1 listed in ICC/ANSI A117.1-2003 - Section 105.2.5.

407.4.4 *Leveling*

Each car shall be equipped with a self-leveling feature that will automatically bring and maintain the car at floor landings within a tolerance of 1/2-inch (12.7mm) under rated loading to zero loading conditions.

407.4.5 *Illumination*

The level of illumination at the car controls, platform, car threshold and car landing sill shall be 5 footcandles (53.8 lux) minimum.

407.4.6 *Elevator Car Controls*

Where provided, elevator car controls shall comply with **407.4.6 - (below & following pages)** *and* **Chapter 55: Operable Parts - 309 - p. 208.**

EXCEPTION:

> *In existing elevators, where a new car operating panel complying with* **407.4.6 - (below & following pages)** *is provided, existing car operating panels shall not be required to comply with* **407.4.6 - (below & following pages).**

407.4.6.1 *Location*

Controls shall be located within one of the reach ranges specified in **Chapter 54: Reach Ranges - 308 - pp. 206 & 207.**

Chapter 31: IBC - ICC/ANSI A117.1 - WAC - Elevators (continued)

EXCEPTIONS:

1. *Where the elevator panel serves more than 16 openings and a parallel approach to the controls is provided, buttons with floor designations shall be permitted to be 54 inches (1372mm) maximum above the floor.*

2. *In existing elevators, where a parallel approach is provided to the controls, car control buttons with floor designations shall be permitted to be located 54 inches (1372mm) maximum above the floor.*

   *Where the panel is changed, it shall comply with **407.4.6.1 - (preceding page & above)**.*

407.4.6.2 **Buttons**

*Car control buttons with floor designations shall be raised or flush, and shall comply with **407.4.6.2 - (below)**.*

EXCEPTION:

In existing elevators, buttons shall be permitted to be recessed.

407.4.6.2.1 **Size**

Buttons shall be 3/4 inches (19.1mm) minimum in their smallest dimension.

1101.2.4 <u>**WAC - 7/01/06**</u>
<u>**ICC/ANSI A117.1 - Section 407.4.6.2.2**</u>

<u>**Arrangement**</u>

<u>This section is not adopted.</u>

407.4.6.3 **Keypads**

*Car control keypads shall be in a standard telephone keypad arrangement and shall comply with this **Chapter - 407.4.7.2 - p. 139**.*

407.4.6.4 **Emergency Controls**

*Emergency controls shall comply with **407.4.6.4 - (following page)**.*

Chapter 31: IBC - ICC/ANSI A117.1 - WAC - Elevators (continued)

407.4.6.4.1   *Height*

Emergency control buttons shall have their centerlines 35 inches (889mm) minimum above the floor.

407.4.6.4.2   *Location*

Emergency controls, including the emergency alarm, shall be grouped at the bottom of the panel.

407.4.7   **Designations and Indicators of Car Controls**

Designations and indicators of car controls shall comply with **407.4.7 - (below & following page)**.

    EXCEPTIONS:

    1.   In existing elevators, where a new car operating panel complying with **407.4.7 - (below & following page)** is provided, existing car operating panels shall not be required to comply with **407.4.7 - (below & following page)**.

    2.   Where existing building floor designations differ from the arrangement required by **407.4.6.2.2 - (preceding page)**, or are alphanumeric, a new operating panel shall be permitted to use such existing building floor designations.

407.4.7.1   *Buttons*

Car control buttons shall comply with **407.4.7.1 - (below & following page)**.

407.4.7.1.1   *Type*

Control buttons shall be identified by tactile characters complying with **Chapter 44: Signage - 703.3 - pp. 176-178.**

407.4.7.1.2   *Location*

Tactile character and Braille designations shall be placed immediately to the left of the control button to which the designations apply.

Where a negative number is used to indicate a negative floor, the Braille designation shall be a cell with the dots 3 and 6 followed by the ordinal number.

    EXCEPTION:

        Where space on an existing car operating panel precludes tactile markings to the left of the control button, markings shall be placed as near to the control button as possible.

Chapter 31: IBC - ICC/ANSI A117.1 - WAC - Elevators (continued)

407.4.7.1.3 *Symbols*

The control button for the emergency stop, alarm, door open, door close, main entry floor, and phone, shall be identified with tactile symbols as shown in **Diagram 49 - p. 354.**

407.4.7.1.4 *Visible Indicators*

Buttons with floor designations shall be provided with visible indicators to show that a call has been registered.

The visible indication shall extinguish when the car arrives at the designated floor.

407.4.7.2 *Keypads*

Keypads shall be shall be identified by visual characters complying with **Chapter 44: Signage - 703.2 - pp. 173-176** *and shall be centered on the corresponding keypad button.*

The number five key shall have a single raised dot.

The dot shall have a base diameter of 0.118-inch (3mm) minimum to 0.120-inch (3.05mm) maximum, and a height of 0.025-inch (0.64mm) minimum to 0.037-inch (0.94mm) maximum.

407.4.8 *Elevator Car Call Sequential Step Scanning*

Elevator car call sequential step scanning shall be provided where car control buttons are provided more than 48 inches (1219mm) above the floor, as permitted by this **Chapter - 407.4.6.1 - EXCEPTION #1 - p. 137.**

Floor selection shall be accomplished by applying momentary or constant pressure to the up or down scan button.

The up scan button shall sequentially select floors above the current floor.

The down scan button shall sequentially select floors below the current floor.

When pressure is removed from the up or down scan button for more than 2 seconds, the last floor selected shall be registered as a car call.

The up and down scan button shall be located adjacent to or immediately above the emergency control buttons.

407.4.9 *Car Position Indicators*

Audible and visible car position indicators shall be provided in elevator cars.

407.4.9.1 *Visible Indicators*

*Visible indicators shall comply with **407.4.9.1 - (below)**.*

407.4.9.1.1 *Size*

Characters shall be 1/2-inch (12.7mm) minimum in height.

407.4.9.1.2 *Location*

Indicators shall be located above the car control panel or above the door.

407.4.9.1.3 *Floor Arrival*

As the car passes a floor and when a car stops at a floor served by the elevator, the corresponding character shall illuminate.

EXCEPTION:

*Destination-oriented elevators shall not be required to comply with **407.4.9.1.3 - (above)**, provided the visible indicators extinguish when the call has been answered.*

407.4.9.1.4 *Destination Indicator*

In destination-oriented elevators, a display shall be provided in the car with visible indicators to show car destinations.

407.4.9.2 *Audible Indicators*

*Audible indicators shall comply with **407.4.9.2 - (below & following page)**.*

407.4.9.2.1 *Signal Type*

The signal shall be an automatic verbal annunciator that announces the floor at which the car is about to stop.

The verbal announcement indicating the floor shall be completed prior to the initiation of the door opening.

Chapter 31: IBC - ICC/ANSI A117.1 - WAC - Elevators (continued)

EXCEPTION:

For elevators other than destination-oriented elevators that have a rated speed of 200 feet per minute (1 m/s) or less, a non-verbal audible signal with a frequency of 1500 Hz maximum that sounds as the car passes or is about to stop at a floor served by the elevator shall be permitted.

407.4.9.2.2 **Signal Level**

The verbal annunciator shall be 10 dBA minimum above ambient, but shall not exceed 80 dBA, measured at the annunciator.

407.4.9.2.3 **Frequency**

The verbal annunciator shall have a frequency of 300 Hz minimum to 3,000 Hz maximum.

407.4.10 **Emergency Communications**

Emergency two-way communication systems between the elevator car and a point outside the hoistway shall comply with **407.4.10 - (below)** *and ASME/ANSI A17.1 listed in ICC/ANSI A117.1-2003 - Section 105.2.5.*

407.4.10.1 **Height**

The highest operable part of a two-way communication system shall comply with **Chapter 54: Reach Ranges - 308 - pp. 206 & 207**.

407.4.10.2 **Identification**

Tactile characters complying with **Chapter 50: Signage - 703.3 - pp. 176-178** *and symbols complying with this* **Chapter - 407.4.7.1.3 - p. 139** *shall be provided adjacent to the device.*

Chapter 32:
ICC/ANSI A117.1
LIMITED-USE/LIMITED-APPLICATION ELEVATORS

ICC/ANSI - Chapter 4 *Accessible Routes*

401 *General*

401.1 *Scope*

Accessible routes required by the scoping provisions adopted by the administrative authority shall comply with the applicable provisions of this **Chapter - 408**.

ICC/ANSI - 408 ***Limited-Use/Limited-Application Elevators***

408.1 *General*

Limited-use/limited-application elevators shall comply with this **Chapter - 408** and ASME A17.1 listed in ICC/ANSI A117.1-2003 - Section 105.2.5.

Elevator operation shall be automatic.

408.2 ***Elevator Landing Requirements***

Landings serving limited-use/limited application elevators shall comply with **408.2 - (below)**.

408.2.1 *Call Controls*

Elevator call buttons and keypads shall comply with **Chapter 31: Elevators - 407.2.1 - pp. 129-131**.

408.2.2 *Hall Signals*

Hall signals shall comply with **Chapter 31: Elevators - 407.2.2 - pp. 131 & 132**.

408.2.3 *Hoistway Signs*

Signs at elevator hoistways shall comply with **Chapter 31: Elevators - 407.2.3 - pp. 132 & 133**.

408.3 ***Elevator Door Requirements***

Elevator hoistway doors shall comply with **408.3 - (following page)**.

Chapter 32: ICC/ANSI A117.1 - Limited-Use/Limited-Application Elevators (continued)

408.3.1   ***Sliding Doors***

*Sliding hoistway and car doors shall comply with **Chapter 31: Elevators - 407.3.1 through 407.3.3 - pp. 133 & 134 and 408.3.3 - (below).***

408.3.2   ***Swinging Doors***

*Swinging hoistway doors shall open and close automatically and shall comply with **408.3.2 - (below), Chapter 56: Doors and Doorways - 404 - pp. 209-216, and Chapter 31: Elevators - 407.3.2 - p. 133.***

408.3.2.1   ***Power Operation***

Swinging doors shall be power-operated and shall comply with ANSI/BHMA A156.19 listed in ICC/ANSI A117.1-2003 - Section 105.2.3.

408.3.2.2   ***Duration***

Power-operated swinging doors shall remain open for 20 seconds minimum when activated.

408.3.3   ***Door Location and Width***

Car doors shall provide a clear opening width of 32 inches (813mm) minimum.

Car doors shall be positioned at a narrow end of the car.

     EXCEPTION:

         Car doors that provide a clear opening width of 36 inches (914mm) minimum shall be permitted to be located on adjacent sides of cars that provide a clear floor area of 51 inches (1295mm) in width and 51 inches (1295mm) in depth.

408.4   ***Elevator Car Requirements***

*Elevator cars shall comply with **408.4 - (below & following page).***

408.4.1   ***Inside Dimensions of Elevator Cars***

Elevator cars shall provide a clear floor area of 42 inches (1067mm) minimum in width, and 54 inches (1372mm) minimum in depth.

See Diagrams 50(a),(b),(c) - p. 355.

Chapter 32: ICC/ANSI A117.1 - Limited-Use/Limited-Application Elevators (continued)

EXCEPTIONS:

1. Cars that provide a 51-inch (1295mm) minimum clear floor width shall be permitted to provide 51 inches (1295mm) minimum clear floor depth.

2. For installations in existing buildings, elevator cars that provide a clear floor area of 15 square feet (1.4m²) minimum, and provide a clear inside dimension of 36 inches (914mm) minimum in width and 54 inches (1372mm) minimum in depth, shall be permitted.

408.4.2   ***Floor Surfaces***

Floor surfaces in elevator cars shall comply with **Chapter 48: Floor Surfaces - 302 - pp. 195 & 196.**

408.4.3   ***Platform to Hoistway Clearance***

The clearance between the car platform sill and the edge of any hoistway landing shall be in compliance with ASME/ANSI A17.1 listed in ICC/ANSI A117.1-2003 - Section 105.2.5.

408.4.4   ***Leveling***

Elevator car leveling shall comply with **Chapter 31: Elevators - 407.4.4 - p. 136.**

408.4.5   ***Illumination***

Elevator car illumination shall comply with **Chapter 31: Elevators - 407.4.5 - p. 136.**

408.4.6   ***Elevator Car Controls***

Elevator car controls shall comply with **Chapter 31: Elevators - 407.4.6 - pp. 136-138.**

Control panels shall be centered on a side wall.

408.4.7   ***Designations and Indicators of Car Controls***

Designations and indicators of car controls shall comply with **Chapter 31: Elevators - 407.4.7 - pp. 138 & 139.**

408.4.8   ***Emergency Communications***

Car emergency signaling devices complying with **Chapter 31: Elevators - 407.4.10 - p. 141** *shall be provided.*

Chapter 33:

ICC/ANSI A117.1
PRIVATE RESIDENCE ELEVATORS

ICC/ANSI - Chapter 4 **Accessible Routes**

401 *General*

401.1 *Scope*

Accessible routes required by the scoping provisions adopted by the administrative authority shall comply with the applicable provisions of this **Chapter - 409**.

ICC/ANSI - 409 **Private Residence Elevators**

409.1 *General*

Private residence elevators shall comply with this **Chapter - 409** *and ASME/ANSI A17.1 listed in ICC/ANSI A117.1-2003 - Section 105.2.5.*

Elevator operation shall be automatic.

> *EXCEPTION:*
>
> > *Elevators complying with* **Chapter 31 - 407 - pp. 128-141** *or* **Chapter 32 - 408 - pp. 142-144**.

409.2 *Call Buttons*

Call buttons at elevator landings shall comply with **Chapter 55: Operable Parts - 309 - p. 208**.

Call buttons shall be 3/4-inch (19.1mm) minimum in their smallest dimension.

409.3 *Doors and Gates*

Elevator car and hoistway doors and gates shall comply with **409.3 - (below & following page)** *and* **Chapter 56: Doors and Doorways - 404 - pp. 209-216**.

> *EXCEPTION:*
>
> > *The maneuvering clearances required by* **Chapter 56: Doors and Doorways - 404.2.3 - pp. 210-212** *shall not apply for approaches to the push side of swinging doors.*

Chapter 33: ICC/ANSI A117.1 - Private Residence Elevators (continued)

409.3.1   ***Power Operation***

Elevator car doors and gates shall be power-operated and shall comply with ANSI/BHMA A156.19 listed in ICC/ANSI A117.1-2003 - Section 105.2.3.

Elevator cars with a single opening shall have low energy power-operated hoistway doors and gates.

    EXCEPTION:

        For elevators with a car that has more than one opening, the hoistway doors and gates shall be permitted to be of the manual-open, self-close type.

409.3.2   ***Duration***

Power-operated doors and gates shall remain open for 20 seconds minimum when activated.

409.3.3   ***Door or Gate Location***

*Car gates or doors shall be positioned at a narrow end of the clear floor area required by **409.4.1** - (below).*

409.4   ***Elevator Car Requirements***

*Elevator cars shall comply with **409.4** - (below & following pages).*

409.4.1   ***Inside Dimension of Elevator Cars***

Elevator cars shall provide a clear floor area 36 inches (914mm) minimum in width and 48 inches (1219mm) minimum in depth.

409.4.2   ***Floor Surfaces***

*Floor surfaces in elevator cars shall comply with **Chapter 48: Floor Surfaces - 302 - pp. 195 & 196**.*

409.4.3   ***Platform ro Hoistway Clearance***

The clearance between the car platform sill and the edge of any hoistway landing shall be 1-1/4 inches (32mm) maximum.

409.4.4   ***Leveling***

Each car shall automatically stop at a floor landing within a tolerance of 1/2-inch (12.7mm) under rated loading to zero loading conditions.

Chapter 33: ICC/ANSI A117.1 - Private Residence Elevators (continued)

409.4.5   *Illumination*

The level of illumination at the car controls, platform, and car threshold and landing sill shall be 5 footcandles (54 lux) minimum.

409.4.6   *Elevator Car Controls*

*Elevator car controls shall comply with **409.4.6 - (below) and Chapter 55: Operable Parts - 309.4 - p. 208**.*

409.4.6.1   *Buttons*

Control buttons shall be 3/4-inch (19.1mm) minimum in their smallest dimension.

Control buttons shall be raised or flush.

409.4.6.2   *Height*

*Buttons with floor designations shall comply with **Chapter 55: Operable Parts - 309.3 - p. 208**.*

409.4.6.3   *Location*

Controls shall be on a sidewall, 12 inches (305mm) minimum from any adjacent wall.

*See **Diagram 51 - p. 356**.*

409.4.7   *Emergency Communications*

*Emergency communications systems shall comply with **409.4.7 - (below & following page)**.*

409.4.7.1   *Type*

A telephone and emergency signal device shall be provided in the car.

409.4.7.2   *Operable Parts*

*The telephone and emergency signaling device shall comply with **Chapter 55: Operable Parts - 309.3 - p. 208**.*

409.4.7.3   *Compartment*

*If the device is in a closed compartment, the compartment door hardware shall comply with **Chapter 55: Operable Parts - 309 - p. 208**.*

409.4.7.4 *Cord*

The telephone cord shall be 29 inches (737mm) in length.

Chapter 34:
IBC - ICC/ANSI A117.1
OTHER FEATURES AND FACILITIES
LIFTS

IBC - Chapter 11   **Accessibility**

1109   **Other Features and Facilities**

1109.1   **General**

See Chapter 24: Other Features and Facilities - 1109.1 - p. 103.

1109.7   **Lifts**

Platform (wheelchair) lifts are permitted to be a part of a required accessible route in new construction where indicated in *Items 1 to 7 - (below).*

Platform (wheelchair) lifts shall be installed in accordance with ASME A18.1.

1. An accessible route to a performing area and speaker's platforms in occupancies in Group A.

2. An accessible route to wheelchair spaces required to comply with the wheelchair space dispersion requirements of *Chapter 20: Assembly Area Seating - 1108.2.2 to 1108.2.4 - pp. 85-87.*

3. An accessible route to spaces that are not open to the general public with an occupant load of not more than five.

4. An accessible route within a dwelling or sleeping unit.

5. An accessible route to wheelchair seating spaces located in outdoor dining terraces in A-5 occupancies where the means of egress from the dining terraces to a public way is open to the outdoors.

6. An accessible route to raised judge's benches, clerk's stations, jury boxes, witness stands, and other raised or depressed areas in a court.

7. An accessible route where existing exterior site constraints make use of a ramp or elevator infeasible.

ICC/ANSI - Chapter 4   **Accessible Routes**

401   **General**

401.1   **Scope**

*Accessible routes required by the scoping provisions adopted by the administrative authority shall comply with the applicable provisions of this **Chapter - 410**.*

ICC/ANSI - 410   **Platform Lifts**

410.1   **General**

*Platform lifts shall comply with this **Chapter - 410** and ASME/ANSI A18.1 listed in ICC/ANSI A117.1-2003 - Section 105.2.6.*

Platform lifts shall not be attendant-operated and shall provide unassisted entry and exit from the lift.

410.2   **Lift Entry**

*Lifts with doors or gates shall comply with **410.2.1** - (below & following page).*

*Lifts with ramps shall comply with **410.2.2** - (following page).*

410.2.1   **Doors and Gates**

*Doors and gates shall be low energy power-operated doors or gates complying with **Chapter 56: Doors and Doorways - 404.3 - pp. 215 & 216**.*

Doors shall remain open for 20 seconds minimum.

End door clear opening width shall be 32 inches (813mm) minimum.

Side door clear opening width shall be 42 inches (1067mm) minimum.

See Diagram 52 - p. 357.

     EXCEPTION:

         Lifts serving two landings maximum and having doors or gates on opposite sides shall be permitted to have self-closing manual doors or gates.

Chapter 34: IBC - ICC/ANSI A117.1 - Lifts (continued)

410.2.2   ***Ramps***

End ramps shall be 32 inches (813mm) minimum in width.

Side ramps shall be 42 inches (1067mm) minimum in width.

410.3   ***Floor Surfaces***

*Floor Surfaces of platform lifts shall comply with **Chapter 48: Floor Surfaces - 302 - pp. 195 & 196**.*

410.4   ***Platform to Runway Clearance***

The clearance between the platform sill and the edge of any runway landing shall be 1-1/4 inches (32mm) maximum.

410.5   ***Clear Floor Space***

*Clear floor space of platform lifts shall comply with **Chapter 51: Clear Floor Space - 305 - pp. 200 & 201**.*

410.6   ***Operable Parts***

*Controls for platform lifts shall comply with **Chapter 55: Operable Parts - 309 - p. 208**.*

Chapter 35:
IBC - ICC/ANSI A117.1
OTHER FEATURES AND FACILITIES
STORAGE

IBC - Chapter 11	**Accessibility**
1109	**Other Features and Facilities**
1109.1	**General**

See Chapter 24: Other Features and Facilities - 1109.1 - p. 103.

1109.8	**Storage**

Where fixed or built-in storage elements such as cabinets, shelves, medicine cabinets, closets and drawers are provided in required accessible spaces, at least one of each type shall contain storage space complying with ICC/ANSI A117.1.

1109.8.1	**Lockers**

Where lockers are provided in accessible spaces, at least five percent, but not less than one, of each type shall be accessible.

1109.8.2	**Shelving and Display Units**

Self-service shelves and display units shall be located on an accessible route.

Such shelving and display units shall not be required to comply with reach-range provisions.

1109.8.3	**Coat Hooks and Folding Shelves**

Where coat hooks and folding shelves are provided in toilet rooms, toilet compartments, or in dressing, fitting or locker rooms, at least one of each type shall be accessible and shall be provided in accessible toilet rooms without toilet compartments, accessible toilet compartments and accessible dressing, fitting and locker rooms.

ICC/ANSI - Chapter 9	*Built-in Furnishings and Equipment*
901	*General*
901.1	*Scope*

*Built-in furnishings and equipment required to be accessible by the scoping provisions adopted by the administrative authority shall comply with the applicable provisions of this **Chapter - 905**.*

Chapter 35: IBC - ICC/ANSI A117.1 - Storage (continued)

ICC/ANSI - 905   ***Storage Facilities***

905.1   ***General***

*Accessible storage facilities shall comply with this **Chapter - 905**.*

905.2   ***Clear Floor Space***

*A clear floor space complying with **Chapter 51: Clear Floor Space - 305 - pp. 200 & 201** shall be provided.*

905.3   ***Height***

*Accessible storage elements shall comply with at least one of the reach ranges specified in **Chapter 54: Reach Ranges - 308 - pp. 206 & 207**.*

905.4   ***Operable Parts***

*Operable parts of storage facilities shall comply with **Chapter 55: Operable Parts - 309.4 - p. 208**.*

Chapter 36:
IBC - ICC/ANSI A117.1 - WAC
OTHER FEATURES AND FACILITIES
DETECTABLE WARNINGS

IBC - Chapter 11		Accessibility
1109		**Other Features and Facilities**
1109.1		*General*

See Chapter 24: Other Features and Facilities - 1109.1 - p. 103.

1109.9 <u>WAC - 7/01/05</u>

<u>**Detectable Warnings**</u>

<u>Passenger transit platform edges bordering a drop-off and not protected by platform screens or guards shall have a detectable warning.</u>

<u>Curb ramps shall have detectable warnings.</u>

<u>EXCEPTION:</u>

<u>Detectable warnings are not required at bus stops.</u>

ICC/ANSI - Chapter 7	**Communication Elements and Features**
701	*General*
701.1	*Scope*

Communications elements and features required to be accessible by the scoping provisions adopted by the administrative authority shall comply with the applicable provisions of this **Chapter - 705.**

ICC/ANSI - 705	*Detectable Warnings*
705.1	*General*

Detectable warning surfaces shall comply with this **Chapter - 705.**

705.2 *Standardization*

Detectable warning surfaces shall be standard within a building, facility, site, or complex of buildings.

Chapter 36: IBC - ICC/ANSI A117.1 - Detectable Warnings (continued)

EXCEPTION:

> *In facilities that have both interior and exterior locations, detectable warnings in exterior locations shall not be required to comply with **705.4 - (below)**.*

705.3   *Contrast*

Detectable warning surfaces shall contrast visually with adjacent surfaces, either light-on-dark or dark-on-light.

705.4   *Interior Locations*

Detectable warning surfaces in interior locations shall differ from adjoining walking surfaces in resiliency or sound-on-cane contact.

705.5   *Truncated Domes*

*Detectable warning surfaces shall have truncated domes complying with **705.5 - (below)**.*

705.5.1   *Size*

Truncated domes shall have a base diameter of 0.9- inch (22.9mm) minimum to 1.4-inch (36mm) maximum, and a top diameter of 50 percent minimum to 65 percent maximum of base diameter.

705.5.2   *Height*

Truncated domes shall have a height of 0.2 inches (5.8mm).

705.5.3   *Spacing*

Truncated domes shall have a center-to-center spacing of 1.6 inches (41mm) minimum and 2.4 inches (61mm) maximum, and a base-to-base spacing of 0.65 inches (16.5mm) minimum, measured between the most adjacent domes on the grid.

705.5.4   *Alignment*

Truncated domes shall be aligned in a square grid pattern.

See Diagrams 53(a),(b) - p. 358.

Chapter 37:

INTERNATIONAL BUILDING CODE
OTHER FEATURES AND FACILITIES
ASSEMBLY AREA SEATING

IBC - Chapter 11   **Accessibility**

1109   **Other Features and Facilities**

1109.1   **General**

See Chapter 24: Other Features and Facilities - 1109.1 - p. 103.

1109.10   **Assembly Area Seating**

Assembly areas with fixed seating in every occupancy shall comply with *Chapter 20: Assembly Area Seating - 1108.2 - pp. 85-89* for accessible seating and assistive listening devices.

Chapter 38:

INTERNATIONAL BUILDING CODE
OTHER FEATURES AND FACILITIES
SEATING AT TABLES - COUNTERS
WORK SURFACES

IBC - Chapter 11   **Accessibility**

1109   **Other Features and Facilities**

1109.1   **General**

See Chapter 24: Other Features and Facilities - 1109.1 - p. 103.

1109.11   **Seating at Tables - Counters - Work Surfaces**

Where seating or standing space at fixed or built-in tables, counters or work surfaces is provided in accessible spaces, at least 5 percent of the seating and standing spaces, but not less than one, shall be accessible.

In Group I-3 Occupancy visiting areas, at least 5 percent, but not less than one, cubicle or counter shall be accessible on both the visitor and detainee sides.

    EXCEPTIONS:

    1. Check-writing surfaces at check-out aisles not required to comply with ***Chapter 39: Service Facilities - 1109.12.2 - pp. 158 & 159*** are not required to be accessible.

    2. In Group I-3 Occupancies, the counter or cubicle on the detainee side is not required to be accessible at noncontact visiting areas or in areas not serving accessible holding cells or sleeping units.

1109.11.1   **Dispersion**

Accessible fixed or built-in seating at tables, counters or work surfaces shall be distributed throughout the space or facility containing such elements.

Chapter 39:
IBC - ICC/ANSI A117.1
OTHER FEATURES AND FACILITIES
SERVICE FACILITIES

IBC - Chapter 11   Accessibility

1109   Other Features and Facilities

1109.1   General

See Chapter 24: Other Features and Facilities - 1109.1 - p. 103.

1109.12   Service Facilities

Service facilities shall provide for accessible features in accordance with *1109.12.1 through 1109.12.5 - (below & following page).*

1109.12.1   Dressing - Fitting - Locker Rooms

Where dressing rooms, fitting rooms, or locker rooms are provided, at least 5 percent, but not less than one, of each type of use in each cluster provided shall be accessible.

1109.12.2   Check-out Aisles

Where check-out aisles are provided, accessible check-out aisles shall be provided in accordance with *Table L - (following page).*

Where check-out aisles serve different functions, at least one accessible check-out aisle shall be provided for each function.

Where check-out aisles serve different functions, accessible check-out aisles shall be provided in accordance with *Table L - (following page)* for each function.

Where check-out aisles are dispersed throughout the building or facility, accessible check-out aisles shall also be dispersed.

Traffic control devices, security devices and turnstiles located in accessible check-out aisles or lanes shall be accessible.

    EXCEPTION:

        Where the area of the selling space is less than 5,000 square feet (465 m²), only one check-out aisle is required to be accessible.

Chapter 39: IBC - ICC/ANSI A117.1 - Service Facilities (continued)

Table L
Accessible Check-out Aisles

Total Check-out Aisles of Each Function	Minimum Number of Accessible Check-out Aisles of Each Function
1 to 4	1
5 to 8	2
9 to 15	3
Over 15	3, plus 20% of additional aisles

1109.12.3 **Point of Sales and Service Counters**

Where counters are provided for sales or distribution of goods or services, at least one of each type provided shall be accessible.

Where such counters are dispersed throughout the building or facility, accessible counters shall also be dispersed.

1109.12.4 **Food Service Lines**

Food service lines shall be accessible.

Where self-service shelves are provided, at least 50 percent, but not less than one, of each type provided shall be accessible.

1109.12.5 **Queue and Waiting Lines**

Queue and waiting lines servicing accessible counters or check-out aisles shall be accessible.

ICC/ANSI - Chapter 8   *Special Rooms and Spaces*

801   *General*

801.1   *Scope*

Special rooms and spaces required to be accessible by the scoping provisions adopted by the administrative authority shall comply with the applicable provisions of this **Chapter - 803.**

Chapter 39: IBC - ICC/ANSI A117.1 - Service Facilities (continued)

ICC/ANSI - 803 **Dressing - Fitting - Locker Rooms**

803.1 *General*

Accessible dressing, fitting, and locker rooms shall comply with this **Chapter - 803**.

803.2 **Turning Space**

A turning space complying with **Chapter 50: Turning Space - 304 - pp. 198 & 199** shall be provided within the room.

803.3 **Door Swing**

Doors shall not swing into the room unless a clear floor space complying with **Chapter 51: Clear Floor Space - 305.3 - p. 200** is provided within the room, beyond the arc of the door swing.

803.4 **Benches**

A bench complying with **903 - (below & following page)** shall be provided within the room.

803.5 **Coat Hooks and Shelves**

Accessible coat hooks provided within the room shall accommodate a forward reach or side reach complying with **Chapter 54: Reach Ranges - 308 - pp. 206 & 207**.

Where provided, a shelf shall be 40 inches (1016mm) minimum and 48 inches (1219mm) maximum above the floor.

ICC/ANSI - Chapter 9 **Built-in Furnishings and Equipment**

901 *General*

901.1 *Scope*

Built-in furnishings and equipment required to be accessible by the scoping provisions adopted by the administrative authority shall comply with the applicable provisions of this **Chapter - 903**.

ICC/ANSI - 903 **Benches**

903.1 *General*

Accessible benches shall comply with this **Chapter - 903**.

See Diagrams 54(a),(b) - p. 359.

Chapter 39: IBC - ICC/ANSI A117.1 - Service Facilities (continued)

903.2 *Clear Floor Space*

*A clear floor space complying with **Chapter 51: Clear Floor Space - 305 - pp. 200 & 201**, positioned for parallel approach to an end of the bench seat, shall be provided.*

903.3 *Size*

Benches shall have seats 42 inches (1067mm) minimum in length, and 20 inches (508mm) minimum and 24 inches (610mm) maximum in depth.

903.4 *Back Support*

The bench shall provide for back support or shall be affixed to a wall.

Back support shall be 42 inches (1067mm) minimum in length and shall extend from a point 2 inches (51mm) maximum above the seat surface to a point 18 inches (457mm) minimum above the seat surface.

Back support shall be 2-1/2 inches (64mm) maximum from the rear edge of the seat measured horizontally.

903.5 *Height*

The top of the bench seat shall be 17 inches (432mm) minimum and 19 inches (483mm) maximum above the floor, measured to the top of the seat.

903.6 *Structural Strength*

Allowable stresses shall not be exceeded for materials used where a vertical or horizontal force of 250 pounds (1112N) is applied at any point on the seat, fastener mounting device, or supporting structure.

903.7 *Wet Locations*

Where provided in wet locations, the surface of the seat shall be slip-resistant and shall not accumulate water.

ICC/ANSI - Chapter 9 ***Built-in Furnishings and Equipment***

901 *General*

901.1 *Scope*

*Built-in furnishings and equipment required to be accessible by the scoping provisions adopted by the administrative authority shall comply with the applicable provisions of this **Chapter - 904**.*

Chapter 39: IBC - ICC/ANSI A117.1 - Service Facilities (continued)

ICC/ANSI - 904   *Sales and Service Counters*

904.1   *General*

*Accessible sales and service counters shall comply with this **Chapter - 904** as applicable.*

904.2   *Approach*

*All portions of counters required to be accessible shall be located adjacent to a walking surface complying with **Chapter 4: Accessible Route - 403 - pp. 13-15.***

904.3   *Sales and Service Counters*

*Sales and service counters shall comply with **904.3.1** or **904.3.2** - (below).*

The accessible portion of the countertop shall extend the same depth as the sales and service countertop.

904.3.1   *Parallel Approach*

A portion of the counter surface 36 inches (914mm) minimum in length and 36 inches (914mm) maximum in height above the floor shall be provided.

Where the counter surface is less than 36 inches (914mm) in length, the entire counter surface shall be 36 inches (914mm) maximum in height above the floor.

*A clear floor space complying with **Chapter 51: Clear Floor Space - 305 - pp. 200 & 201**, positioned for a parallel approach adjacent to the accessible counter, shall be provided.*

904.3.2   *Forward Approach*

A portion of the counter surface 30 inches minimum in length and 36 inches maximum in height above the floor shall be provided.

*A clear floor space complying with **Chapter 51: Clear Floor Space - 305 - pp. 200 & 201**, positioned for a forward approach to the accessible counter, shall be provided.*

*Knee and toe clearance complying with **Chapter 52: Knee and Toe Clearance - 306 - pp. 202 & 203** shall be provided under the accessible counter.*

904.4   *Check-out Aisles*

*Check-out aisles shall comply with **904.4** - (following page).*

Chapter 39: IBC - ICC/ANSI A117.1 - Service Facilities (continued)

904.4.1 *Aisle*

Aisles shall comply with **Chapter 4: Accessible Route - 403 - pp. 13-15.**

904.4.2 *Check-out Counters*

The check-out counter surface shall be 38 inches (965mm) maximum in height above the floor.

The top of the counter edge protection shall be 2 inches (51mm) maximum above the top of the counter surface on the aisle side of the check-out counter.

See Diagram 55 - p. 360.

904.4.3 *Check Writing Surfaces*

Where provided, check writing surfaces shall comply with **Chapter 21: Dining Areas - 902.3 - p. 96.**

904.5 *Food Service Lines*

Counters in food service lines shall comply with **904.5 - (below).**

904.5.1 *Self-Service Shelves and Dispensing Devices*

Self-service shelves and dispensing devices for tableware, dishware, condiments, food and beverages shall comply with **Chapter 54: Reach Ranges - 308 - pp. 206 & 207.**

904.5.2 *Tray Slides*

The tops of tray slides shall be 28 inches (711mm) minimum and 34 inches (864mm) maximum above the floor.

904.6 *Security Glazing*

Where counters or teller windows have security glazing to separate personnel from the public, a method to facilitate voice communication shall be provided.

Telephone handset devices, if provided, shall comply with **Chapter 65: Telephones - 704.3 - p. 241.**

Chapter 40:

INTERNATIONAL BUILDING CODE
OTHER FEATURES AND FACILITIES
CONTROLS - OPERATING MECHANISMS
HARDWARE

IBC - Chapter 11	Accessibility
1109	Other Features and Facilities
1109.1	General

See Chapter 24: Other Features and Facilities - 1109.1 - p. 103.

1109.13 **Controls - Operating Mechanisms - Hardware**

Controls, operating mechanisms and hardware intended for operation by the occupant, including switches that control lighting and ventilation, and electrical convenience outlets, in accessible spaces, along accessible routes or as parts of accessible elements shall be accessible.

EXCEPTIONS:

1. Operable parts that are intended for use only by service or maintenance personnel shall not be required to be accessible.

2. Electrical or communication receptacles serving a dedicated use shall not be required to be accessible.

3. Where two or more outlets are provided in a kitchen above a length of countertop that is uninterrupted by a sink or appliance, one outlet shall not be required to be accessible.

4. Floor electrical receptacles shall not be required to be accessible.

5. HVAC diffusers shall not be required to be accessible.

6. Except for light switches, where redundant controls are provided for a single element, one control in each space shall not be required to be accessible.

Chapter 41:
IBC - ICC/ANSI A117.1
OTHER FEATURES AND FACILITIES
OPERABLE WINDOWS

IBC - Chapter 11	**Accessibility**
1109	**Other Features and Facilities**
1109.1	**General**

See Chapter 24: Other Features and Facilities - 1109.1 - p. 103.

1109.13.1	**Operable Windows**

Where operable windows are provided in rooms that are required to be accessible in accordance with *Chapter 9: Group I Occupancies - 1107.5.1.1, 1107.5.2.1, 1107.5.3.1, 1107.5.4 - pp. 29 & 30 and Chapter 10: Group R Occupancies - 1107.6.1.1 - pp. 32 & 33, 1107.6.2.2.1 - p. 35, and 1107.6.4.1 - p. 35,* at least one window in each room shall be accessible and each required operable window shall be accessible.

    EXCEPTION:

        Accessible windows are not required in bathrooms or kitchens.

ICC/ANSI - Chapter 5	*General Site and Building Elements*
501	*General*
501.1	*Scope*

*General site and building elements required to be accessible by the scoping provisions adopted by the administrative authority shall comply with the applicable provisions of this **Chapter - 506.***

ICC/ANSI - 506	*Windows*

*Accessible windows shall have operable parts complying with **Chapter 55: Operable Parts - 309 - p. 208.***

Chapter 42:

IBC - WAC
OTHER FEATURES AND FACILITIES
RECREATIONAL FACILITIES

IBC - Chapter 11   **Accessibility**

1109   **Other Features and Facilities**

1109.1   **General**

See Chapter 24: Other Features and Facilities - 1109.1 - p. 103.

1109.14   **Recreational Facilities**

Recreational facilities shall be provided with accessible features in accordance with *1109.14.1 through 1109.14.3 - (below).*

1109.14.1   **Facilities Serving a Single Building**

In Group R-2 and R-3 Occupancies where recreational facilities are provided serving a single building containing Type A or Type B units, 25 percent, but not less than one, of each type of recreational facility shall be accessible.

Every recreational facility of each type on a site shall be considered to determine the total number of each type that is required to be accessible.

1109.14.2   **Facilities Serving Multiple Buildings**

In Group R-2 and R-3 Occupancies on a single site where multiple buildings containing Type A or Type B units are served by recreational facilities, 25 percent, but not less than one, of each type of recreational facility serving each building shall be accessible.

The total number of each type of recreational facility that is required to be accessible shall be determined by considering every recreational facility of each type serving each building on the site.

<u>1109.14.3</u>   <u>**WAC - 7/01/05**</u>

<u>**Other Occupancies**</u>

<u>All recreational facilities not falling within the purview of *1109.14.1 or 1109.14.2 - (above)* shall be accessible as required by *Chapter 71: Recreation Facilities - Federal Final Rule - pp. 267-305.*</u>

Chapter 43:
IBC - ICC/ANSI A117.1
OTHER FEATURES AND FACILITIES
STAIRWAYS

IBC - Chapter 11   **Accessibility**

1109   **Other Features and Facilities**

1109.1   **General**

See Chapter 24: Other Features and Facilities - 1109.1 - p. 103.

1109.15   **Stairways**

Stairways located along accessible routes connecting floor levels that are not connected by an elevator shall be designed and constructed to comply with 2003 International Building Code - Chapter 10, and ICC/ANSI A117.1.

ICC/ANSI - Chapter 5   ***General Site and Building Elements***

501   ***General***

501.1   ***Scope***

*General site and building elements required to be accessible by the scoping provisions adopted by the administrative authority shall comply with the applicable provisions of this **Chapter - 504**.*

ICC/ANSI - 504   ***Stairways***

504.1   ***General***

*Accessible stairs shall comply with this **Chapter - 504**.*

504.2   ***Treads and Risers***

All steps on a flight of stairs shall have uniform riser height and uniform tread depth.

Risers shall be 4 inches (102mm) minimum and 7 inches (178mm) maximum in height.

Treads shall be 11 inches (279mm) minimum in depth.

See Diagram 56 - p. 361.

Chapter 43: IBC - ICC/ANSI A117.1 - Stairways (continued)

504.3 *Open Risers*

Open risers shall not be permitted.

504.4 *Tread Surface*

Stair treads shall comply with **Chapter 48: Floor Surfaces - 302 - pp. 195 & 196** *and shall have a slope not steeper than 1:48.*

504.5 *Nosings*

The radius of curvature at the leading edge of the tread shall be 1/2-inch (13mm) maximum.

Nosings that project beyond risers shall have the underside of the leading edge curved or beveled.

Risers shall be permitted to slope under the tread at an angle of 30 degrees maximum from vertical.

The permitted projection of the nosing shall be 1-1/2 inches (38mm) maximum over the tread or floor below.

The leading 2 inches (51mm) of the tread shall have visual contrast of dark-on-light or light-on-dark from the remainder of the tread.

See Diagrams 57(a),(b),(c),(d) - p. 362.

504.6 *Handrails*

Stairs shall have handrails complying with **Chapter 17: Means of Egress - Handrails - pp. 77-80.**

504.7 *Wet Conditions*

Stair treads and landings subject to wet conditions shall be designed to prevent the accumulation of water.

504.8 *Lighting*

Lighting for interior stairways shall comply with **504.8 - *(below & following page)*.**

504.8.1 *Luminance Level*

Lighting facilities shall be capable of providing 10 footcandles (108 lux) of luminance measured at the center of tread surfaces and on landing surfaces within 24 inches (610mm) of step nosings.

Chapter 43: IBC - ICC/ANSI A117.1 - Stairways (continued)

504.8.2 *Lighting Controls*

*If provided, occupancy-sensing automatic controls shall activate the stairway lighting so the luminance level required by **504.8.1 - (preceding page)** is provided on the entrance landing, each stair flight adjacent to the entrance landing, and on the landings above and below the entrance landing prior to any step being used.*

504.9 *Stair Level Identification*

*Stair level identification signs in tactile characters complying with **Chapter 44: Signage - 703.3 - pp. 176-178** shall be located at each floor level landing in all enclosed stairways adjacent to the door leading from the stairwell into the corridor to identify the floor level.*

The exit door discharging to the outside or to the level of exit discharge shall have a tactile sign stating "EXIT."

Chapter 44:

IBC - ICC/ANSI A117.1 - WAC
SIGNAGE

IBC - Chapter 11	**Accessibility**
1110	**Signage**
1110.1	**Signs**

Required accessible elements shall be identified by the International Symbol of Accessibility *(Diagram 58(a) - p. 363)* at the following locations:

1. Accessible parking spaces as required by *Chapter 6: Parking - 1106.1 - pp. 18 & 19* except where the total number of parking spaces provided is four or less.

2. Accessible passenger loading zones.

3. Accessible areas of refuge required by the 2003 International Building Code - Section 1007.6 and *1007.6.3 through 1007.6.5 - (following pages).*

4. Accessible rooms where multiple single-user toilet or bathing rooms are clustered at a single location.

5. Accessible entrances where not all entrances are accessible.

6. Accessible check-out aisles where not all aisles are accessible.

    The sign, where provided, shall be above the check-out aisle in the same location as the check-out aisle number or type of check-out identification.

7. Unisex toilet and bathing rooms.

8. Accessible dressing, fitting and locker rooms where not all such rooms are accessible.

1110.2	**Directional Signage**

Directional signage indicating the route to the nearest like accessible element shall be provided at the following locations.

These directional signs shall include the International Symbol of Accessibility:

1. Inaccessible building entrances.

Chapter 44: IBC - ICC/ANSI A117.1 - WAC - Signage (continued)

2. Inaccessible public toilets and bathing facilities.

3. Elevators not serving an accessible route.

4. At each separate-sex toilet and bathing room indicating the location of the nearest unisex toilet or bathing room where provided in accordance with *Chapter 26: Unisex Toilet and Bathing Rooms - 1109.2.1 - pp. 107 & 108.*

5. At exits and elevators serving a required accessible space, but not providing an approved accessible means of egress, signage shall be provided in accordance with *1007.7 - (following page).*

1110.3 **Other Signs**

Signage indicating special accessibility provisions shall be provided as shown:

1. Each assembly area required to comply with *Chapter 20: Assembly Area Seating - 1108.2.7 - pp. 87 & 88,* shall provide a sign notifying patrons of the availability of assistive listening systems. shall be provided at ticket offices or similar locations.

    EXCEPTION:

    Where ticket offices or windows are provided, signs are not required at each assembly area provided that signs are displayed at each ticket office or window informing patrons of the availability of assistive listening systems.

2. At each door to an egress stairway, exit passageway and exit discharge, signage shall be provided in accordance with this *Chapter - 1011.3 - p. 173.*

3. At areas of refuge, signage shall be provided in accordance with *1007.6.3 through 1007.6.5 - (below & following page).*

4. At areas for assisted rescue, signage shall be provided in accordance with *1007.8.3 - (following page).*

1007.6.3 **Two-Way Communication**

Areas of refuge shall be provided with a two-way communication system between the area of refuge and a central control point.

If the central control point is not constantly attended, the area of refuge shall also have controlled access to a public telephone system.

Chapter 44: IBC - ICC/ANSI A117.1 - WAC - Signage (continued)

Location of the central control point shall be approved by the fire department.

The two-way communication system shall include both audible and visible signals.

1007.6.4 **Instructions**

In areas of refuge that have a two-way emergency communications system, instructions on the use of the area under emergency conditions shall be posted adjoining the communications system.

The instructions shall include all of the following:

1. Directions to find other means of egress.

2. Persons able to use the exit stairway do so as soon as possible, unless they are assisting others.

3. Information on planned availability of assistance in the use of stairs or supervised operation of elevators and how to summon such assistance.

4. Directions for use of the emergency communications system.

1007.6.5 **Identification**

Each door providing access to an area of refuge from an adjacent floor area shall be identified by a sign complying with ICC/ANSI A117.1, stating: AREA OF REFUGE, and including the International Symbol of Accessibility.

See Diagram 58(a) - p. 363.

Where exit sign illumination is required by *1011.2 - (following page),* the area of refuge sign shall be illuminated.

Additionally, tactile signage complying with ICC/ANSI A117.1 shall be located at each door to an area of refuge.

1007.7 **Signage**

At exits and elevators serving a required accessible space but not providing an approved accessible means of egress, signage shall be installed indicating the location of accessible means of egress.

1007.8.3 **Identification**

Exterior areas for assisted rescue shall have identification as required for area of refuge that complies with *1007.6.5 - (above).*

Chapter 44: IBC - ICC/ANSI A117.1 - WAC - Signage (continued)

1011.2 **Illumination**

Exit signs shall be internally or externally illuminated.

> EXCEPTION:
>
> > Tactile signs required by *1011.3 - (below)* need not be provided with illumination.

1011.3 **Tactile Exit Signs**

A tactile sign stating EXIT and complying with ICC/ANSI A117.1 shall be provided adjacent to each door to an egress stairway, an exit passageway and the exit discharge.

ICC/ANSI - Chapter 7   *Communication Elements and Features*

701   *General*

701.1   *Scope*

*Communications elements and features required to be accessible by the scoping provisions adopted by the administrative authority shall comply with the applicable provisions of this **Chapter - 703**.*

ICC/ANSI - 703   *Signs*

703.1   *General*

*Accessible signs shall comply with this **Chapter - 703**.*

703.2   *Visual Characters*

703.2.1   *General*

*Visual characters shall comply with **703.2** - (below & following pages).*

> EXCEPTION:
>
> > *Visual characters complying with this **Chapter - 703.3** - pp. 176-178, shall not be required to comply with **703.2** - (above, below & following pages).*

703.2.2   *Case*

Characters shall be uppercase, lowercase, or a combination of both.

Chapter 44: IBC - ICC/ANSI A117.1 - WAC - Signage (continued)

703.2.3 *Style*

Characters shall be conventional in form.

Characters shall not be italic, oblique, script, highly decorative, or of other unusual forms.

703.2.4 ***Character Height***

The uppercase letter "I" shall be used to determine the allowable height of all characters of a font.

The uppercase letter "I" of the font shall have a minimum height complying with **Table M - (below).**

Viewing distance shall be measured as the horizontal distance between the character and an obstruction preventing further approach toward the sign.

Table M
Visual Character Height

Height above Floor to Baseline of Character	*Horizontal Viewing Distance*	*Minimum Character Height*
40 inches (1016mm) to less than or equal to 70 inches (1778mm)	*Less than 6 feet (1829mm)*	*5/8-inch (15.9mm)*
	6 feet (1829mm) and greater	*5/8-inch (15.9mm), plus 1/8-inch (3.2mm) per foot (305mm) of viewing distance above 6 feet (1829mm)*
Greater than 70 inches (1778mm) to less than or equal to 120 inches (3048mm)	*Less than 15 feet (4572mm)*	*2 inches (51mm)*
	15 feet (4572mm) and greater	*2 inches (51mm), plus 1/8-inch (3.2mm) per foot (305mm) of viewing distance above 15 feet (4572mm)*
Greater than 120 inches (3048mm)	*Less than 21 feet (6400mm)*	*3 inches (76mm)*
	21 feet (6400mm) and greater	*3 inches (76mm), plus 1/8-inch (3.2mm) per foot (305mm) of viewing distance above 21 feet (6400mm)*

Chapter 44: IBC - ICC/ANSI A117.1 - WAC - Signage (continued)

703.2.5   ***Character Width***

The uppercase letter "O" shall be used to determine the allowable width of all characters of a font.

The width of the uppercase letter "O" of the font shall be 55 percent minimum and 110 percent maximum of the height of the uppercase "I" of the font.

703.2.6   ***Stroke Width***

The uppercase letter "I" shall be used to determine the allowable stroke width of all characters of a font.

The stroke width shall be 10 percent minimum and 30 percent maximum of the height of the uppercase "I" of the font.

703.2.7   ***Character Spacing***

Spacing shall be measured between the two closest points of adjacent characters within a message, excluding word spaces.

Spacing between individual characters shall be 10 percent minimum and 35 percent maximum of the character height.

703.2.8   ***Line Spacing***

Spacing between the baselines of separate lines of characters within a message shall be 135 percent minimum to 170 percent maximum of the character height.

703.2.9   ***Height above Floor***

Visual characters shall be 40 inches (1016mm) minimum above the floor of the viewing position, measured to the baseline of the character.

*Heights shall comply with **Table M - (preceding page)**, based on the size of the characters on the sign.*

> *EXCEPTION:*
>
> *Visual characters indicating elevator car controls shall not be required to comply with **703.2.9 - (above)**.*

703.2.10   ***Finish and Contrast***

Characters and their background shall have a non-glare finish.

Chapter 44: IBC - ICC/ANSI A117.1 - WAC - Signage (continued)

Characters shall contrast with their background, with either light characters on a dark background, or dark characters on a light background.

703.3 **Tactile Characters**

703.3.1 **General**

*Tactile characters shall comply with **703.3 - (below & following pages)**, and shall be duplicated in Braille complying with this **Chapter - 703.4 - pp. 179 & 180**.*

703.3.2 **Depth**

Tactile characters shall be raised 1/32-inch (0.794mm) minimum above their background.

703.3.3 **Case**

Characters shall be uppercase.

703.3.4 **Style**

Characters shall be sans serif.

Characters shall not be italic, oblique, script, highly decorative, or of other unusual forms.

703.3.5 **Character Height**

The uppercase letter "I" shall be used to determine the allowable height of all characters of a font.

The height of the uppercase letter "I" of the font, measured vertically from the baseline of the character, shall be 5/8-inch (16mm) minimum, and 2 inches (51mm) maximum.

See Diagram 59 - p. 364.

    EXCEPTION:

        Where separate tactile and visual characters with the same information are provided, the height of the tactile uppercase letter "I" shall be permitted to be 1/2-inch (12.7mm) minimum.

703.3.6 **Character Width**

The uppercase letter "O" shall be used to determine the allowable width of all characters of a font.

Chapter 44: IBC - ICC/ANSI A117.1 - WAC - Signage (continued)

The width of the uppercase letter "O" of the font shall be 55 percent minimum, and 110 percent maximum the height of the uppercase "I" of the font.

703.3.7 **Stroke Width**

*Tactile character stroke width shall comply with **703.3.7 - (below)**.*

The uppercase letter "I" of the font shall be used to determine the allowable stroke width of all characters of a font.

703.3.7.1 **Maximum**

The stroke width shall be 15 percent maximum of the height of the uppercase letter "I" measured at the top surface of the character, and 30 percent maximum of the height of the uppercase letter "I" measured at the base of the character.

703.3.7.2 **Minimum**

Where characters are both visual and tactile, the stroke width shall be 10 percent minimum of the height of the uppercase letter "I."

703.3.8 **Character Spacing**

Character spacing shall be measured between the two closest points of adjacent tactile characters within a message, excluding word spaces.

Spacing between individual tactile characters shall be 1/8-inch (3.2mm) minimum measured at the top surface of the characters, 1/16-inch (1.6mm) minimum measured at the base of the characters, and four times the tactile character stroke width maximum.

Characters shall be separated from raised borders and decorative elements 3/8-inch (9.5mm) minimum.

703.3.9 **Line Spacing**

Spacing between the baselines of separate lines of tactile characters within a message shall be 135 percent minimum and 170 percent maximum of the tactile character height.

703.3.10 **Height above Floor**

Tactile characters shall be 48 inches (1219mm) minimum above the floor, measured to the baseline of the lowest tactile character and 60 inches (1524mm) maximum above the floor, measured to the baseline of the highest tactile character.

See Diagram 60 - p. 365.

Chapter 44: IBC - ICC/ANSI A117.1 - WAC - Signage (continued)

EXCEPTION:

Tactile characters for elevator car controls shall not be required to comply with **703.3.10 - (preceding page).**

703.3.11   **Location**

Where a tactile sign is provided at a door, the sign shall be alongside the door at the latch side.

Where a tactile sign is provided at double doors with one active leaf, the sign shall be located on the inactive leaf.

Where a tactile sign is provided at double doors with two active leaves, the sign shall be to the right of the right-hand door.

Where there is no wall space on the latch side of a single door, or to the right side of double doors, signs shall be on the nearest adjacent wall.

Signs containing tactile characters shall be located so that a clear floor area 18-inches (457mm) minimum by 18-inches (457mm) minimum, centered on the tactile characters, is provided beyond the arc of any door swing between the closed position and 45 degrees open position.

See Diagram 61 - p. 366.

EXCEPTION:

Signs with tactile characters shall be permitted on the push side of doors with closers and without hold-open devices.

703.3.12   **Finish and Contrast**

Characters and their backgrounds shall have a non-glare finish.

Characters shall contrast with their background with either light characters on a dark background, or dark characters on a light background.

EXCEPTION:

Where separate tactile characters and visual characters with the same information are provided, tactile characters are not required to have non-glare finish or to contrast with their background.

Chapter 44: IBC - ICC/ANSI A117.1 - WAC - Signage (continued)

703.4 *Braille*

703.4.1 *General*

*Braille shall be contracted (Grade 2) Braille and shall comply with **703.4 - (below & following page)**.*

703.4.2 *Uppercase Letters*

The indication of an uppercase letter or letters shall only be used before the first word of sentences, proper nouns and names, individual letters of the alphabet, initials, or acronyms.

703.4.3 *Dimensions*

*Braille dots shall have a domed or rounded shape and shall comply with **Table N - (below)**.*

See Diagram 62 - p. 367.

Table N
Braille Dimensions

Measurement Range	Minimum in inches	Maximum in inches
Dot base diameter	0.059-inch (1.5mm)	0.063-inch (1.6mm)
Distance between two dots in the same cell	0.090-inch (2.3mm)	0.100-inch (2.5mm)
Distance between corresponding dots in adjacent cells[1]	0.241-inch (6.1mm)	0.300-inch (7.6mm)
Dot Height	0.025-inch (0.6mm)	0.037-inch (0.9mm)
Distance between corresponding dots from one cell directly below[1]	0.395-inch (10.0mm)	0.400-inch (10.1mm)

[1]Measured center to center

703.4.4 *Position*

Braille shall be below the corresponding text.

If text is multilined, Braille shall be placed below entire text.

Chapter 44: IBC - ICC/ANSI A117.1 - WAC - Signage (continued)

Braille shall be separated 3/8-inch (9.5mm) minimum from any other tactile characters and 3/8-inch (9.5mm) minimum from raised borders and decorative elements.

Braille provided on elevator car controls shall be separated 3/16-inch (4.8mm) minimum either directly below or adjacent to the corresponding raised characters or symbols.

See Diagram 63 - p. 368.

703.4.5 **Mounting Height**

Braille shall be 48 inches (1219mm) minimum and 60 inches (1524mm) maximum above the floor, measured to the baseline of the Braille cells.

　　EXCEPTION:

　　　　*Elevator car controls shall not be required to comply with **703.4.5 - (above)**.*

703.5 ***Pictograms***

703.5.1 ***General***

*Pictograms shall comply with **703.5 - (below)**.*

703.5.2 ***Pictogram Field***

Pictograms shall have a field of 6 inches (152mm) minimum in height.

Characters or Braille shall not be located in the pictogram field.

703.5.3 ***Finish and Contrast***

Pictograms and their fields shall have a non-glare finish.

Pictograms shall contrast with their fields, with either a light pictogram on a dark field or a dark pictogram on a light field.

703.5.4 ***Text Descriptors***

Where text descriptors for pictograms are required, they shall be located directly below the pictogram field.

*Text descriptors shall comply with **703.3 and 703.4 - (preceding pages & above)**.*

See Diagram 64 - p. 369.

Chapter 44: IBC - ICC/ANSI A117.1 - WAC - Signage (continued)

703.6   ***Symbols of Accessibility***

703.6.1   ***General***

*Symbols of accessibility shall comply with **703.6 - (below)**.*

703.6.2   ***Finish and Contrast***

Symbols of accessibility and their backgrounds shall have a non-glare finish.

Symbols of accessibility shall contrast with their backgrounds, with either a light symbol on a dark background or a dark symbol on a light background.

703.6.3   ***Symbols***

703.6.3.1   ***International Symbol of Accessibility***

*The International Symbol of Accessibility shall comply with **Diagram 58(a) - p. 363**.*

1101.2.9   **WAC - 7/01/06**
                       ICC/ANSI A117.1 - Section 703.6.3.1

                        International Symbol of Accessibility

Where the International Symbol of Accessibility is required, it shall be proportioned complying with ***Diagram 58(a) - p. 363**.*

All interior and exterior signs depicting the International Symbol of Accessibility shall be white on a blue background.

703.6.3.2   ***International Symbol of TTY***

*The International Symbol of TTY shall comply with **Diagram 58(b) - p. 363**.*

703.6.3.3   ***Assistive Listening Systems***

*Assistive listening systems shall be identified by the International Symbol of Access for Hearing Loss complying with **Diagram 58(d) - p. 363**.*

703.6.3.4   ***Volume-Controlled Telephones***

*Telephones with volume controls shall be identified by a pictogram of a telephone handset with radiating sound waves on a square field complying with **Diagram 58(c) - p. 363**.*

Chapter 44: IBC - ICC/ANSI A117.1 - WAC - Signage (continued)

703.7   ***Remote Infrared Audible Sign (RIAS) System***

703.7.1   ***General***

*Remote Infrared Audible Sign Systems shall comply with **703.7 - (below)**.*

703.7.2   ***Transmitters***

*Where provided, Remote Infrared Audible Sign Transmitters shall be designed to communicate with receivers complying with **703.7.3 - (below)**.*

703.7.3   ***Remote Infrared Audible Sign Receivers***

703.7.3.1   ***Frequency***

Basic speech messages shall be frequency modulated at 25 kHz, with a +/- 2.5 kHz deviation, and shall have an infrared wavelength from 850 to 950 nanometer (nm).

703.7.3.2   ***Optical Power Density***

Receiver shall produce a 12 decibel (dB) signal-plus-noise-to-noise ratio with a 1 kHz modulation tone at +/- 2.5 kHz deviation of the 25 kHz subcarrier at an optical power density of 26 picowatts per square millimeter measured at the receiver photosensor aperture.

703.7.3.3   ***Audio Output***

The audio output from an internal speaker shall be at 75 dBA minimum at 18 inches (457mm) with a maximum distortion of 10 percent.

703.7.3.4   ***Reception Range***

The receiver shall be designed for a high dynamic range and capable of operating in full-sun background illumination.

703.7.3.5   ***Multiple Signals***

A receiver provided for the capture of the stronger of two signals in the receiver field of view shall provide a received power ratio on the order of 20 dB for negligible interference.

703.8   ***Pedestrian Signals***

Accessible pedestrian signals shall comply with Section 4E.06 - Accessible Pedestrian Signals, and Section 4E.08 - Accessible Pedestrian Signal Detectors, of the Manual on Uniform Traffic Control Devices listed in ICC/ANSI A117.1-2003 - Section 105.2.1.

Chapter 44: IBC - ICC/ANSI A117.1 - WAC - Signage (continued)

EXCEPTION:

Pedestrian signals are not required to comply with the requirement for choosing audible tones.

Chapter 45:

IBC - APPENDIX (E107)
SUPPLEMENTARY ACCESSIBILITY REQUIREMENTS
SIGNAGE

IBC - E107 **Signage**

E107.1 **Signs**

Required accessible portable toilets and bathing facilities shall be identified by the International Symbol of Accessibility.

See Diagram 58(a) - p. 363.

E107.2 **Designations**

Interior and exterior signs identifying permanent rooms and spaces shall be tactile.

Where pictograms are provided as designations of interior rooms and spaces, the pictograms shall have tactile text descriptors.

Signs required to provide tactile characters and pictograms shall comply with ICC/ANSI A117.1.

EXCEPTIONS:

1. Exterior signs that are not located at the door to the space they serve are not required to comply.

2. Building directories, menus, seat and row designations in assembly areas, occupant names, building addresses and company names and logos are not required to comply.

3. Signs in parking facilities are not required to comply.

4. Temporary (seven days or less) signs are not required to comply.

E107.3 **Directional and Informational Signs**

Signs that provide direction to, or information about, permanent interior spaces of the site and facilities shall contain visual characters complying with ICC/ANSI A117.1.

Chapter 45: IBC - Appendix (E107) - Signage (continued)

EXCEPTION:

> Building directories, personnel names, company or occupant names and logos, menus and temporary (seven days or less) signs are not required to comply with ICC/ANSI A117.1.

E107.4 **Other Signs**

Signage indicating special accessibility provisions shall be provided as follows:

1. At bus stops and terminals, signage must be provided in accordance with *E108.4 - (below)*.

2. At fixed facilities and stations, signage must be provided in accordance with *E109.2.2 through E109.2.2.3 - (below & following page)*.

3. At airports, terminal information systems must be provided in accordance with *E110.3 - (following page)*.

E108 **Bus Stops**

E108.4 **Signs**

New bus route identification signs shall have finish and contrast complying with *Chapter 44: Signage - 703.4.1 - p. 179*.

Additionally, to the maximum extent practicable, new bus route identification signs shall provide visual characters complying with *Chapter 44: Signage - 703.4 - pp. 179 & 180*.

EXCEPTION:

> Bus schedules, timetables and maps that are posted at the bus stop or bus bay are not required to meet this requirement.

E109 **Transportation Facilities and Stations**

E109.2.2 **Signs**

Signage in fixed transportation facilities and stations shall comply with *E109.2.2.1 through E109.2.2.3 - (below & following page)*.

E109.2.2.1 **Tactile Signs**

Where signs are provided at entrances to stations identifying the station or the entrance, or both, at least one sign at each entrance shall be tactile.

Chapter 45: IBC - Appendix (E107) - Signage (continued)

A minimum of one tactile sign identifying the specific station shall be provided on each platform or boarding area.

Such signs shall be placed in uniform locations at entrances and on platforms or boarding areas within the transit system to the maximum extent practicable.

Tactile signs shall comply with ***Chapter 44: Signage - 1011.3 - p. 171.***

> EXCEPTIONS:
>
> 1. Where the station has no defined entrance but signs are provided, the tactile signs shall be placed in a central location.
>
> 2. Signs are not required to be tactile where audible signs are remotely transmitted to hand-held receivers, or are user or proximity actuated.

E109.2.2.2 **Identification Signs**

Stations covered by this chapter shall have identification signs containing visual characters complying with ***Chapter 44: Signage - 703.4 - pp. 179 & 180.***

Signs shall be clearly visible and within the sightlines of a standing or sitting passenger from within the train on both sides when not obstructed by another train.

E109.2.2.3 **Informational Signs**

Lists of stations, routes and destinations served by the station which are located on boarding areas, platforms or mezzanines shall provide visual characters complying with ***Chapter 44: Signage - 703.4 - pp. 179 & 180.***

Signs covered by this provision shall, to the maximum extent practicable, be placed in uniform locations within the transit system.

E110 **Airports**

E110.3 **Terminal Information Systems**

Where terminal information systems convey audible information to the public, the same or equivalent information shall be provided in a visual format.

Chapter 46:

IBC - WAC
ACCESSIBILITY FOR EXISTING BUILDINGS

IBC - 3409   **Accessibility for Existing Buildings**

3409.1   **Scope**

The provisions of *3409.1 to 3409.7.12 - (below & following pages) and Chapter 47: Historic Buildings - 3409.8 through 3409.8.5 - pp. 193 & 194* apply to the maintenance, change of occupancy, additions and alterations to existing buildings, including those identified as historic buildings.

    EXCEPTION:

        Type B dwelling or sleeping units required by *Chapters 8-11 - 1107 - pp. 27-38* are not required to be provided in existing buildings and facilities.

3409.2   **Maintenance of Facilities**

A building, facility or element that is constructed or altered to be accessible shall be maintained accessible during occupancy.

3409.3   **Change of Occupancy**

Existing buildings, or portions thereof, that undergo a change of group or occupancy shall have all of the following accessible features:

1. At least one accessible building entrance.

2. At least one accessible route from an accessible building entrance to primary function areas.

3. Signage complying with *Chapter 44: Signage - 1110 - pp. 170 & 171.*

4. Accessible parking, where parking is being provided.

5. At least one accessible passenger loading zone, when loading zones are provided.

6. At least one accessible route connecting accessible parking and accessible passenger loading zones to an accessible entrance.

Chapter 46: IBC - WAC - Accessibility for Existing Buildings (continued)

Where it is technically infeasible to comply with the new construction standards for any of these requirements for a change of group or occupancy, the above items shall conform to the requirements to the maximum extent technically feasible.

Change of group or occupancy that incorporates any alterations or additions shall comply with *3409.1 through 3409.7 - (preceding page, above, below & following pages)*.

3409.4 **Additions**

Provisions for new construction shall apply to additions.

An addition that affects the accessibility to, or contains an area of primary function, shall comply with the requirements in *3409.6 - (following page)* for accessible routes.

3409.5 <u>**WAC - 7/01/05**</u>

<u>**Alterations**</u>

<u>A building, facility or element that is altered shall comply with the applicable provisions in the 2003 International Building Code - Chapter 11, and ICC/ANSI A117.1, unless technically infeasible.</u>

<u>Where compliance with this chapter and *Chapter 47: Historic Buildings - 3409.8 - pp. 193 & 194* is technically infeasible, the alteration shall provide access to the maximum extent technically feasible.</u>

<u>Where alterations would increase the number of public pay telephones to four, with at least one in the interior, or where the facility has four or more public pay telephones and one or more is altered; at least one interior text telephone shall be provided.</u>

EXCEPTIONS:

<u>1.</u> <u>The altered element or space is not required to be on an accessible route, unless required by *3409.6 - (following page)*.</u>

<u>2.</u> <u>Accessible means of egress required by the 2003 International Building Code - Chapter 10, are not required to be provided in existing buildings and facilities.</u>

<u>3.</u> <u>In alterations, accessibility to raised or sunken dining areas, or to all parts of outdoor seating areas is not required provided that the same services and amenities are provided in an accessible space usable by the general public and not restricted to use by people with disabilities.</u>

Chapter 46: IBC - WAC - Accessibility for Existing Buildings (continued)

3409.5.1   **Extent of Application**

An alteration of an existing element, space, or area of a building or facility shall not impose a requirement for greater accessibility than that which would be required for new construction.

Alterations shall not reduce or have the effect of reducing accessibility of a building, portion of a building, or facility.

3409.6   **WAC - 7/01/05**

Alterations Affecting an Area Containing a Primary Function

Where an alteration affects the accessibility to, or contains an area of primary function, the route to the primary function area shall be accessible.

The accessible route to the primary function area shall include toilet facilities, telephones or drinking fountains serving the area of primary function.

EXCEPTIONS:

1. The costs of providing the accessible route are not required to exceed 20 percent of the costs of the alteration affecting the area of primary function.

2. This provision does not apply to alterations limited solely to windows, hardware, operating controls, electrical outlets and signs.

3. This provision does not apply to alterations limited solely to mechanical systems, electrical systems, installation or alteration of fire-protection systems and abatement of hazardous materials.

4. This provision does not apply to alterations undertaken for the primary purpose of increasing the accessibility of an existing building, facility or element.

3409.7   **WAC - 7/01/05**

Scoping for Alterations

The provisions of *3409.7.1 through 3409.7.12 - (following pages)* shall apply to alterations to existing buildings and facilities.

Where an escalator or new stairway is planned or installed requiring major structural changes, then a means of vertical transportation (e.g. elevator, platform lift) shall be provided in accordance with this chapter, *Chapter 47: Historic Buildings - 3409.8 - pp. 193 & 194,* and Chapter 34 of the 2003 International Building Code.

Chapter 46: IBC - WAC - Accessibility for Existing Buildings (continued)

3409.7.1 **Entrances**

Accessible entrances shall be provided in accordance with *Chapter 5: Accessible Entrances - 1105 - pp. 16 & 17.*

EXCEPTION:

Where an alteration includes alterations to an entrance, and the building or facility has an accessible entrance, the altered entrance is not required to be accessible, unless required by *3409.6 - (preceding page).*

Signs complying with *Chapter 44: Signage - 1110 - pp. 170 & 171* shall be provided.

3409.7.2 **WAC - 7/01/05**

Elevators

Altered elements of existing elevators shall comply with ASME A17.1 and ICC/ANSI A117.1.

Such elements shall also be altered in elevators programmed to respond to the same hall call control as the altered elevator.

Elevators shall comply with Chapter 296-96 WAC.

3409.7.3 **WAC - 7/01/05**

Platform Lifts

Platform (wheelchair) lifts complying with ICC/ANSI A117.1 and installed in accordance with ASME A18.1 shall be permitted as a component of an accessible route.

Platform lifts shall comply with Chapter 296-96 WAC.

3409.7.4 **Stairs and Escalators in Existing Buildings**

In alterations where an escalator or stair is added where none existed previously, an accessible route shall be provided in accordance with *Chapter 4: Accessible Route - 1104.4 and 1104.5 - pp. 11 & 12.*

3409.7.5 **Ramps**

Where steeper slopes than allowed by *Chapter 16: Means of Egress - Ramps - 1010.2 - p. 69* are necessitated by space limitations, the slope of ramps in or providing access to existing buildings or facilities shall comply with *Table O - (following page).*

Chapter 46: IBC - WAC - Accessibility for Existing Buildings (continued)

Table O
Ramps - Existing Buildings

Slope	Maximum Rise
Steeper than 1:10 but not steeper than 1:8	3 inches (76mm)
Steeper than 1:12 but not steeper than 1:10	6 inches (152mm)

3409.7.6 **Performance Areas**

Where it is technically infeasible to alter performance areas to be on an accessible route, at least one of each type of performance area shall be made accessible.

3409.7.7 **WAC - 7/01/05**

Dwelling or Sleeping Units

Where I-1, I-2, I-3, R-1, R-2 or R-4 dwelling or sleeping units are being altered or added, the requirements of *Chapters 8-11 - 1107 - pp. 27-38* for Accessible or Type A units, the 2003 International Building Code - Chapter 9, and *Chapter 18: Fire Protections Systems - Alarms - pp. 81-83* for accessible alarms apply only to the quantity of spaces being altered or added.

At least one sleeping room for each 25 sleeping rooms, or fraction thereof, being added or altered, shall have telephones and visible notification devices complying with *E104.3.4 - (below)*, as well as visible alarms.

E104.3.4 **Notification Devices**

Visual notification devices shall be provided to alert room occupants of incoming telephone calls and a door knock or bell.

Notification devices shall not be connected to visual alarm signal appliances.

Permanently installed telephones shall have volume controls and an electrical outlet complying with ICC/ANSI A117.1 located within 48 inches (1219mm) of the telephone to facilitate the use of TTY.

3409.7.8 **Jury Boxes and Witness Stands**

In alterations, accessible wheelchair spaces are not required to be located within the defined area of raised jury boxes or witness stands and shall be permitted to be located outside these spaces where the ramp or lift access restricts or projects into the means of egress.

Chapter 46: IBC - WAC - Accessibility for Existing Buildings (continued)

3409.7.9 <u>WAC - 7/01/05</u>

<u>Toilet Rooms</u>

<u>Where it is technically infeasible to alter existing toilet and bathing facilities to be accessible, an accessible unisex toilet or bathing facility is permitted.</u>

<u>The unisex facility shall be located on the same floor and in the same area as the existing facility.</u>

<u>The number of toilet facilities and water closets required by the State Building Code is permitted to be reduced by one, in order to provide accessible features.</u>

3409.7.10 **Dressing - Fitting - Locker Rooms**

Where it is technically infeasible to provide accessible dressing, fitting or locker rooms at the same location as similar types of rooms, one accessible room on the same level shall be provided.

Where separate-sex facilities are provided, accessible rooms for each sex shall be provided.

Separate-sex facilities are not required where only unisex rooms are provided.

3409.7.11 **Check-out Aisles**

Where check-out aisles are altered, at least one of each check-out aisle serving each function shall be made accessible until the number of accessible check-out aisles complies with *Chapter 39: Service Facilities - 1109.12.2 - pp. 158 & 159.*

3409.7.12 **Thresholds**

The maximum height of thresholds at doorways shall be 3/4 inches (19.1mm).

Such threshold shall have beveled edges on each side.

Chapter 47:

INTERNATIONAL BUILDING CODE ACCESSIBILITY FOR EXISTING BUILDINGS HISTORIC BUILDINGS

IBC - 3409   Accessibility for Existing Buildings

3409.1   Scope

See Chapter 46: Accessibility for Existing Buildings - 3409.1 - p. 187.

3409.8   Historic Buildings

These provisions shall apply to buildings and facilities designated as historic structures that undergo alterations or a change of occupancy, unless technically infeasible.

Where compliance with the requirements for accessible routes, ramps, entrances, or toilet facilities would threaten or destroy the historic significance of the building or facility, as determined by the authority having jurisdiction, the alternative requirements of *3409.8.1 through 3409.8.5 - (below & following page)* for that element shall be permitted.

3409.8.1   Site Arrival Points

At least one accessible route from a site arrival point to an accessible entrance shall be provided.

3409.8.2   Multilevel Buildings and Facilities

An accessible route from an accessible entrance to public spaces on the level of the accessible entrance shall be provided.

3409.8.3   Entrances

At least one main entrance shall be accessible.

    EXCEPTIONS:

    1.   If a main entrance cannot be made accessible, an accessible nonpublic entrance that is unlocked while the building is occupied shall be provided;

           or

    2.   If a main entrance cannot be made accessible, a locked accessible entrance with a notification system or remote monitoring shall be provided.

Chapter 47: IBC - Historic Buildings (continued)

Signs complying with *Chapter 44: Signage - 1110 - pp. 170 & 171* shall be provided at the primary entrance and the accessible entrance.

3409.8.4 **Toilet and Bathing Facilities**

Where toilet rooms are provided, at least one accessible toilet room complying with *Chapter 26: Unisex Toilet and Bathing Rooms - 1109.2.1 - pp. 107 & 108* shall be provided.

3409.8.5 **Ramps**

The slope of a ramp run of 24 inches (610mm) maximum shall not be steeper than one unit vertical in eight units horizontal (12 percent slope).

Chapter 48:

ICC/ANSI A117.1
FLOOR SURFACES

ICC/ANSI - Chapter 3		***Building Blocks***

301   ***General***

301.1   ***Scope***

*The provisions of this **Chapter - 302** shall apply where required by the scoping provisions adopted by the administrative authority or by ICC/ANSI A117.1-2003 - Chapters 4 through 10.*

ICC/ANSI - 302   ***Floor Surfaces***

302.1   ***General***

*Floor surfaces shall be stable, firm, and slip resistant, and shall comply with this **Chapter - 302**.*

*Changes in level in floor surfaces shall comply with **Chapter 49: Changes in Level - 303 - p. 197**.*

302.2   ***Carpet***

Carpet or carpet tile shall be securely attached and shall have a firm cushion, pad, or backing or no cushion or pad.

Carpet or carpet tile shall have a level loop, textured loop, level cut pile, or level cut/uncut pile texture.

The pile shall be 1/2-inch (13mm) maximum in height.

Exposed edges of carpet shall be fastened to the floor and shall have trim along the entire length of the exposed edge.

*Carpet edge trim shall comply with **Chapter 49: Changes in Level - 303 - p. 197**.*

See Diagram 65(a) - p. 370.

302.3   ***Openings***

*Openings in floor surfaces shall be of a size that does not permit the passage of a 1/2-inch (13mm) diameter sphere, except as allowed in **Chapter 31 - 407.4.3 - p. 136, Chapter 32 - 408.4.3 - p. 144, Chapter 33 - 409.4.3 - p. 146, Chapter 34 - 410.4 - p. 151 and Chapter 69: Transportation Facilities - 805.10 - p. 253**.*

Chapter 48: ICC/ANSI A117.1 - Floor Surfaces (continued)

Elongated openings shall be placed so that the long dimension is perpendicular to the dominant direction of travel.

Diagram 65(b) - p. 370.

Chapter 49:

ICC/ANSI A117.1
CHANGES IN LEVEL

ICC/ANSI - Chapter 3   **Building Blocks**

301   *General*

301.1   *Scope*

*The provisions of this **Chapter - 303** shall apply where required by the scoping provisions adopted by the administrative authority or by ICC/ANSI A117.1-2003 - Chapters 4 through 10.*

ICC/ANSI - 303   **Changes in Level**

303.1   *General*

*Changes in level in floor surfaces shall comply with this **Chapter - 303**.*

303.2   *Vertical*

Changes in level of 1/4-inch (6.4mm) maximum in height shall be permitted to be vertical.

See Diagram 66 - p. 371.

303.3   *Beveled*

Changes in level greater than 1/4-inch (6.4mm) in height and not more than 1/2-inch (13mm) maximum in height shall be beveled with a slope not steeper than 1:2.

See Diagram 67 - p. 372.

303.4   *Ramped*

*Changes in level greater than 1/2-inch (13mm) in height shall be ramped and shall comply with **Chapter 16: Means of Egress - Ramps - 405 - pp. 73-76** or **Chapter 57: Curb Ramps - 406 - pp. 217-220**.*

Chapter 50:

ICC/ANSI A117.1
TURNING SPACE

ICC/ANSI - Chapter 3   **Building Blocks**

301   *General*

301.1   *Scope*

*The provisions of this **Chapter - 304** shall apply where required by the scoping provisions adopted by the administrative authority or by ICC/ANSI A117.1-2003 - Chapters 4 through 10.*

ICC/ANSI - 304   ***Turning Space***

304.1   *General*

*A turning space shall comply with this **Chapter - 304**.*

304.2   ***Floor Surfaces***

*Floor surfaces of a turning space shall have a slope not steeper than 1:48 and shall comply with **Chapter 48: Floor Surfaces - 302 - pp. 195 & 196**.*

304.3   *Size*

*Turning spaces shall comply with **304.3.1** or **304.3.2** - (below & following page).*

304.3.1   ***Circular Space***

The turning space shall be a circular space with a 60-inch (1524mm) minimum diameter.

See Diagram 3(a) - p. 308.

*The turning space shall be permitted to include knee and toe clearance complying with **Chapter 52: Knee and Toe Clearance - 306 - pp. 202 & 203**.*

304.3.2   ***T-Shaped Space***

The turning space shall be a T-shaped space within a 60-inch (1524mm) minimum square, with arms and base 36 inches (914mm) minimum in width.

Each arm of the T shall be clear of obstructions 12 inches (305mm) minimum in each direction, and the base shall be clear of obstructions 24 inches (610mm) minimum.

Chapter 50: ICC/ANSI A117.1 - Turning Space (continued)

See Diagram 3(b) - p. 308.

*The turning space shall be permitted to include knee and toe clearance complying with **Chapter 52: Knee and Toe Clearance - 306 - pp. 202 & 203** only at the end of either the base or one arm.*

304.4   ***Door Swing***

Unless otherwise specified, doors shall be permitted to swing into turning spaces.

Chapter 51:

ICC/ANSI A117.1
CLEAR FLOOR SPACE

ICC/ANSI - Chapter 3 **Building Blocks**

301 *General*

301.1 *Scope*

The provisions of this **Chapter - 305** *shall apply where required by the scoping provisions adopted by the administrative authority or by ICC/ANSI A117.1-2003 - Chapters 4 through 10.*

ICC/ANSI - 305 **Clear Floor Space**

305.1 *General*

Clear floor space shall comply with this **Chapter - 305.**

305.2 *Floor Surfaces*

Floor surfaces of a clear floor space shall have a slope not steeper than 1:48 and shall comply with **Chapter 48: Floor Surfaces - 302 - pp. 195 & 196.**

305.3 *Size*

The clear floor space shall be 48 inches (1219mm) minimum in length and 30 inches (762mm) minimum in width.

See Diagram 68 - p. 373.

305.4 **Knee and Toe Clearance**

Unless otherwise specified, clear floor space shall be permitted to include knee and toe clearance complying with **Chapter 52: Knee and Toe Clearance - 306 - pp. 202 & 203.**

305.5 *Position*

Unless otherwise specified, the clear floor space shall be positioned for either forward or parallel approach to an element.

See Diagrams 69(a),(b) - p. 374.

Chapter 51: ICC/ANSI A117.1 - Clear Floor Space (continued)

305.6 *Approach*

One full, unobstructed side of the clear floor space shall adjoin or overlap an accessible route or adjoin another clear floor space.

305.7 *Alcoves*

*If a clear floor space is in an alcove or otherwise confined on all or part of three sides, additional maneuvering clearances complying with **305.7.1 and 305.7.2 - (below)** shall be provided, as applicable.*

305.7.1 *Parallel Approach*

Where the clear floor space is positioned for a parallel approach, the alcove shall be 60 inches (1524mm) minimum in width where the depth exceeds 15 inches (381mm).

See Diagram 70(b) - p. 375.

305.7.2 *Forward Approach*

Where the clear floor space is positioned for a forward approach, the alcove shall be 36 inches (914mm) minimum in width where the depth exceeds 24 inches (610mm).

See Diagram 70(a) - p. 375.

Chapter 52:

ICC/ANSI A117.1
KNEE AND TOE CLEARANCE

ICC/ANSI - Chapter 3   **Building Blocks**

301   *General*

301.1   *Scope*

*The provisions of this **Chapter - 306** shall apply where required by the scoping provisions adopted by the administrative authority or by ICC/ANSI A117.1-2003 - Chapters 4 through 10.*

ICC/ANSI - 306   **Knee and Toe Clearance**

306.1   *General*

*Where space beneath an element is included as part of clear floor space at an element, clearance at an element, or a turning space, the space shall comply with this **Chapter - 306.***

Additional space beyond knee and toe clearance shall be permitted beneath elements.

306.2   *Toe Clearance*

306.2.1   *General*

*Space beneath an element between the floor and 9 inches (229mm) above the floor shall be considered toe clearance and shall comply with **306.2 - (below & following page)**.*

306.2.2   *Maximum Depth*

Toe clearance shall be permitted to extend 25 inches (635mm) maximum under an element.

306.2.3   *Minimum Depth*

Where toe clearance is required at an element as part of a clear floor space, the toe clearance shall extend 17 inches (432mm) minimum beneath the element.

306.2.4   *Additional Clearance*

Space extending greater than 6 inches (152mm) beyond the available knee clearance at 9 inches (229mm) above the floor shall not be considered toe clearance.

Chapter 52: ICC/ANSI A117.1 - Knee and Toe Clearance (continued)

306.2.5   ***Width***

Toe clearance shall be 30 inches (762mm) minimum in width.

See Diagrams 71(a),(b) - p. 376.

306.3   ***Knee Clearance***

306.3.1   ***General***

*Space beneath an element between 9 inches (229mm) and 27 inches (686mm) above the floor shall be considered knee clearance and shall comply with **306.3 - (below)**.*

306.3.2   ***Maximum Depth***

Knee clearance shall be permitted to extend 25 inches (635mm) under an element at 9 inches (229mm) above the floor.

306.3.3   ***Minimum Depth***

Where knee clearance is required beneath an element as part of a clear floor space, the knee clearance shall be 11 inches (279mm) minimum in depth at 9 inches (229mm) above the floor, and 8 inches (203mm) minimum in depth at 27 inches (686mm) above the floor.

306.3.4   ***Clearance Reduction***

Between 9 inches (229mm) and 27 inches (686mm) above the floor, the knee clearance shall be permitted to be reduced at a rate of 1-inch (25.4mm) for each 6 inches (152mm) in height.

306.3.5   ***Width***

Knee clearance shall be 30 inches (762mm) minimum in width.

See Diagrams 72(a),(b) - p. 377.

Chapter 53:

ICC/ANSI A117.1
PROTRUDING OBJECTS

ICC/ANSI - Chapter 3   ***Building Blocks***

301   *General*

301.1   *Scope*

*The provisions of this **Chapter - 307** shall apply where required by the scoping provisions adopted by the administrative authority or by ICC/ANSI A117.1-2003 - Chapters 4 through 10.*

ICC/ANSI - 307   ***Protruding Objects***

307.1   *General*

*Protruding objects on circulation paths shall comply with this **Chapter - 307**.*

307.2   ***Protrusion Limits***

Objects with leading edges more than 27 inches (686mm) and not more than 80 inches (2032mm) above the floor shall protrude 4 inches (102mm) maximum horizontally into the circulation path.

*See **Diagram 73** - p. 378.*

    EXCEPTIONS:

    1.   *Handrails shall be permitted to protrude 4-1/2 inches (114mm) maximum.*

    2.   *Door closers and door stops shall be permitted to be 78 inches (1981mm) minimum above the floor.*

307.3   ***Post-Mounted Objects***

Objects on posts or pylons shall be permitted to overhang 4 inches (102mm) maximum where more than 27 inches (686mm) and not more than 80 inches (2032mm) is above the floor.

Objects on multiple posts or pylons where the clear distance between the posts or pylons is greater than 12 inches (305mm), shall have the lowest edge of such object either 27 inches (686mm) maximum or 80 inches (2032mm) minimum above the floor.

*See **Diagrams 74(a),(b)** - p. 379.*

Chapter 53: ICC/ANSI A117.1 - Protruding Objects (continued)

307.4   ***Reduced Vertical Clearance***

*Guardrails or other barriers shall be provided where object protrusion is beyond the limits allowed by **307.2 and 307.3 - (preceding page),** and where the vertical clearance is less than 80 inches (2032mm) above the floor.*

The leading edge of such guardrail or barrier shall be 27 inches (686mm) maximum above the floor.

See Diagram 75 - p. 380.

307.5   **Required Clear Width**

Protruding objects shall not reduce the clear width required for accessible routes.

Chapter 54:

ICC/ANSI A117.1
REACH RANGES

ICC/ANSI - Chapter 3   **Building Blocks**

301   **General**

301.1   **Scope**

*The provisions of this **Chapter - 308** shall apply where required by the scoping provisions adopted by the administrative authority or by ICC/ANSI A117.1-2003 - Chapters 4 through 10.*

ICC/ANSI - 308   **Reach Ranges**

308.1   **General**

*Reach ranges shall comply with this **Chapter - 308**.*

308.2   **Forward Reach**

308.2.1   **Unobstructed**

Where a forward reach is unobstructed, the high forward reach shall be 48 inches (1219mm) maximum and the low forward reach shall be 15 inches (381mm) minimum above the floor.

See Diagram 76 - p. 381.

308.2.2   **Obstructed High Reach**

Where a high forward reach is over an obstruction, the clear floor space shall extend beneath the element for a distance not less than the required reach depth over the obstruction.

The high forward reach shall be 48 inches (1219mm) maximum where the reach depth is 20 inches (508mm) maximum.

Where the reach depth exceeds 20 inches (508mm), the high forward reach shall be 44 inches (1118mm) maximum, and the reach depth shall be 25 inches (635mm) maximum.

See Diagrams 77(a),(b) - p. 382.

Chapter 54: ICC/ANSI A117.1 - Reach Ranges (continued)

308.3   ***Side Reach***

308.3.1   ***Unobstructed***

Where a clear floor space allows a parallel approach to an element and the side reach is unobstructed, the high side reach shall be 48 inches (1219mm) maximum and the low side reach shall be 15 inches (381mm) minimum above the floor.

*See **Diagram 78** - p. 383.*

    EXCEPTION:

        Existing elements shall be permitted at 54 inches (1372mm) maximum above the floor.

308.3.2   ***Obstructed High Reach***

Where a clear floor space allows a parallel approach to an object and the high side reach is over an obstruction, the height of the obstruction shall be 34 inches (864mm) maximum and the depth of the obstruction shall be 24 inches (610mm) maximum.

The high side reach shall be 48 inches (1219mm) maximum for a reach depth of 10 inches (254mm) maximum.

Where the reach depth exceeds 10 inches (254mm), the high side reach shall be 46 inches (1168mm) maximum for a reach depth of 24 inches (610mm) maximum.

*See **Diagrams 79(a),(b)** - p. 384.*

Chapter 55:

ICC/ANSI A117.1
OPERABLE PARTS

ICC/ANSI - Chapter 3 — **Building Blocks**

301 — *General*

301.1 — *Scope*

*The provisions of this **Chapter - 309** shall apply where required by the scoping provisions adopted by the administrative authority or by ICC/ANSI A117.1-2003 - Chapters 4 through 10.*

ICC/ANSI - 309 — **Operable Parts**

309.1 — *General*

*Operable parts required to be accessible shall comply with this **Chapter - 309**.*

309.2 — *Clear Floor Space*

*A clear floor space complying with **Chapter 51: Clear Floor Space - 305 - pp. 200 & 201** shall be provided.*

309.3 — *Height*

*Operable parts shall be placed within one or more of the reach ranges specified in **Chapter 54: Reach Ranges - 308 - pp. 206 & 207**.*

309.4 — *Operation*

Operable parts shall be operable with one hand and shall not require tight grasping, pinching, or twisting of the wrist.

The force required to activate operable parts shall be 5 pounds (22.2N) maximum.

> *EXCEPTION:*
>
> *Gas pump nozzles shall not be required to provide operable parts that have an activating force of 5 pounds (22.2N) maximum.*

Chapter 56:

ICC/ANSI A117.1 - WAC
DOORS AND DOORWAYS

ICC/ANSI - Chapter 4 *Accessible Routes*

401 *General*

401.1 *Scope*

Accessible routes required by the scoping provisions adopted by the administrative authority shall comply with the applicable provisions of this **Chapter - 404.**

ICC/ANSI - 404 **Doors and Doorways**

404.1 *General*

Doors and doorways that are part of an accessible route shall comply with this **Chapter - 404.**

404.2 **Manual Doors**

Manual doors and doorways, and manual gates, including ticket gates, shall comply with the requirements of **404.2 - (below & following pages).**

    EXCEPTION:

    Doors, doorways, and gates designed to be operated only by security personnel shall not be required to comply with this **Chapter - 404.2.6 through 404.2.8 - pp. 213 & 214.**

404.2.1 **Double-Leaf Doors and Gates**

At least one of the active leaves of doorways with two leaves shall comply with **404.2.2 and 404.2.3 - (below & following pages).**

404.2.2 **Clear Width**

Doorways shall have a clear opening width of 32 inches (813mm) minimum.

Clear opening width of doorways with swinging doors shall be measured between the face of the door and stop, with the door open 90 degrees.

Openings, doors and doorways without doors more than 24 inches (610mm) in depth shall provide a clear opening width of 36 inches (914mm) minimum.

Chapter 56: ICC/ANSI A117.1 - WAC - Doors and Doorways (continued)

There shall be no projections into the clear opening width lower than 34 inches (864mm) above the floor.

Projections into the clear opening width between 34 inches (864mm) and 80 inches (2032mm) above the floor shall not exceed 4 inches (102mm).

See Diagrams 80(a),(b),(c),(d) - p. 385.

    EXCEPTIONS:

        1.   Door closers and door stops shall be permitted to be 78 inches (1981mm) minimum above the floor.

        2.   In alterations, a projection of 5/8-inch (15.9mm) maximum into the required clear opening width shall be permitted for the latch side stop.

404.2.3   **Maneuvering Clearances at Doors**

*Minimum maneuvering clearances at doors shall comply with **404.2.3 - (below & following pages)** and shall include the full clear opening width of the doorway.*

404.2.3.1   **Swinging Doors**

*Swinging doors shall have maneuvering clearances complying with **Table P - (following page)**.*

See Diagrams 81(a),(b),(c),(d),(e),(f),(g) - p. 386.

Chapter 56: ICC/ANSI A117.1 - WAC - Doors and Doorways (continued)

Table P
Maneuvering Clearances at Manual Swinging Doors

Type of Use		Minimum Maneuvering Clearances	
Approach Direction	Door Side	Perpendicular to Doorway	Parallel to Doorway (beyond latch unless noted)
From front	Pull	60 inches (1524mm)	18 inches (457mm)
From front	Push	48 inches (1219mm)	0 inches (0mm)[3]
From hinge side	Pull Pull	60 inches (1524mm) 54 inches (1372mm)	36 inches (914mm) 42 inches (1067mm)
From hinge side	Push	42 inches (1067mm)[1]	22 inches (559mm)[3] & [4]
From latch side	Pull	48 inches (1219mm)[2]	24 inches (610mm)
From latch side	Push	42 inches (1067mm)[2]	24 inches (610mm)

[1]   Add 6 inches (152mm) if closer and latch provided..
[2]   Add 6 inches (152mm) if closer provided.
[3]   Add 12 inches (305mm) beyond latch if closer and latch provided.
[4]   Beyond hinge side.

404.2.3.2   *Sliding and Folding Doors*

Sliding doors and folding doors shall have maneuvering clearances complying with **Table Q** - *(following page).*

See Diagrams 82(a),(b),(c) - p. 387.

Chapter 56: ICC/ANSI A117.1 - WAC - Doors and Doorways (continued)

Table Q
Maneuvering Clearances at Sliding and Folding Doors

Approach Direction	Minimum Maneuvering Clearances	
	Perpendicular to Doorway	*Parallel to Doorway (beyond stop or latch side unless noted)*
From front	*48 inches (1219mm)*	*0 inches (0mm)*
From nonlatch side	*42 inches (1067mm)*	*22 inches (559mm)[1]*
From latch side	*42 inches (1067mm)*	*24 inches (610mm)*

[1] Beyond pocket or hinge side.

404.2.3.3   **Doorways without Doors**

Doorways without doors that are less than 36 inches (914mm) in width shall have maneuvering clearances complying with **Table R - (below) and Diagrams 83(a),(b) - p. 388.**

Table R
Maneuvering Clearances for Doorways without Doors

	Minimum Maneuvering Clearances
Approach Direction	*Perpendicular to Doorway*
From front	*48 inches (1219mm)*
From side	*42 inches (1067mm)*

404.2.3.4   **Recessed Doors**

Where any obstruction within 18 inches (457mm) of the latch side of a doorway projects more than 8 inches (203mm) beyond the face of the door, measured perpendicular to the face of the door, maneuvering clearances for a forward approach shall be provided.

See Diagrams 84(a),(b),(c) - p. 389.

404.2.3.5   **Floor Surface**

Floor surface within the maneuvering clearances shall have a slope not steeper than 1:48 and shall comply with **Chapter 48: Floor Surfaces - 302 - pp. 195 & 196.**

Chapter 56: ICC/ANSI A117.1 - WAC - Doors and Doorways (continued)

404.2.4   *Thresholds at Doorways*

If provided, thresholds at doorways shall be 1/2-inch (13mm) maximum in height.

*Raised thresholds and changes in level at doorways shall comply with **Chapter 48: Floor Surfaces - 302 - pp. 195 & 196 and Chapter 49: Changes in Level - 303 - p. 197.***

EXCEPTION:

> ***404.2.4 - (above)*** *shall not apply to existing thresholds or altered thresholds 3/4 inches (19.1mm) maximum in height that have a beveled edge on each side with a maximum slope of 1:2 for the height exceeding 1/4-inch (6.4mm).*

404.2.5   *Two Doors in Series*

Distance between two hinged or pivoted doors in series shall be 48 inches (1219mm) minimum plus the width of any door swinging into the space.

*The space between the doors shall provide a turning space complying with **Chapter 50: Turning Space - 304 - pp. 198 & 199.***

See Diagrams 85(a),(b),(c) - p. 390.

404.2.6   *Door Hardware*

Handles, pulls, latches, locks, and other operable parts on accessible doors shall have a shape that is easy to grasp with one hand and does not require tight grasping, pinching, or twisting of the wrist to operate.

Operable parts of such hardware shall be 34 inches (864mm) minimum and 48 inches (1219mm) maximum above the floor.

Where sliding doors are in the fully open position, operating hardware shall be exposed and usable from both sides.

EXCEPTION:

> *Locks used only for security purposes and not used for normal operation are permitted in any location.*

Chapter 56: ICC/ANSI A117.1 - WAC - Doors and Doorways (continued)

404.2.7   *Closing Speed*

404.2.7.1   *Door Closers*

Door closers shall be adjusted so that from an open position of 90 degrees, the time required to move the door to an open position of 12 degrees shall be 5 seconds minimum.

404.2.7.2   *Spring Hinges*

Door spring hinges shall be adjusted so that from the open position of 70 degrees, the door shall move to the closed position in 1.5 seconds minimum.

1101.2.3   **WAC - 7/01/06**
                                 ICC/ANSI A117.1 - Section 404.2.8

Door-Opening Force

Fire doors shall have the minimum opening force allowable by the appropriate administrative authority.

The maximum force for pushing open or pulling open doors other than fire doors shall be as follows:

    Interior hinged door: 5.0 pounds (22.2N)

    Sliding or folding doors: 5.0 pounds (22.2N)

At exterior doors where environmental conditions require a closing pressure greater than 8.5 pounds (37.8N), power-operated doors shall be used within the accessible route of travel.

These forces do not apply to the force required to retract latch bolts or disengage other devices that hold the door in a closed position.

404.2.9   *Door Surface*

Door surfaces within 10 inches (254mm) of the floor, measured vertically, shall be a smooth surface on the push side extending the full width of the door.

Parts creating horizontal or vertical joints in such surface shall be within 1/16-inch (1.6mm) of the same plane as the other.

Cavities created by added kick plates shall be capped.

Chapter 56: ICC/ANSI A117.1 - WAC - Doors and Doorways (continued)

EXCEPTIONS:

1. *Sliding doors.*

2. *Tempered glass doors without stiles and having a bottom rail or shoe with the top leading edge tapered at no less than 60 degrees from the horizontal shall not be required to meet the 10-inch (254mm) bottom rail height requirement.*

3. *Doors that do not extend to within 10 inches (254mm) of the floor.*

404.2.10 **Vision Lites**

Doors and sidelites adjacent to doors containing one or more glazing panels that permit viewing through the panels shall have the bottom of at least one panel on either the door or an adjacent sidelite 43 inches (1092mm) maximum above the floor.

EXCEPTION:

*Vision lites with the lowest part more than 66 inches (1676mm) above the floor are not required to comply with **404.2.10 - (above).***

404.3 **Automatic Doors**

*Automatic doors and automatic gates shall comply with **404.3 - (below & following page).***

Full powered automatic doors shall comply with ANSI/BHMA A156.10 listed in ICC/ANSI A117.1-2003 - Section 105.2.4.

Power-assisted and low-energy doors shall comply with ANSI/BHMA A156.19 as listed in ICC/ANSI A117.1-2003 - Section 105.2.3.

404.3.1 **Clear Opening Width**

Doorways shall have a clear opening width of 32 inches (813mm) in power-on and power-off mode.

The minimum clear opening width for automatic door systems shall be based on the clear opening width provided with all leafs in the open position.

404.3.2 **Maneuvering Clearances**

*Maneuvering clearances at power-assisted doors shall comply with this **Chapter - 404.2.3 - pp. 210-212.***

Chapter 56: ICC/ANSI A117.1 - WAC - Doors and Doorways (continued)

404.3.3   *Thresholds*

*Thresholds and changes in level at doorways shall comply with this **Chapter - 404.2.4 - p. 213**.*

404.3.4   *Two Doors in Series*

*Doors in series shall comply with this **Chapter - 404.2.5 - p. 213**.*

404.3.5   *Control Switches*

*Manually operated control switches shall comply with **Chapter 55: Operable Parts - 309 - p. 208**.*

The clear floor space adjacent to the control switch shall be located beyond the arc of the door swing.

1101.2.11   **WAC - 7/01/06**
           ICC/ANSI A117.1 - Section 404.3.5

             Control Switches

Controls switches shall be mounted 32 inches to 40 inches (813mm to 1016mm) above the floor and not less than 18 inches (457mm) nor more than 36 inches (914mm) horizontally from the nearest point of travel of the moving doors.

Chapter 57:

ICC/ANSI A117.1
CURB RAMPS

ICC/ANSI - Chapter 4   *Accessible Routes*

401   *General*

401.1   *Scope*

Accessible routes required by the scoping provisions adopted by the administrative authority shall comply with the applicable provisions of this **Chapter - 406.**

ICC/ANSI - 406   *Curb Ramps*

406.1   *General*

Curb ramps on accessible routes shall comply with this **Chapter - 406 and Chapter 16: Means of Egress - Ramps 405.2, 405.3 - p. 74 and 405.10 - p. 76.**

406.2   *Counter Slope*

Counter slopes of adjoining gutters and road surfaces immediately adjacent to the curb ramp shall not be steeper than 1:20.

See Diagram 86 - p. 391.

The adjacent surfaces at transitions at curb ramps to walks, gutters or streets shall be at the same level.

406.3   *Sides of Curb Ramps*

Where provided, curb ramp flares shall not be steeper than 1:10.

See Diagram 87 - p. 392.

406.4   *Width*

Curb ramps shall be 36 inches (914mm) minimum in width, exclusive of flared sides.

406.5   *Floor Surfaces*

Floor surfaces of curb ramps shall comply with **Chapter 48: Floor Surfaces - 302 - pp. 195 & 196.**

Chapter 57: ICC/ANSI A117.1 - Curb Ramps (continued)

406.6 *Location*

Curb ramps and the flared sides of curb ramps shall be located so they do not project into vehicular traffic lanes, parking spaces, or parking access aisles.

Curb ramps at marked crossings shall be wholly contained within the markings, excluding any flared sides.

406.7 *Landings*

Landings shall be provided at the tops of curb ramps.

The clear width of the landing shall be 36 inches (914mm) minimum.

The clear width of the landing shall be at least as wide as the curb ramp, excluding flared sides, leading to the landing.

EXCEPTION:

In alterations, where there is no landing at the top of curb ramps, curb ramp flares shall be provided and shall not be steeper than 1:12.

406.8 *Obstructions*

Curb ramps shall be located or protected to prevent their obstruction by parked vehicles.

406.9 *Handrails*

Handrails are not required on curb ramps.

406.10 *Diagonal Curb Ramps*

Diagonal or corner-type curb ramps with returned curbs or other well-defined edges shall have the edges parallel to the direction of pedestrian flow.

The bottoms of diagonal curb ramps shall have 48 inches (1219mm) minimum clear space outside active traffic lanes of the roadway.

Diagonal curb ramps provided at marked crossings shall provide the 48 inches (1219mm) minimum clear space within the markings.

Diagonal curb ramps with flared sides shall have a segment of curb 24 inches (610mm) minimum in length on each side of the curb ramp and within the marked crossing.

See Diagrams 88(a),(b) - p. 393.

Chapter 57: ICC/ANSI A117.1 - Curb Ramps (continued)

406.11   ***Islands***

Raised islands in crossings shall be cut-through level with the street or have curb ramps at both sides.

Each curb ramp shall have a level area 48 inches (1219mm) minimum in length and 36 inches (914mm) minimum in width at the top of the curb ramp in the part of the island intersected by the crossings.

Each 48-inch (1219mm) by 36-inch (914mm) area shall be oriented so the 48-inch (1219mm) length is in the direction of the running slope of the curb ramp it serves.

The 48-inch (1219mm) by 36-inch (914mm) areas and the accessible route shall be permitted to overlap.

See Diagrams 89(a),(b) - p. 394.

406.12   ***Detectable Warnings at Raised Marked Crossings***

*Marked crossings that are raised to the same level as the adjoining sidewalk shall be preceded by a 24-inch (610mm) deep detectable warning complying with **Chapter 36: Detectable Warnings - 705 - pp. 154 & 155**, extending the full width of the marked crossing.*

406.13   ***Detectable Warnings at Curb Ramps***

*Where detectable warnings are provided on curb ramps, they shall comply with **406.13- (below) and Chapter 36: Detectable Warnings - 705 - pp. 154 & 155**.*

406.13.1   ***Area Covered***

Detectable warnings shall be 24 inches (610mm) minimum in the direction of travel and extend the full width of the curb ramp or flush surface.

406.13.2   ***Location***

The detectable warning shall be located so the edge nearest the curb line is 6 inches (152mm) to 8 inches (203mm) from the curb line.

406.14   ***Detectable Warnings at Islands or Cut-Through Medians***

*Where detectable warnings are provided on curb ramps or at raised marked crossings leading to islands or cut-through medians, the island or cut-through median shall also be provided with detectable warnings complying with **Chapter 36: Detectable Warnings - 705 - pp. 154 & 155**, are 24 inches (610mm) in depth, and extend the full width of the pedestrian route or cut-through.*

Chapter 57: ICC/ANSI A117.1 - Curb Ramps (continued)

Where such island or cut-through median is less than 48 inches (1219mm) in depth, the entire width and depth of the pedestrian route or cut-through shall have detectable warnings.

Chapter 58:
ICC/ANSI A117.1
WATER CLOSETS AND TOILET COMPARTMENTS FOR CHILDREN'S USE

ICC/ANSI - Chapter 6   *Plumbing Elements and Facilities*

601   *General*

601.1   *Scope*

*Plumbing elements and facilities required to be accessible by scoping provisions adopted by the administrative authority shall comply with the applicable provisions of this **Chapter - 604.10**.*

ICC/ANSI - 604.10   *Water Closets and Toilet Compartments for Children's Use*

604.10.1   *General*

*Accessible water closets and toilet compartments primarily for children's use shall comply with this **Chapter - 604.10**.*

604.10.2   *Location*

The water closet shall be located with a wall or partition to the rear and to one side.

The centerline of the water closet shall be 12 inches (305mm) minimum to 18 inches (457mm) maximum from the side wall or partition.

*Water closets located in ambulatory accessible toilet compartments specified in **Chapter 27: Water Closet Compartment - 604.9 - pp. 116 & 117** shall be located as specified in **Chapter 27: Water Closet Compartment - 604.2 - p. 110**.*

*See **Diagram 90 - p. 395**.*

604.10.3   *Clearance*

*A clearance around a water closet complying with **Chapter 27: Water Closet Compartment - 604.3 - p. 110** shall be provided.*

604.10.4   *Height*

The height of water closet seats shall be 11 inches (279mm) minimum and 17 inches (432mm) maximum above the floor, measured to the top of the seat.

Chapter 58: ICC/ANSI A117.1 - Compartments for Children Use (continued)

Seats shall not be sprung to return to a lifted position.

See Diagram 91(a) - p. 396.

604.10.5 **Grab Bars**

Grab bars for water closets shall comply with **Chapter 27: Water Closet Compartment - 604.5 - pp. 111-113.**

604.10.6 **Flush Controls**

Flush controls shall be hand-operated or automatic.

Hand-operated flush controls shall comply with **Chapter 55: Operable Parts - 309.2 and 309.4 - p. 208** *and shall be installed 36 inches (914mm) maximum above the floor.*

Flush controls shall be located on the open side of the water closet.

EXCEPTION:

> *In ambulatory accessible compartments complying with* **Chapter 27: Water Closet Compartment - 604.9 - pp. 116 & 117,** *flush controls shall be permitted to be located on either side of the water closet.*

604.10.7 **Dispensers**

Toilet paper dispensers shall comply with **Chapter 55: Operable Parts - 309.4 - p. 208** *and shall be 7 inches (178mm) minimum and 9 inches (229mm) maximum in front of the water closet measured to the centerline of the dispenser.*

The outlet of the dispenser shall be 14 inches (356mm) minimum and 19 inches (483mm) maximum above the floor.

There shall be a clearance of 1-1/2 inches (38mm) minimum below the grab bar.

Dispensers shall not be of a type that control delivery or do not allow continuous paper flow.

See Diagram 91(b) - p. 396.

604.10.8 **Toilet Compartments**

Toilet compartments shall comply with **Chapter 27: Water Closet Compartment - 604.8 - pp. 114-116 and Chapter 27: Water Closet Compartment - 604.9 - pp. 116 & 117,** *as applicable.*

Chapter 59:

ICC/ANSI A117.1
URINALS

ICC/ANSI - Chapter 6 *Plumbing Elements and Facilities*

601 *General*

601.1 *Scope*

*Plumbing elements and facilities required to be accessible by scoping provisions adopted by the administrative authority shall comply with the applicable provisions of this **Chapter - 605.***

ICC/ANSI - 605 *Urinals*

605.1 *General*

*Accessible urinals shall comply with this **Chapter - 605.***

605.2 *Height*

Urinals shall be of the stall-type or shall be of the wall-hung type with the rim at 17 inches (432mm) maximum above the floor.

See Diagrams 92(a),(b) - p. 397.

605.3 *Clear Floor Space*

*A clear floor space complying with **Chapter 51: Clear Floor Space - 305 - pp. 200 & 201**, positioned for forward approach, shall be provided.*

605.4 *Flush Controls*

Flush controls shall be hand-operated or automatic.

*Hand-operated flush controls shall comply with **Chapter 55: Operable Parts - 309 - p. 208.***

Chapter 60:

ICC/ANSI A117.1
BATHTUBS

ICC/ANSI - Chapter 6	*Plumbing Elements and Facilities*
601	*General*
601.1	*Scope*

*Plumbing elements and facilities required to be accessible by scoping provisions adopted by the administrative authority shall comply with the applicable provisions of this **Chapter - 607.***

ICC/ANSI - 607	**Bathtubs**
607.1	*General*

*Accessible bathtubs shall comply with this **Chapter - 607.***

607.2   *Clearance*

A clearance in front of bathtubs shall extending the length of the bathtub and 30 inches (762mm) minimum in depth shall be provided.

Where a permanent seat is provided at the head end of the bathtub, the clearance shall extend 12 inches (305mm) minimum beyond the wall at the head end of the bathtub.

See Diagrams 93(a),(b) - p. 398.

607.3   *Seat*

A permanent seat at the head end of the bathtub or a removable in-tub seat shall be provided.

*Seats shall comply with **Chapter 63: Seats - 610 - pp. 237 & 238.***

607.4   *Grab Bars*

*Grab bars shall comply with **Chapter 62: Grab Bars - 609 - pp. 234-236** and shall be provided in accordance with **607.4.1** or **607.4.2** - (following pages).*

Chapter 60: ICC/ANSI A117.1 - Bathtubs (continued)

EXCEPTIONS:

1. *Grab bars shall not be required to be installed in a bathing facility for a single occupant accessed only through a private office and not for common use or public use, provided reinforcement has been installed in walls and located so as to permit the installation of grab bars complying with **607.4** - (preceding page, below & following page).*

2. *In Type A units, grab bars are not required to be installed where reinforcement complying with **Chapter 13: Type A Units - 1003.11.9 - p. 49** is installed for the future installation of grab bars.*

607.4.1 Bathtubs with Permanent Seats

For bathtubs with permanent seats, grab bars complying with **607.4.1 - (below & following page)** shall be provided.

607.4.1.1 Back Wall

Two horizontal grab bars shall be provided on the back wall, one complying with **Chapter 62: Grab Bars - 609.4 - p. 235** and the other 9 inches (229mm) above the rim of the bathtub.

Each grab bar shall be located 15 inches (381mm) maximum from the head end wall and extend to 12 inches (305mm) maximum from the control end wall.

607.4.1.2 Control End Wall

Control end wall grab bars shall comply with **607.4.1.2 - (below & following page)**.

EXCEPTION:

An L-shaped continuous grab bar of equivalent dimensions and positioning shall be permitted to serve the function of separate vertical and horizontal grab bars.

607.4.1.2.1 Horizontal Grab Bar

A horizontal grab bar 24 inches (610mm) minimum in length shall be provided on the control end wall at the front edge of the bathtub.

607.4.1.2.2 Vertical Grab Bar

A vertical grab bar 18 inches (457mm) minimum in length shall be provided on the control end wall 3 inches (76mm) minimum to 6 inches (152mm) maximum above the horizontal grab bar, and 4 inches (102mm) maximum inward from the front edge of the bathtub.

Chapter 60: ICC/ANSI A117.1 - Bathtubs (continued)

See Diagrams 94(a),(b) - p. 399.

607.4.2 **Bathtubs without Permanent Seats**

For bathtubs without permanent seats, grab bars complying with **607.4.2 - (below)** *shall be provided.*

607.4.2.1 **Back Wall**

Two horizontal grab bars shall be provided on the back wall, one complying with **Chapter 62: Grab Bars - 609.4 - p. 235** *and the other 9 inches (229mm) above the rim of the bathtub.*

Each grab bar shall be 24 inches (610mm) minimum in length, located 24 inches (610mm) maximum from the head end wall and extend to 12 inches (305mm) maximum from the control end wall.

607.4.2.2 **Control End Wall**

Control end wall grab bars shall comply with **607.4.2.2 - (below).**

EXCEPTION:

An L-shaped continuous grab bar of equivalent dimensions and positioning shall be permitted to serve the function of separate vertical and horizontal grab bars.

607.4.2.2.1 **Horizontal Grab Bar**

A horizontal grab bar 24 inches (610mm) minimum in length shall be provided on the control end wall beginning near the front edge of the bathtub and extend toward the inside corner of the bathtub.

607.4.2.2.2 **Vertical Grab Bar**

A vertical grab bar 18 inches (457mm) minimum in length shall be provided on the control end wall 3 inches (76mm) minimum to 6 inches (152mm) maximum above the horizontal grab bar, and 4 inches (102mm) maximum inward from the front edge of the bathtub.

607.4.2.3 **Head End Wall**

A horizontal grab bar 12 inches (305mm) minimum in length shall be provided on the head end wall at the front edge of the bathtub.

See Diagrams 95(a),(b) - p. 400.

Chapter 60: ICC/ANSI A117.1 - Bathtubs (continued)

607.5 *Controls*

Controls, other than drain stoppers, shall be provided on an end wall, located between the bathtub rim and grab bar, and between the open side of the bathtub and the midpoint of the width of the bathtub.

Controls shall comply with **Chapter 55: Operable Parts - 309.4 - p. 208.**

See **Diagram 96 - p. 401.**

607.6 ***Hand Shower***

A hand shower with a hose 59 inches (1499mm) minimum in length, that can be used as both a fixed shower head and as a hand-held shower, shall be provided.

The hand shower shall have a control with a nonpositive shut-off feature.

An adjustable-height hand shower mounted on a vertical bar shall be installed so as to not obstruct the use of grab bars.

607.7 ***Bathtub Enclosures***

Enclosures for bathtubs shall not obstruct controls or transfer from wheelchairs onto bathtub seats or into bathtubs.

Enclosures on bathtubs shall not have tracks installed on the rim of the bathtub.

607.8 ***Water Temperature***

Bathtubs shall deliver water that is 120 degrees F (49 degrees C) maximum.

Chapter 61:

ICC/ANSI A117.1
SHOWER COMPARTMENTS

ICC/ANSI - Chapter 6   *Plumbing Elements and Facilities*

601   *General*

601.1   *Scope*

Plumbing elements and facilities required to be accessible by scoping provisions adopted by the administrative authority shall comply with the applicable provisions of this **Chapter - 608.**

ICC/ANSI - 608   *Shower Compartments*

608.1   *General*

Accessible shower compartments shall comply with this **Chapter - 608.**

608.2   *Size and Clearances*

608.2.1   *Transfer-Type Shower Compartments*

Transfer-type shower compartments shall have a clear inside dimension of 36 inches (914mm) in width and 36 inches (914mm) in depth, measured at the center point of opposing sides.

An entry 36 inches (914mm) minimum in width shall be provided.

A clearance of 48 inches (1219mm) minimum in length measured perpendicular from the control wall, and 36 inches (914mm) minimum in depth shall be provided adjacent to the open face of the compartment.

See Diagram 97 - p. 402.

608.2.2   *Standard Roll-in-Type Shower Compartments*

Standard roll-in-type shower compartments shall have a clear inside dimension of 60 inches (1524mm) minimum in width and 30 inches (762mm) minimum in depth, measured at the center point of opposing sides.

An entry 60-inches (1524mm) minimum in width shall be provided.

Chapter 61: ICC/ANSI A117.1 - Shower Compartments (continued)

A clearance of 60 inches (1524mm) minimum in length adjacent to the 60-inch (1524mm) width of the open face of the shower compartment, and 30 inches (762mm) minimum in depth, shall be provided.

*A lavatory complying with **Chapter 28: Sinks - 606 - pp. 118-120** shall be permitted at the end of the clearance opposite the shower compartment side where shower controls are positioned.*

See Diagram 98 - p. 403.

608.2.3 *Alternate Roll-in-Type Shower Compartment*

Alternate roll-in shower compartments shall have a clear inside dimension of 60 inches (1524mm) minimum in width, and 36 inches (914mm) in depth, measured at the center point of opposing sides.

An entry 36 inches (914mm) minimum in width shall be provided at one end of the 60-inch (1524mm) width of the compartment.

A seat wall, 24 inches (610mm) minimum and 36 inches (914mm) maximum in length, shall be provided on the entry side of the compartment.

See Diagram 99 - p. 404.

608.3 *Grab Bars*

*Grab bars shall comply with **Chapter 62: Grab Bars - 609 - pp. 234-236** and shall be provided in accordance with **608.3 - (below & following pages)**.*

Where multiple grab bars are used, required horizontal grab bars shall be installed at the same height above the floor.

EXCEPTIONS:

1. *Grab bars are not required to be installed in a shower facility for a single occupant, accessed only through a private office and not for common use or public use, provided reinforcement has been installed in walls and located so as to permit the installation of grab bars complying with **608.3 - (above, below & following pages)**.*

2. *In Type A units, grab bars are not required to be installed where reinforcement complying with **Chapter 13: Type A Units - 1003.11.9 - p. 49** is installed for the future installation of grab bars.*

Chapter 61: ICC/ANSI A117.1 - Shower Compartments (continued)

608.3.1   *Transfer-Type Showers*

*Grab bars for transfer-type showers shall comply with **608.3.1 - (below)**.*

608.3.1.1   *Horizontal Grab Bars*

Horizontal grab bars shall be provided across the control wall and on the back wall to a point 18 inches (457mm) from the control wall.

608.3.1.2   *Vertical Grab Bar*

A vertical grab bar 18 inches (457mm) minimum in length shall be provided on the control end wall 3 inches (76mm) minimum to 6 inches (152mm) maximum above the horizontal grab bar, and 4 inches (102mm) maximum inward from the front edge of the shower.

608.3.1.3   *Grab Bar Configuration*

*Grab bars complying with **608.3.1.1 and 608.3.1.2 - (above)** shall be permitted to be separate bars, a single piece bar, or combination thereof.*

See Diagram 100 - p. 405.

608.3.2   *Standard Roll-in-Type Showers*

In standard roll-in-type showers, grab bars shall be provided on three walls of showers without seats.

Where a seat is provided in a standard roll-in-type shower, grab bars shall be provided on the back wall and on the wall opposite the seat.

Grab bars shall not be provided above the seat.

Grab bars shall be 6 inches (152mm) maximum from the adjacent wall.

See Diagrams 101(a),(b) - p. 406.

608.3.3   *Alternate Roll-in-Type Showers*

In alternate roll-in-type showers, grab bars shall be provided on the back wall and the end wall adjacent to the seat.

Grab bars shall not be provided above the seat.

Grab bars shall be 6 inches (152mm) maximum from the adjacent wall.

Chapter 61: ICC/ANSI A117.1 - Shower Compartments (continued)

See Diagram 102 - p. 407.

608.4   ***Seats***

A folding or nonfolding seat shall be provided in transfer-type shower compartments.

A seat shall be provided in an alternate roll-in-type shower compartment.

*In standard and alternate roll-in-type showers where a seat is provided, if the seat extends over the minimum clear inside dimension required by this **Chapter - 608.2.2 or 608.2.3 - pp. 228 & 229**, the seat shall be a folding seat.*

*Seats shall comply with **Chapter 63: Seats - 610 - pp. 237 & 238**.*

> *EXCEPTIONS:*
>
> 1. *A shower seat is not required to be installed in a shower facility for a single occupant, accessed only through a private office and not for common use or public use, provided reinforcement has been installed in walls and located so as to permit the installation of grab bars complying with **608.4 - (above)**.*
>
> 2. *In Type A units, a shower seat is not required to be installed where reinforcement complying with **Chapter 13: Type A Units - 1003.11.9 - p. 49** is installed for the future installation of a shower seat.*

608.5   ***Controls***

*Controls and hand showers shall comply with **608.5 - (below & following page)** and **Chapter 55: Operable Parts - 309.4 - p. 208**.*

608.5.1   ***Transfer-Type Showers***

In transfer-type showers, the controls and hand shower shall be located on the control wall opposite the seat, 38 inches (965mm) minimum and 48 inches (1219mm) maximum above the shower floor, within 15 inches (381mm), left or right, of the centerline of the seat.

See Diagram 103 - p. 408.

608.5.2   ***Standard Roll-in Showers***

In standard roll-in showers, the controls and hand shower shall be located 38 inches (965mm) minimum and 48 inches (1219mm) maximum above the shower floor.

In standard roll-in showers with seats, the controls and hand shower shall be located on the back wall, no more than 27 inches (686mm) maximum from the end wall behind the seat.

Chapter 61: ICC/ANSI A117.1 - Shower Compartments (continued)

See Diagrams 104(a),(b) - p. 409.

608.5.3   *Alternate Roll-in Showers*

In alternate roll-in showers, the controls and hand shower shall be located 38 inches (965mm) minimum and 48 inches (1219mm) maximum above the shower floor.

In alternate roll-in showers with controls and hand shower located on the end wall adjacent to the seat, the controls and hand shower shall be 27 inches (686mm) maximum from the seat wall.

In alternate roll-in showers with the controls and hand shower located on the back wall opposite the seat, the controls and hand shower shall be located within 15 inches (381mm), left or right, of the centerline of the seat.

    EXCEPTION:

        A fixed shower head with the controls and shower head located on the back wall opposite the seat shall be permitted.

See Diagrams 105(a),(b),(c),(d) - p. 410.

608.6   *Hand Showers*

A hand shower with a hose 59 inches (1499mm) minimum in length, that can be used both as a fixed shower head and as a hand-held shower, shall be provided.

The hand shower shall have a control with a nonpositive shut-off feature.

An adjustable-height shower head mounted on a vertical bar shall be installed so as to not obstruct the use of grab bars.

    EXCEPTION:

        A fixed shower head shall be permitted in lieu of a hand shower where the scoping provisions of the administrative authority require a fixed shower head.

608.7   *Thresholds*

*Thresholds in roll-in-type shower compartments 1/2-inch (13mm) maximum in height in accordance with **Chapter 49: Changes in Level - 303 - p. 197.***

In transfer-type shower compartments, thresholds 1/2-inch (12.7mm) maximum in height shall be beveled, rounded, or vertical.

Chapter 61: ICC/ANSI A117.1 - Shower Compartments (continued)

EXCEPTION:

> *In existing facilities, in transfer-type shower compartments where provision of a threshold 1/2-inch (12.7mm) in height would disturb the structural reinforcement of the floor slab, a threshold 2 inches (51mm) maximum in height shall be permitted.*

608.8 **Shower Enclosures**

Shower compartment enclosures for shower compartments shall not obstruct controls or obstruct transfer from wheelchairs onto shower seats.

608.9 **Water Temperature**

Showers shall deliver water that is 120 degrees F (49 degrees C) maximum.

Chapter 62:

ICC/ANSI A117.1
GRAB BARS

ICC/ANSI - Chapter 6   ***Plumbing Elements and Facilities***

601   ***General***

601.1   ***Scope***

*Plumbing elements and facilities required to be accessible by scoping provisions adopted by the administrative authority shall comply with the applicable provisions of this **Chapter - 609**.*

ICC/ANSI - 609   ***Grab Bars***

609.1   ***General***

*Grab bars in accessible toilet or bathing facilities shall comply with this **Chapter - 609**.*

609.2   ***Cross Section***

*Grab bars shall have a cross section complying with **609.2.1 or 609.2.2** - (below).*

609.2.1   ***Circular Cross Section***

Grab bars with a circular cross section shall have an outside diameter of 1-1/4 inches (32mm) minimum and 2 inches (51mm) maximum.

609.2.2   ***Non-Circular Cross Section***

Grab bars with a non-circular cross section shall have a cross section dimension of 2 inches (51mm) maximum, and a perimeter dimension of 4 inches (102mm) minimum and 4.8 inches (122mm) maximum.

See Diagrams 106(b),(c) - p. 411.

609.3   ***Spacing***

The space between the wall and the grab bar shall be 1-1/2 inches (38mm).

The space between the grab bar and projecting objects below and at the ends of the grab bar shall be 1-1/2 inches (38mm) minimum.

Chapter 62: ICC/ANSI A117.1 - Grab Bars (continued)

The space between the grab bar and projecting objects above the grab bar shall be 12 inches (305mm) minimum.

EXCEPTIONS:

1. *The space between the grab bars and shower controls, shower fittings, and other grab bars above the grab bar shall be permitted to be 1-1/2 inches (38mm) minimum.*

2. *Swing-up grab bars shall not be required to comply with **609.3** - (preceding page & above).*

See Diagram 106(d) - p. 411.

609.4   ***Position of Grab Bars***

Grab bars shall be installed in a horizontal position, 33 inches (838mm) minimum and 36 inches (914mm) maximum above the floor measured to the top of the gripping surface.

*At water closets primarily for children's use complying with **Chapter 58: Water Closets and Toilet Compartments for Children's Use - 604.10 - pp. 221 & 222**, grab bars shall be installed in a horizontal position 18 inches (457mm) minimum to 27 inches (686mm) maximum above the floor measured to the top of the gripping surface.*

EXCEPTIONS:

1. *The lower grab bar on the back wall of a bathtub required by **Chapter 60: Bathtubs - 607.4.1.1 and 607.4.2.1 - pp. 225 & 226**.*

2. *Vertical grab bars required by **Chapter 27: Water Closet Compartment - 604.5.1 - p. 112, Chapter 60: Bathtubs - 607.4.1.2.2 and 607.4.2.2.2 - pp. 225 & 226, and Chapter 61: Shower Compartments - 608.3.1.2 - p. 230**.*

609.5   ***Surface Hazards***

Grab bars, and any wall or other surfaces adjacent to grab bars, shall be free of sharp or abrasive elements.

Edges shall be rounded.

609.6   ***Fittings***

Grab bars shall not rotate within their fittings.

Chapter 62: ICC/ANSI A117.1 - Grab Bars (continued)

609.7   *Installation*

Grab bars shall be installed in any manner that provides a gripping surface at the locations specified in ICC/ANSI A117.1-2003 and does not obstruct the clear floor space.

609.8   ***Structural Strength***

Allowable stresses shall not be exceeded for materials used where a vertical or horizontal force of 250 pounds (1112N) is applied at any point on the grab bar, fastener mounting device, or supporting structure.

Chapter 63:

ICC/ANSI A117.1
SEATS

ICC/ANSI - Chapter 6   *Plumbing Elements and Facilities*

601   *General*

601.1   *Scope*

*Plumbing elements and facilities required to be accessible by scoping provisions adopted by the administrative authority shall comply with the applicable provisions of this **Chapter - 610**.*

ICC/ANSI - 610   *Seats*

610.1   *General*

*Seats in accessible bathtubs and shower compartments shall comply with this **Chapter - 610**.*

610.2   **Bathtub Seats**

The height of bathtub seats shall be 17 inches (432mm) minimum to 19 inches (483mm) maximum above the bathroom floor, measured to the top of the seat.

Removable in-tub seats shall be 15 inches (381mm) minimum and 16 inches (406mm) maximum in depth.

Removable in-tub seats shall be capable of secure placement.

Permanent seats shall be 15 inches (381mm) minimum in depth and shall extend from the back wall to or beyond the outer edge of the bathtub.

Permanent seats shall be positioned at the head end of the bathtub.

See Diagrams 107(a),(b) - p. 412.

610.3   **Shower Compartment Seats**

Where a seat is provided in a standard roll-in shower compartment, it shall be a folding type and shall be on the wall adjacent to the controls.

The height of the seat shall be 17 inches (432mm) minimum and 19 inches (483mm) maximum above the bathroom floor, measured to the top of the seat.

Chapter 63: ICC/ANSI A117.1 - Seats (continued)

In a transfer-type and alternate roll-in-type showers, the seat shall extend along the seat wall to a point within 3 inches (76mm) of the compartment entry.

In standard roll-in-type showers, the seat shall extend from the control wall to a point within 3 inches (76mm) of the compartment entry.

*Seats shall comply with **610.3.1 or 610.3.2 - (below).***

610.3.1   ***Rectangular Seats***

The rear edge of a rectangular seat shall be 2-1/2 inches (64mm) maximum and the front edge 15 inches (381mm) minimum to 16 inches (406mm) maximum from the seat wall.

The side edge of the seat shall be 1-1/2 inches (38mm) maximum from the back wall of a transfer-type shower and 1-1/2 inches (38mm) maximum from the control wall of a roll-in-type shower.

See Diagram 108(a) - p. 413.

610.3.2   ***L-Shaped Seats***

The rear edge of an L-shaped seat shall be 2-1/2 inches (64mm) maximum and the front edge 15 inches (381mm) minimum to 16 inches (406mm) maximum from the seat wall.

The rear edge of the "L" portion of the seat shall be 1-1/2 inches (38mm) maximum from the wall and the front edge shall be 14 inches (356mm) minimum and 15 inches (381mm) maximum from the wall.

The end of the "L" shall be 22 inches (559mm) minimum and 23 inches (584mm) maximum from the main seat wall.

See Diagram 108(b) - p. 413.

610.4   ***Structural Strength***

Allowable stresses shall not be exceeded for materials used where a vertical or horizontal force of 250 pounds (1112N) is applied at any point on the seat, fastener mounting device, or supporting structure.

Chapter 64:

ICC/ANSI A117.1
WASHING MACHINES AND CLOTHES DRYERS

ICC/ANSI - Chapter 6   **Plumbing Elements and Facilities**

601   **General**

601.1   **Scope**

Plumbing elements and facilities required to be accessible by scoping provisions adopted by the administrative authority shall comply with the applicable provisions of this **Chapter - 611.**

ICC/ANSI - 611   **Washing Machines and Clothes Dryers**

611.1   **General**

Accessible washing machines and clothes dryers shall comply with this **Chapter - 611.**

611.2   **Clear Floor Space**

A clear floor space complying with **Chapter 51: Clear Floor Space - 305 - pp. 200 & 201,** *positioned for parallel approach, shall be provided.*

The clear floor space shall be centered on the appliance.

611.3   **Operable Parts**

Operable parts, including doors, lint screens, detergent and bleach compartments, shall comply with **Chapter 55: Operable Parts - 309 - p. 208.**

611.4   **Height**

Top loading machines shall have the door to the laundry compartment 36 inches (914mm) maximum above the floor.

Front loading machines shall have the bottom of the opening to the laundry compartment 15 inches (381mm) minimum and 34 inches (864mm) maximum above the floor.

See Diagrams 109(a),(b) - p. 414.

Chapter 65:

ICC/ANSI A117.1
TELEPHONES

ICC/ANSI - Chapter 7   *Communication Elements and Features*

701   *General*

701.1   *Scope*

Communications elements and features required to be accessible by the scoping provisions adopted by the administrative authority shall comply with the applicable provisions of this **Chapter - 704.**

ICC/ANSI - 704   *Telephones*

704.1   *General*

Accessible public telephones shall comply with this **Chapter - 704.**

704.2   *Wheelchair Accessible Telephones*

Wheelchair accessible public telephones shall comply with **704.2 - (below & following page).**

704.2.1   *Clear Floor Space*

A clear floor space complying with **Chapter 51: Clear Floor Space - 305 - pp. 200 & 201** shall be provided.

The clear floor space shall not be obstructed by bases, enclosures, or seats.

704.2.1.1   *Parallel Approach*

Where a parallel approach is provided, the distance from the edge of the telephone enclosure to the face of the telephone shall be 10 inches (254mm) maximum.

See Diagram 110(a) - p. 415.

704.2.1.2   *Forward Approach*

Where a forward approach is provided, the distance from the front edge of a counter within the enclosure to the face of the telephone shall be 20 inches (508mm) maximum.

See Diagram 110(b) - p. 415.

Chapter 65: ICC/ANSI A117.1 - Telephones (continued)

704.2.2   ***Operable Parts***

*The highest operable part of the telephone shall comply with **Chapter 54: Reach Ranges - 308 - pp. 206 & 207**.*

Telephones shall have push button controls where service for such equipment is available.

704.2.3   ***Telephone Directories***

*Where provided, telephone directories shall comply with **Chapter 55: Operable Parts - 309 - p. 208**.*

704.2.4   ***Cord Length***

The telephone handset cord shall be 29 inches (737mm) minimum in length.

704.2.5   ***Hearing-Aid Compatibility***

Telephones shall be hearing-aid compatible.

704.3   ***Volume-Control Telephones***

Public telephones required to have volume controls shall be equipped with a receiver volume control that provides a gain adjustable up to 20 dB minimum.

Incremental volume controls shall provide at least one intermediate step of gain of 12 dB minimum.

An automatic reset shall be provided.

704.4   ***TTY***

TTY's required at a public pay telephone shall be permanently affixed within, or adjacent to, the telephone enclosure.

Where an acoustic coupler is used, the telephone cord shall be of sufficient length to allow connection of the TTY and the telephone handset.

704.5   ***Height***

When is use, the touch surface of TTY keypads shall be 34 inches (864mm) minimum above the floor.

Chapter 65: ICC/ANSI A117.1 - Telephones (continued)

EXCEPTION:

> *Where seats are provided, TTY's shall not be required to comply with 704.5 - (preceding page & below).*

704.5   **Shelf**

Where pay telephones designed to accommodate a portable TTY are provided, they shall be equipped with a shelf and an electrical outlet within or adjacent to the telephone enclosure.

The telephone handset shall be capable of being placed flush on the surface of the shelf.

The shelf shall be capable of accommodating a TTY and shall have a vertical clearance of 6 inches (152mm) minimum in height above the area where the TTY is placed.

704.7   **Protruding Objects**

*Telephones, enclosures, and related equipment shall comply with **Chapter 53: Protruding Objects - 307 - pp. 204 & 205**.*

Chapter 66:

ICC/ANSI A117.1
ASSISTIVE LISTENING SYSTEMS

ICC/ANSI - Chapter 7 **Communication Elements and Features**

701 **General**

701.1 **Scope**

Communications elements and features required to be accessible by the scoping provisions adopted by the administrative authority shall comply with the applicable provisions of this **Chapter - 706.**

ICC/ANSI - 706 **Assistive Listening Systems**

706.1 **General**

Accessible assistive listening systems in assembly areas shall comply with this **Chapter - 706.**

706.2 **Receiver Jacks**

Receivers required for use with an assistive listening system shall include a 1/8-inch (3.2mm) standard mono jack.

706.3 **Receiver Hearing-Aid Compatibility**

Receivers required to be hearing-aid compatible shall interface with telecoils in hearing-aids through the provision of neck loops.

706.4 **Sound Pressure Level**

Assistive listening systems shall be capable of providing a sound pressure level of 110 dB minimum and 118 dB maximum, with a dynamic range on the volume control of 50 dB.

706.5 **Signal-to-Noise Ratio**

The signal-to-noise ratio for internally generated noise in assistive listening systems shall be 18 dB minimum.

706.6 **Peak Clipping Level**

Peak clipping shall not exceed 18 dB of clipping relative to the peaks of speech.

Chapter 67:
ICC/ANSI A117.1
AUTOMATIC TELLER MACHINES (ATM's) AND FAIR MACHINES

ICC/ANSI - Chapter 7   *Communication Elements and Features*

701   *General*

701.1   *Scope*

*Communications elements and features required to be accessible by the scoping provisions adopted by the administrative authority shall comply with the applicable provisions of this **Chapter - 707**.*

ICC/ANSI - 707   *Automatic Teller Machines (ATMs) and Fare Machines*

707.1   *General*

*Accessible automatic teller machines and fare machines shall comply with this **Chapter - 707**.*

707.2   *Clear Floor Space*

*A clear floor space complying with **Chapter 51: Clear Floor Space - 305 - pp. 200 & 201** shall be provided in front of the machine.*

> EXCEPTION:
>
> *Clear floor space is not required at drive-up only automatic teller machines and fare machines.*

707.3   *Operable Parts*

*Operable parts shall comply with **Chapter 55: Operable Parts - 309 - p. 208**.*

Each operable part shall be able to be differentiated by sound or touch, without activation.

> EXCEPTION:
>
> *Drive-up only automatic teller machines and fare machines shall not be required to comply with **Chapter 55: Operable Parts - 309.2 or 309.3 - p. 208**.*

707.4   *Privacy*

Automatic teller machines shall provide the opportunity for the same degree of privacy of input and output available to all individuals.

Chapter 67: ICC/ANSI A117.1 - (ATMs) and Fare Machines (continued)

707.5 *Numeric Keys*

Numeric keys shall be arranged in a 12-key ascending or descending telephone keypad layout.

The number Five key shall have a single raised dot.

See Diagrams 111(a),(b) - p. 416.

707.6 *Function Keys*

*Function keys shall comply with **707.6 - (below)**.*

707.6.1 *Tactile Symbols*

*Function key surfaces shall have raised tactile symbols as shown in **Table S - (below)**.*

Table S
Tactile Symbols

Key Function	Description of Tactile Symbol	Tactile Symbol
Enter or Proceed:	CIRCLE	○
Clear or Correct:	LEFT ARROW	←
Cancel:	"X"	x
Add Value:	PLUS SIGN	+
Decrease Value:	MINUS SIGN	-

707.6.2 *Contrast*

Function keys shall contrast visually from background surfaces.

Characters and symbols on key surfaces shall contrast visually from key surfaces.

Visual contrast shall be either light-on-dark or dark-on-light.

 EXCEPTION:

  *Tactile symbols required by **707.6.1 - (above)** shall not be required to comply with **707.6.2 - (above)**.*

707.7   **Display Screen**

*The display screen shall comply with **707.7 - (below)**.*

707.7.1   **Visibility**

The display screen shall be visible from a point located 40 inches (1016mm) above the center of the clear floor space in front of the machine.

> *EXCEPTION:*
>
>> *Drive-up only automatic teller machines and fare machines shall not be required to comply with **707.7.1 - (above)**.*

707.7.2   **Characters**

Characters displayed on the screen shall be in a sans serif font.

The uppercase letter "I" shall be used to determine the allowable height of all characters of the font.

The uppercase letter "I" of the font shall be 3/16-inch (4.8mm) minimum in height.

Characters shall contrast with the background with either light characters on a dark background, or dark characters on a light background.

707.8   **Speech Output**

Machines shall be speech enabled.

Operating instructions and orientation, visible transaction prompts, user input verification, error messages, and all displayed information for full use shall be accessible to and independently usable by individuals with vision impairments.

Speech shall be delivered through a mechanism that is readily available to all users including, but not limited to, an industry standard connector or a telephone handset.

Speech shall be recorded or digitized human, or synthesized.

> *EXCEPTIONS:*
>
> 1. *Audible tones shall be permitted in lieu of speech for visible output that is not displayed for security purposes, including, but not limited to, asterisks representing personal identification numbers.*

Chapter 67: ICC/ANSI A117.1 - (ATMs) and Fare Machines (continued)

2. *Advertisements and other similar information shall not be required to be audible unless they convey information that can be used in the transaction being conducted.*

3. *Where speech synthesis cannot be supported, dynamic alphabetic output shall not be required to be audible.*

707.8.1 User Control

Speech shall be capable of being repeated and interrupted by the user.

There shall be a volume control for the speech function.

EXCEPTION:

Speech output for any single function shall be permitted to be automatically interrupted when a transaction is selected.

707.8.2 Receipts

Where receipts are provided, speech output devices shall provide audible balance inquiry information, error messages, and all other information on the printed receipt necessary to complete or verify the transaction.

EXCEPTIONS:

1. *Machine location, date and time of transaction, customer account number, and the machine identifier shall not be required to be audible.*

2. *Information on printed receipts that duplicates audible information available on-screen shall not be required to be presented in the form of an audible receipt.*

3. *Printed copies of bank statements and checks shall not be required to be audible.*

707.9 Input Controls

At least one tactually discernible input control shall be provided for each function.

Where provided, key surfaces not on active areas of display screens shall be raised above surrounding surfaces.

Where membrane keys are the only method of input, each shall be tactually discernible from surrounding surfaces and adjacent keys.

Chapter 67: ICC/ANSI A117.1 - (ATMs) and Fare Machines (continued)

707.10 *Braille Instructions*

Braille instructions for initiating the speech mode shall be provided.

*Braille shall comply with **Chapter 44: Signage - 703.4 - pp. 179 & 180**.*

Chapter 68:

ICC/ANSI A117.1
TWO-WAY COMMUNICATION SYSTEMS

ICC/ANSI - Chapter 7   ***Communication Elements and Features***

701   ***General***

701.1   ***Scope***

Communications elements and features required to be accessible by the scoping provisions adopted by the administrative authority shall comply with the applicable provisions of this **Chapter - 708.**

ICC/ANSI - 708   ***Two-Way Communication Systems***

708.1   ***General***

Accessible two-way communication systems shall comply with this **Chapter - 708.**

708.2   ***Audible and Visual Indicators***

The system shall provide both visual and audible signals.

708.3   ***Handsets***

Handset cords, if provided, shall be 29 inches (737mm) minimum in length.

Chapter 69:

ICC/ANSI A117.1
TRANSPORTATION FACILITIES

ICC/ANSI - Chapter 8 **Special Rooms and Spaces**

801 *General*

801.1 *Scope*

Special rooms and spaces required to be accessible by the scoping provisions adopted by the administrative authority shall comply with the applicable provisions of this **Chapter - 805.**

ICC/ANSI - 805 **Transportation Facilities**

805.1 *General*

Transportation facilities shall comply with this **Chapter - 805.**

805.2 **Bus Boarding and Alighting Areas**

Bus boarding and alighting areas shall comply with 805.2 - (below & following page).

805.2.1 *Surface*

Bus stop boarding and alighting areas shall have a firm, stable surface.

805.2.2 *Dimensions*

Bus stop boarding and alighting areas shall have a 96 inches (2438mm) minimum clear length, measured perpendicular to the curb or vehicle roadway edge, and a 60 inches (1524mm) minimum clear width, measured parallel to the vehicle roadway.

See Diagram 112 - p. 417.

805.2.3 *Slope*

The slope of the bus stop boarding and alighting area parallel to the vehicle roadway shall be the same as the roadway, to the maximum extent practicable.

The slope of the bus stop boarding and alighting area perpendicular to the vehicle roadway shall be 1:48 maximum.

Chapter 69: ICC/ANSI A117.1 - Transportation Facilities (continued)

805.2.4 *Connection*

*Bus stop boarding and alighting areas shall be connected to streets, sidewalks, or pedestrian paths by an accessible route complying with **Chapter 4: Accessible Route - 402 - pp. 12 & 13**.*

805.3 ***Bus Shelters***

*Bus shelters shall provide a minimum clear floor space complying with **Chapter 51: Clear Floor Space - 305 - pp. 200 & 201** entirely within the shelter.*

*Bus shelters shall be connected by an accessible route complying with **Chapter 4: Accessible Route - 402 - pp. 12 & 13** to a boarding and alighting area complying with **805.2 - (preceding page & above)**.*

See Diagram 113 - p. 418.

805.4 ***Bus Signs***

*Bus route identification signs shall have visual characters complying with **Chapter 44: Signage - 703.2.2, 703.2.3, and 703.2.5 through 703.2.8 - pp. 173-175**.*

*In addition, bus route identification numbers shall be visual characters complying with **Chapter 44: Signage - 703.2.4 - p. 174**.*

EXCEPTION:

*Bus schedules, timetables and maps that are posted at the bus stop or bus bay shall not be required to comply with **805.4 - (above)**.*

805.5 ***Rail Platforms***

*Rail platforms shall comply with **805.5 - (below & following page)**.*

805.5.1 *Slope*

Rail platforms shall not exceed a slope of 1:48 in all directions.

EXCEPTION:

Where platforms serve vehicles operating on existing track or track laid in existing roadway, the slope of the platform parallel to the track shall be permitted to be equal to the slope (grade) of the roadway or existing track.

Chapter 69: ICC/ANSI A117.1 - Transportation Facilities (continued)

805.5.2   *Detectable Warnings*

*Platform boarding edges not protected by platform screens or guards shall have a detectable warning complying with **Chapter 36: Detectable Warnings - 705 - pp. 154 & 155**, 24 inches (610mm) in width, along the full length of the public use area of the platform.*

805.6   *Rail Station Signs*

*Rail station signs shall comply with **805.6 - (below)**.*

    EXCEPTION:

        *Signs shall not be required to comply with **805.6.1 and 805.6.2 - (below)** where audible signs are remotely transmitted to hand-held receivers, or are user- or proximity-actuated.*

805.6.1   *Entrances*

*Where signs identify a station or a station entrance, at least one sign with tactile characters complying with **Chapter 44: Signage - 703.3 - pp. 176-178** shall be provided at each entrance.*

805.6.2   *Routes and Destinations*

*Lists of stations, routes and destinations served by the station that are located on boarding areas, platforms, or mezzanines shall have visual characters complying with **Chapter 44: Signage - 703.2 - pp. 173-176**.*

*A minimum of one tactile sign complying with **Chapter 44: Signage - 703.3 - pp. 176-178** shall be provided on each platform or boarding area to identify the specific station.*

    EXCEPTION:

        Where sign space is limited, characters shall not be required to exceed 3 inches (76mm) in height.

805.6.3   *Station Names*

*Stations covered by this chapter shall have identification signs with visual characters complying with **Chapter 44: Signage - 703.2 - pp. 173-176**.*

The signs shall be clearly visible and within the sightlines of a standing or sitting passenger from within the vehicle on both sides when not obstructed by another vehicle.

Chapter 69: ICC/ANSI A117.1 - Transportation Facilities (continued)

805.7   *Public Address Systems*

Where public address systems convey audible information to the public, the same or equivalent information shall be provided in a visual format.

805.8   *Clocks*

Where clocks are provided for use by the public, the clock face shall be uncluttered so that its elements are clearly visible.

Hands, numerals and digits shall contrast with the background either light-on-dark or dark-on-light.

*Where clocks are installed overhead, numerals and digits shall be visual characters complying with **Chapter 44: Signage - 703.2 - pp. 173-176.***

805.9   *Escalators*

Where provided, escalators shall have a 32-inch (813mm) minimum clear width, and shall comply with Requirements 6.1.3.5.6 - Step Demarcations, and 6.1.3.6.5 - Flat Steps of ASME A17.1 listed in ICC/ANSI A117-2003 - Section 105.2.5.

805.10   *Track Crossings*

*Where a circulation path serving boarding platforms crosses tracks, it shall comply with **Chapter 4: Accessible Route - 402 - pp. 12 & 13.***

*See **Diagram 114** - p. 419.*

    EXCEPTION:

        Openings for wheel flanges shall be permitted to be 2-1/2 inches (64mm) maximum.

Chapter 70:

FAIR HOUSING ACCESSIBILITY GUIDELINES (FHAG)

Application of the Guidelines

The design specifications (guidelines) presented *(below & following pages)* apply to new construction of "covered multifamily dwellings", as defined *(below):*

These guidelines are recommended for designing dwellings that comply with the requirements of the Fair Housing Amendments Act of 1988.

Definition

"Covered multifamily dwellings" or "covered multifamily dwellings subject to the Fair Housing Amendments" means buildings consisting of four or more dwelling units if such buildings have one or more elevators; and ground floor dwelling units in other buildings consisting of four or more dwelling units.

Dwelling units within a single structure separated by firewalls do not constitute separate buildings.

Guidelines
Accessible Building Entrance on an Accessible Route

Under section FHAG 100.205(a), covered multifamily dwellings shall be designed and constructed to have at least one building entrance on an accessible route, unless it is impractical to do so because of terrain or unusual characteristics of the site.

(1)   **Building Entrance**

Each building on a site shall have at least one building entrance on an accessible route unless prohibited by the terrain, as provided in this *Chapter - (2)(a)(i) or (2)(a)(ii) - pp. 256 & 257,* or unusual characteristics of the site, as provided in this *Chapter - (2)(b) - p. 257.*

This guideline applies both to a single building on a site and to multiple buildings on a site.

Separate Ground Floor Unit Entrances

(a)   When a ground floor unit of a building has a separate entrance, each such ground floor unit shall be served by an accessible route, except for any unit where the terrain or unusual characteristics of the site prohibit the provision of an accessible route to the entrance of that unit.

Chapter 70: Fair Housing Accessibility Guidelines (FHAG) (continued)

Multiple Entrances

(b) Only one entrance is required to be accessible to any one ground floor of a building, except in cases where an individual dwelling unit has a separate exterior entrance, or where the building contains clusters of dwelling units, with each cluster sharing a different exterior entrance.

In these cases, more than one entrance may be required to be accessible, as determined by analysis of the site.

In every case, the accessible entrance should be on an accessible route to the covered dwelling unit it serves.

(2) **Site Impracticality**

Covered multifamily dwellings with elevators shall be designed and constructed to provide at least one accessible entrance on an accessible route, regardless of terrain or unusual characteristics of the site.

Covered multifamily dwellings without elevators shall be designed and constructed to provide at least one accessible entrance on an accessible route unless terrain or unusual characteristics of the site are such that the following conditions are found to exist:

Site Impracticality Due to Terrain

(a) There are two alternative tests for determining site impracticality due to terrain: the individual building test provided in *(2)(a)(i) - (following page),* or the site analysis test provided in *(2)(a)(ii) - (following pages).*

These tests may be used as follows.

A site with a single building having a common entrance for all units may be analyzed only as described in *(2)(a)(i) - (following page).*

All other sites, including a site with a single building having multiple entrances serving either individual dwelling units or clusters of dwelling units, may be analyzed using the methodology in either *(2)(a)(i) - (following page) or (2)(a)(ii) - (following pages).*

For these sites for which either test is applicable, regardless of which test selected, at least 20 percent of the total ground floor units in non-elevator buildings, on any site, must comply with the guidelines.

Chapter 70: Fair Housing Accessibility Guidelines (FHAG) (continued)

Individual Building Test

(i) It is impractical to provide an accessible entrance served by an accessible route when the terrain of the site is such that:

    (A) The slopes of the undisturbed site measured between the planned entrance and all vehicular or pedestrian arrival points within 50 feet (15 240mm) of the planned entrance exceed 10 percent; and

    (B) The slopes of the planned finished grade measured between the entrance and all vehicular or pedestrian arrival points within 50 feet (15 240mm) of the planned entrance also exceed 10 percent.

If there are no vehicular or pedestrian arrival points within 50 feet (15 240mm) of the planned entrance, the slope for the purposes of this *(2)(a)(i) - (above)* will be measured to the closest vehicular or pedestrian arrival point.

For purposes of these guidelines, vehicular or pedestrian arrival points include public or resident parking areas; public transportation stops; passenger loading zones; and public streets or sidewalks.

To determine site impracticality, the slope would be measured at ground level from the point of the planned entrance on a straight line to (i) each vehicular or pedestrian arrival point that is within 50 feet (15 240mm) of the planned entrance, or (ii) if there are no vehicular or pedestrian arrival points within that specified area, the vehicular or pedestrian arrival point closest to the planned entrance.

In the case of sidewalks, the closest point to the entrance will be where a public sidewalk entering the site intersects with the sidewalk to the entrance.

In the case of resident parking areas, the closest point to the planned entrance will be measured from the entry point to the parking area that is located closest to the planned entrance.

Site Analysis Test

(ii) Alternatively, for a site having multiple buildings, or a site with a single building with multiple entrances, impracticality of providing an accessible entrance served by an accessible route can be established by the following steps:

    (A) The percentage of the total buildable area of the undisturbed site with a natural grade less than 10 percent shall be calculated.

    The analysis of the existing slope (before grading) shall be done on a topographic survey with 2-foot (610mm) contour intervals with slope determination made between each successive interval.

Chapter 70: Fair Housing Accessibility Guidelines (FHAG) (continued)

The accuracy of the slope analysis shall be certified by a professional licensed engineer, landscape architect, architect or surveyor.

(B) To determine the practicality of providing accessibility to planned multifamily dwellings based on the topography of the existing natural terrain, the minimum percentage of ground floor units to be made accessible should equal the percentage of the total buildable area (not including floodplains, wetlands, or other restricted use areas) of the undisturbed site that has an existing natural grade of less than 10 percent slope.

(C) In addition to the percentage established in *(B) - (above),* all ground floor units in a building, or ground floor units served by a particular entrance, shall be made accessible if the entrance to the units is on an accessible route, defined as a walkway with a slope between the planned entrance and a pedestrian or vehicular arrival point that is no greater than 8.33 percent.

Site Impracticality Due to Unusual Characteristics

(b) Unusual characteristics include sites located in a federally-designated floodplain or coastal high-hazard area and sites subject to other similar requirements of law or code that the lowest floor or the lowest structural member of the lowest floor must be raised to a specified level at or above the base flood elevation.

An accessible route to a building entrance is impractical due to unusual characteristics of the site when:

(i) the unusual site characteristics result in a difference in finished grade elevation exceeding 30 inches (762mm) and 10 percent measured between an entrance and all vehicular or pedestrian arrival points within 50 feet (15 240mm) of the planned entrance;
or
(ii) if there are no vehicular or pedestrian arrival points within 50 feet (15 240mm) of the planned entrance, the unusual characteristics result in a difference in finished grade elevation exceeding 30 inches (762mm) and 10 percent measured between an entrance and the closest vehicular or pedestrian arrival point.

(3) **Exceptions to Site Impracticality**

Regardless of site considerations described in *(1) and (2) - (preceding pages & above),* an accessible entrance on an accessible route is practical when:

(a) There is an elevator connecting the parking area with the dwelling units on a ground floor.

Chapter 70: Fair Housing Accessibility Guidelines (FHAG) (continued)

(In this case, those dwelling units on the ground floor served by an elevator, and at least one of each type of public and common use areas, would be subject to these guidelines.)

However:

(i) Where a building elevator is provided only as a means of creating an accessible route to dwelling units on a ground floor, the building is not considered an elevator building for purposes of these guidelines; hence, only the ground floor dwelling units would be covered.

(ii) If the building elevator is provided as a means of access to dwelling units other than dwelling units on a ground floor, then the building is an elevator building which is a covered multifamily dwelling, and the elevator in that building must provide accessibility to all dwelling units in the building regardless of the slope of the natural terrain;

or

(b) An elevated walkway is planned between a building entrance and a vehicular or pedestrian arrival point and the planned walkway has a slope no greater than 10 percent.

(4) **Accessible Entrance**

An entrance that complies with ADAAG - "Entrances" meets FHAG section 100.205(a).

(5) **Accessible Route**

An accessible route that complies with ADAAG - "Accessible Routes" would meet FHAG section 100.205(a).

If the slope of the finished grade between covered multifamily dwellings and a public or common use facility (including parking) exceeds 8.33 percent, or where other physical barriers (natural or manmade) or legal restrictions, all of which are outside the control of the owner, prevent the installation of an accessible pedestrian route, an acceptable alternative is to provide access via a vehicular route, so long as necessary site provisions such as parking spaces and curb ramps are provided at the public or common use facility.

Accessible and Usable Public and Common Use Areas

FHAG section 100.205(c)(1) provides that covered multifamily dwellings with a building entrance on an accessible route shall be designed in such a manner that the public and common use areas are readily accessible to and usable by handicapped persons.

Chapter 70: Fair Housing Accessibility Guidelines (FHAG) (continued)

Usable Doors

FHAG section 100.205(c)(2) provides that covered multifamily dwellings with a building entrance on an accessible route shall be designed in such a manner that all the doors designed to allow passage into and within all premises are sufficiently wide to allow passage by handicapped persons in wheelchairs.

Guideline

FHAG section 100.205(c)(2) would apply to doors that are a part of an accessible route in the public and common use areas of multifamily dwellings and to doors into and within individual dwelling units.

(1)   On accessible routes in public and common use areas, and for primary entry doors to covered units, doors that comply with ADAAG - "Doors and Doorways" would meet this requirement.

(2)   Within individual dwelling units, doors intended for user passage through the unit which have a clear opening of at least 32 inches (813mm) nominal width when the door is open 90 degrees, measured between the face of the door and the stop, would meet this requirement.

Openings more than 24 inches (610mm) in depth are not considered doorways.

NOTE:

A 34-inch (864mm) door, hung in the standard manner, provides an acceptable nominal 32-inch (813mm) clear opening.

This door can be adapted to provide a wider opening by using offset hinges, by removing lower portions of the door stop, or both.

Pocket or sliding doors are acceptable doors in covered dwelling units and have the added advantage of not impinging on clear floor space in small rooms.

The nominal 32-inch (813mm) clear opening provided by a standard 6-foot (1829mm) sliding patio door assembly is acceptable.

Accessible Route into and through the Covered Dwelling Unit

FHAG section 100.205(c)(3)(I) provides that all covered multifamily dwellings with a building entrance on an accessible route shall be designed and constructed in such a manner that all premises within covered multifamily dwelling units contain an accessible route into and through the covered dwelling unit.

Chapter 70: Fair Housing Accessibility Guidelines (FHAG) (continued)

Guideline

Accessible routes into and through dwelling units would meet FHAG section 100.205(c)(3)(I) if:

(1) A minimum clear width of 36 inches (914mm) is provided.

(2) In single-story dwelling units, changes in level within the dwelling unit with heights between 1/4-inch and 1/2-inch (6.4mm and 12.7mm) are beveled with a slope no greater than 1:2.

Except for design features, such as a loft or an area on a different level within a room (e.g., a sunken living room), changes in level greater than 1/2-inch (12.7mm) are ramped or have other means of access.

Where single-story dwelling units has special design features, all portions of the single-story unit, except the loft or the sunken or raised area, are on an accessible route; and

    (a) In single-story dwelling units with lofts, all spaces other than the loft are on an accessible route.

    (b) Design features such as sunken or raised functional areas do not interrupt the accessible route through the remainder of the dwelling unit.

(3) In multistory dwelling units in buildings with elevators, the story of the unit that is served by the building elevator (a) is the primary entry to the unit, (b) complies with this *Chapter - pp. 254-266* with respect to the rooms located on the entry/accessible floor; and (c) contains a bathroom or powder room which complies with this *Chapter - Usable Kitchens and Bathrooms - pp. 263-266.*

(Note: multistory dwelling units in non-elevator buildings are not covered dwelling units because, in such cases, there is no ground floor unit.)

(4) Except as provided in *(5) and (6) - (below & following page),* thresholds at exterior doors, including sliding door tracks, are no higher than 3/4-inch (19.1mm).

Thresholds and changes in level at these locations are beveled with a slope no greater than 1:2.

(5) Exterior deck, patio, or balcony surfaces are no more than 1/2-inch (12.7mm) below the floor level of the interior of the dwelling unit, unless they are constructed of impervious material such as concrete, brick or flagstone.

In such case, the surface is no more than 4 inches (102mm) below the floor level of the interior of the dwelling unit, or lower if required by local building code.

Chapter 70: Fair Housing Accessibility Guidelines (FHAG) (continued)

(6) At the primary entry door to dwelling units with direct exterior access, outside landing surfaces constructed of impervious materials such as concrete, brick or flagstone, are no more than 1/2-inch (12.7mm) below the floor level of the interior of the dwelling unit.

The finished surface of this area that is located immediately outside the entry may be sloped, up to 1/8-inch (3.2mm) per foot (12 inches) (305mm), for drainage.

Light Switches - Electrical Outlets - Thermostats and other Environmental Controls in Accessible Locations

FHAG section 100.205(c)(3)(ii) requires that all covered multifamily dwellings with a building entrance on an accessible route shall be designed and constructed in such a manner that all premises within covered multifamily dwelling units contain light switches, electrical outlets, thermostats, and other environmental controls in accessible locations.

Guideline

Light switches, electrical outlets, thermostats and other environmental controls would meet FHAG section 100.205(c)(3)(ii) if operable parts of the controls are located no higher than 48 inches (1219mm), and no lower than 15 inches (381mm), above the floor.

See Diagram 115(a) - p. 420.

If the reach is over an obstruction (for example, an overhanging shelf) between 20 and 25 inches (508mm and 635mm) in depth, the maximum height is reduced to 44 inches (1118mm) for forward approach; or 46 inches (1168mm) for side approach, provided the obstruction (for example, a kitchen base cabinet) is more than 24 inches (610mm) in depth.

See Diagrams 115(b) and 116 - pp. 420 & 421.

Obstructions should not extend more than 25 inches (635mm) from the wall beneath a control.

See Diagrams 115(b) and 116 - pp. 420 & 421.

NOTE:

Controls or outlets that do not satisfy these specifications are acceptable provided that comparable controls or outlets (i.e., that perform the same functions) are provided within the same area and are accessible, in accordance with the *guideline - (above)*.

Chapter 70: Fair Housing Accessibility Guidelines (FHAG) (continued)

Reinforced Walls for Grab Bars

FHAG section 100.205(c)(3)(iii) requires that covered multifamily dwellings with a building entrance on an accessible route shall be designed and constructed in such a manner that all premises within covered multifamily dwelling units contain reinforcements in bathroom walls to allow later installation of grab bars around toilet, tub, shower stall and shower seat, where such facilities are provided.

Guideline

Reinforced bathroom walls to allow later installation of grab bars around the toilet, tub, shower stall and shower seat, where such facilities are provided, would meet FHAG section 100.205(c)(3)(iii) if reinforced areas are provided at least at those points where grab bars will be mounted.

(For example, see Diagrams 117 through 119 - pp. 422-424).

Where the toilet is not place adjacent to a side wall, the bathroom would comply if provision was made for installation of floor-mounted, foldaway or similar alternative grab bars.

Where the powder room (a room with a toilet and sink) is the only toilet facility located on an accessible level of a multistory dwelling unit, it must comply with this requirement for reinforced walls for grab bars.

NOTE:

> Installation of bathtubs is not limited by the illustrative *diagrams;* a tub may have shelves or benches at either end; or a tub may be installed without surrounding walls, if there is provision for alternative mounting of grab bars.
>
> For example, a sunken tub placed away from walls could have reinforced areas for installation of floor-mounted grab bars.
>
> The same principle applies to shower stalls -- e.g., glass-walled stalls could be planned to allow floor-mounted grab bars to be installed later.
>
> Reinforcement for grab bars may be provided in a variety of ways (for example, by plywood or wood blocking) so long as the necessary reinforcement is placed so as to permit later installation of appropriate grab bars.

Chapter 70: Fair Housing Accessibility Guidelines (FHAG) (continued)

Usable Kitchens and Bathrooms

FHAG section 100.205(c)(3)(iv) requires that covered multifamily dwellings with a building entrance on an accessible route shall be designed and constructed in such a manner that all premises within covered multifamily dwelling units contain usable kitchens and bathrooms such that an individual in a wheelchair can maneuver about the space.

Guideline

(1) **Usable Kitchens**

Usable kitchens would meet FHAG section 100.205(c)(3(iv) if:

(a) A clear floor space at least 30 inches by 48 inches (762mm by 1219mm) that allows a parallel approach by a person in a wheelchair is provided at the range or cooktop and sink, and either a parallel or forward approach is provided at oven, dishwasher, refrigerator/freezer or trash compactor.

(b) Clearance between counters and all opposing base cabinets, countertops, appliances or walls is at least 40 inches (1016mm).

(c) In U-shaped kitchens with sink or range or cooktop at the base of the "U", a 60-inch (1524mm) turning radius is provided to allow parallel approach, or base cabinets are removable at that location to allow knee space for a forward approach.

(2) **Usable Bathrooms**

To meet the requirements of FHAG section 100.205(c)(3)(iv) either:

All bathrooms in the dwelling unit comply with the provisions of *(2)(a) - (following page);*

or

At least one bathroom in the dwelling unit complies with the provisions of *(2)(b) - (following pages),* and all other bathrooms and powder rooms within the dwelling unit must be on an accessible route with usable entry door in accordance with the guidelines in this *Chapter - Usable Doors and Accessible Routes - pp. 258-261.*

However, in multistory dwelling units, only those bathrooms on the accessible level are subject to the requirements of FHAG section 100.205(c)(3)(iv).

Where a powder room is the only facility provided on the accessible level of a multistory dwelling unit, the powder room must comply with provisions of *(2)(a) or (2)(b) - (following pages).*

Chapter 70: Fair Housing Accessibility Guidelines (FHAG) (continued)

Powder rooms that are subject to the requirements of FHAG section 100.205(c)(3)(iv) must have reinforcements for grab bars as provided in the guideline in this *Chapter - Reinforced Walls for Grab Bars - p. 262.*

(a) Bathrooms that have reinforced walls for grab bars would meet FHAG section 100.205(c)(3)(iv) if:

 (i) Sufficient maneuvering space is provided within the bathroom for a person using a wheelchair or other mobility aid to enter and close the door, use the fixtures, reopen the door and exit.

 Doors may swing into the clear floor space provided at any fixture if the maneuvering space is provided.

 Maneuvering spaces may include any knee space or toe space available below bathroom fixtures.

 (ii) Clear floor space is provided at fixtures as shown in *Diagrams 120 through 122 - pp. 425-427.*

 Clear floor space at fixtures may overlap.

 (iii) If the shower stall is the only bathing facility provided in the covered dwelling unit, the shower stall measures at least 36 inches by 36 inches (914mm by 914mm).

 See Diagram 122(a) - p. 427.

NOTE:

 Cabinets under lavatories are acceptable provided the bathroom has space to allow a parallel approach by a person in a wheelchair; if parallel approach is not possible within the space, any cabinets provided would have to be removable to afford the necessary knee clearance for forward approach.

(b) Bathrooms that have reinforced walls for grab bars would meet FHAG section 100.205(c)(3)(iv) if:

 (i) Where the door swings into the bathroom, there is a clear space (approximately, 30 inches by 48 inches) (762mm by 1219mm) within the room to position a wheelchair or other mobility aid clear of the path of the door as it is closed and to permit use of fixtures.

 This clear space can include any knee space and toe space available below bathroom fixtures.

Chapter 70: Fair Housing Accessibility Guidelines (FHAG) (continued)

(ii) Where the door swings out, a clear space is provided within the bathroom for a person using a wheelchair or other mobility aid to position the wheelchair such that the person is allowed the use of the fixtures.

There also shall be clear space to allow persons using wheelchairs to reopen the door to exit.

(iii) When both tub and shower fixtures are provided in the bathroom, at least one is accessible.

When two or more lavatories in a bathroom are provided, at least one is made accessible.

(iv) Toilets are located within bathrooms in a manner that permits a grab bar to be installed on one side of the fixture.

In locations where toilets are adjacent to walls or bathtubs, the centerline of the fixture is a minimum of 18 inches (457mm) from the obstacle.

The other (non-grab bar) side of the toilet fixture is a minimum of 15 inches (381mm) from the finished surface of adjoining walls, vanities or from the edge of a lavatory.

See Diagram 120(a) - p. 425.

(v) Vanities and lavatories are installed with the centerline of the fixture a minimum of 15 inches (381mm) horizontally from an adjoining wall or fixture.

The top of the fixture rim is a maximum height of 34 inches (864mm) above the finished floor.

If knee space is provided below the vanity, the bottom of the apron is at least 27 inches (686mm) above the floor.

If provided, full knee space (for front approach) is at least 17 inches (432mm) deep.

See Diagram 121(a) - p. 426.

(vi) Bathtubs and tub/showers located in the bathroom provide a clear access aisle adjacent to the lavatory that is at least 30 inches (762mm) wide and extends for a length of 48 inches (1219mm) (measured from the foot of the bathtub).

See Diagrams 122(a),(b) - p. 427.

Chapter 70: Fair Housing Accessibility Guidelines (FHAG) (continued)

(vii) Stall showers in the bathroom may be of any size or configuration.

A minimum clear floor space 30 inches by 48 inches (762mm by 1219mm) should be available outside the stall.

See Diagram 122(a) - p. 427.

If the shower stall is the only bathing facility provided in the covered dwelling unit, or on the accessible level of a covered multistory unit, and measures a nominal 36 inches by 36 inches (914mm by 914mm), the shower stall must have reinforcing to allow for installation of an optional wall hung bench seat.

Chapter 71:

RECREATION FACILITIES
FEDERAL FINAL RULE

15 **Recreation Facilities**

Newly designed or newly constructed and altered recreation facilities shall comply with the applicable requirements of ADAAG - 4.1 through 4.35, and the special application sections ADAAG - 5 through 10, except as modified or otherwise provided in this chapter.

15.1 **Amusement Rides**

15.1.1 **General**

Newly designed or newly constructed and altered amusement rides shall comply with this *Chapter - 15.1 - pp. 267-272*.

EXCEPTION 1:

Mobile or portable amusement rides shall not be required to comply with this *Chapter - 15.1 - pp. 267-272*.

EXCEPTION 2:

Amusement rides which are controlled or operated by the rider shall be required to comply only with *15.1.4 and 15.1.5 - (following pages)*.

EXCEPTION 3:

Amusement rides designed primarily for children, where children are assisted on and off the ride by an adult, shall be required to comply only with *15.1.4 and 15.1.5 - (following pages)*.

EXCEPTION 4:

Amusement rides without amusement ride seats shall be required to comply only with *15.1.4 and 15.1.5 - (following pages)*.

15.1.2 **Alterations to Amusement Rides**

A modification to an existing amusement ride is an alteration subject to this *Chapter - 15.1 - pp. 267-272* if one or more of the following conditions apply:

Chapter 71: Recreation Facilities - Federal Final Rule (continued)

(1) The amusement ride's structural or operational characteristics are changed to the extent that the ride's performance differs from that specified by the manufacturer or the original design criteria;

or

(2) The load and unload area of the amusement ride is newly designed and constructed.

15.1.3 Number Required

Each amusement ride shall provide at least one wheelchair space complying with *15.1.7 - (following pages)*, or at least one amusement ride seat designed for transfer complying with this *Chapter - 15.1.8 - pp. 271 & 272*, or at least one transfer device complying with this *Chapter - 15.1.9 - p. 272*.

15.1.4 Accessible Route

When in the load and unload position, amusement rides required to comply with this *Chapter - 15.1 - pp. 267-272* shall be served by an accessible route complying with ADAAG - 4.3 and ADAAG - 4.3.11.

Any part of an accessible route serving amusement rides with a slope greater than 1:20 shall be considered a ramp and shall comply with ADAAG - 4.8.

EXCEPTION 1:

The maximum slope specified in ADAAG - 4.8.2 shall not apply in the load and unload areas or on the amusement ride where compliance is structurally or operationally infeasible, provided that the slope of the ramp shall not exceed 1:8.

EXCEPTION 2:

Handrails shall not be required in the load and unload areas or on the amusement ride where compliance is structurally or operationally infeasible.

EXCEPTION 3:

Limited use/limited-application elevators and platform lifts complying with ADAAG - 4.11 shall be permitted to be part of an accessible route serving the load and unload area.

15.1.5 Load and Unload Areas

Load and unload areas serving amusement rides required to comply with this *Chapter - 15.1 - pp. 267-272* shall provide a maneuvering space complying with ADAAG - 4.2.3.

Chapter 71: Recreation Facilities - Federal Final Rule (continued)

The maneuvering space shall have a slope not steeper than 1:48.

15.1.6 Signage

Signage shall be provided at the entrance of the queue or waiting line for each amusement ride to identify the type of access provided.

Where an accessible unload area also serves as the accessible load area, signage shall be provided at the entrance to the queue or waiting line indicating the location of the accessible load and unload area.

15.1.7 Amusement Rides with Wheelchair Spaces

Amusement rides with wheelchair spaces shall comply with *15.1.7 - (below & following pages)*.

Floor or Ground Surface

(1) The floor or ground surface of wheelchair spaces shall comply with *15.1.7(1) - (below)*.

Slope

1. The floor or ground surface of wheelchair spaces shall have a slope not steeper than 1:48 when in the load and unload position and shall be stable and firm.

Gaps

2. Floors of amusement rides with wheelchair spaces and floors of load and unload areas shall be coordinated so that, when the amusement rides are at rest in the load and unload position, the vertical difference between the floors shall be within plus or minus 5/8 inches (15.9mm) and the horizontal gap shall be no greater than 3 inches (76mm) under normal passenger load conditions.

EXCEPTION:

> Where compliance is not operationally or structurally feasible, ramps, bridge plates, or similar devices complying with the applicable requirements of 36 CFR 1192.83(c) shall be provided.

Clearances

(2) Clearances for wheelchair spaces shall comply with *15.1.7(2) - (following page)*.

EXCEPTION 1:

>   Where provided, securement devices shall be permitted to overlap required clearances.

EXCEPTION 2:

>   Wheelchair spaces shall be permitted to be mechanically or manually repositioned.

EXCEPTION 3:

>   Wheelchair spaces shall not be required to comply with ADAAG - 4.4.2.

Width and Length

1. Wheelchair spaces shall provide a clear width of 30 inches (762mm) and a clear length of 48 inches (1219mm) minimum measured to 9 inches (229mm) minimum above the floor surface.

Wheelchair Spaces - Side Entry

2. Where the wheelchair space can be entered only from the side, the ride shall be designed to permit sufficient maneuvering space for individuals using a wheelchair or mobility device to enter and exit the ride.

Protrusions in Wheelchair Spaces

3. Objects are permitted to protrude a distance of 6 inches (152mm) maximum along the front of the wheelchair space where located 9 inches (229mm) minimum and 27 inches (686mm) maximum above the floor or ground surface of the wheelchair space.

   Objects are permitted to protrude a distance of 25 inches (635mm) maximum along the front of the wheelchair space, where located more than 27 inches (686mm) above the floor or ground surface of the wheelchair space.

See Diagram 123 - p. 428.

Openings

(3) Where openings are provided to access wheelchair spaces on amusement rides, the entry shall provide a 32-inch (813mm) minimum clear opening.

Chapter 71: Recreation Facilities - Federal Final Rule (continued)

Approach

(4) One side of the wheelchair space shall adjoin an accessible route.

Companion Seats

(5) Where the interior width of the amusement ride is greater than 53 inches (1346mm), seating is provided for more than one rider, and the wheelchair is not required to be centered within the amusement ride, a companion seat shall be provided for each wheelchair space.

Shoulder-to-Shoulder Seating

1. Where an amusement ride provides shoulder-to-shoulder seating, companion seats shall be shoulder-to-shoulder with the adjacent wheelchair space.

EXCEPTION:

> Where shoulder-to-shoulder companion seating is not operationally or structurally feasible, compliance with this provision shall be required to the maximum extent feasible.

15.1.8 **Amusement Ride Seats Designed for Transfer**

Amusement ride seats designed for transfer shall comply with *15.1.8 - (below & following page).* when positioned for loading and unloading.

Clear Floor or Ground Space

(1) Clear floor or ground space complying with ADAAG - 4.2.4 shall be provided in the load and unload area adjacent to the amusement ride seats designed for transfer.

Transfer Height

(2) The height of the amusement ride seats shall be 14 inches (356mm) minimum to 24 inches (610mm) maximum measured above the load and unload surface.

Transfer Entry

(3) Where openings are provided to transfer to amusement ride seats, the space shall be designed to provide clearance for transfer from a wheelchair or mobility device to the amusement ride seat.

Chapter 71: Recreation Facilities - Federal Final Rule (continued)

Wheelchair Storage Space

(4) Wheelchair storage spaces complying with ADAAG - 4.2.4 shall be provided in or adjacent to unload areas for each required amusement ride seat designed for transfer and shall not overlap any required means of egress or accessible route.

15.1.9 **Transfer Devices for Use with Amusement Rides**

Transfer devices for use with amusement rides shall comply with *15.1.9 - (below)* when positioned for loading and unloading.

Clear Floor or Ground Space

(1) Clear floor or ground space complying with ADAAG - 4.2.4 shall be provided in the load and unload area adjacent to the transfer devices.

Transfer Height

(2) The height of the transfer device seats shall be 14 inches (356mm) minimum to 24 inches (610mm) maximum measured above the load and unload surface.

Wheelchair Storage Space

(3) Wheelchair storage spaces complying with ADAAG - 4.2.4 shall be provided in or adjacent to unload areas for each required transfer device and shall not overlap any required means of egress or accessible route.

15.2 **Boating Facilities**

15.2.1 **General**

Newly designed or newly constructed and altered boating facilities shall comply with *15.2 - (below & following pages)*.

15.2.2 **Accessible Route**

Accessible routes, including gangways that are part of accessible routes, shall comply with ADAAG - 4.3 and ADAAG - 4.3.11.

EXCEPTION 1:

Where an existing gangway or series of gangways is replaced or altered, an increase in the length of the gangway is not required to comply with *15.2.2 - (above & following page),* unless required by ADAAG - 4.1.6(2).

Chapter 71: Recreation Facilities - Federal Final Rule (continued)

EXCEPTION 2:

The maximum rise specified in ADAAG - 4.8.2 shall not apply to gangways.

EXCEPTION 3:

Where the total length of the gangway or series of gangways serving as part of a required accessible route is at least 80 feet (24 384mm), the maximum slope specified in ADAAG - 4.8.2 shall not apply to gangways.

EXCEPTION 4:

In facilities containing fewer than 25 boat slips and where the total length of the gangways or series of gangways serving as part of a required accessible route is at least 30 feet (9144mm), the maximum slope specified in ADAAG - 4.8.2 shall not apply to the gangways.

EXCEPTION 5:

Where gangways connect to transition plates, landings specified by ADAAG - 4.8.4 shall not be required.

EXCEPTION 6:

Where gangways and transition plates connect and are required to have handrails, handrail extensions specified by ADAAG - 4.8.5 shall not be required.

Where handrail extensions are provided on gangways or transition plates, such extensions are not required to be parallel with the ground or floor surface.

EXCEPTION 7:

The cross slope of gangways, transition plates, and floating piers that are part of an accessible route shall be 1:50 maximum measured in the static position.

EXCEPTION 8:

Limited-use/limited-application elevators or platform lifts complying with ADAAG - 4.11 shall be permitted in lieu of gangways complying with ADAAG - 4.3 and ADAAG - 4.3.11.

15.2.3 **Boat Slips - Minimum Number**

Where boat slips are provided, boat slips complying with this *Chapter - 15.2.5 - pp. 275 & 276* shall be provided in accordance with *Table T - (following page)*.

Where the number of boat slips is not identified, each 40 feet (12 192mm) of boat slip edge provided along the perimeter of the pier shall be counted as one boat slip for the purpose of this section.

Table T
Boat Slips - Minimum Number

Total Boat Slips in Facility	Minimum Number of Required Accessible Boat Slips
1 to 25	1
26 to 50	2
51 to 100	3
101 to 150	4
151 to 300	5
301 to 400	6
401 to 500	7
501 to 600	8
601 to 700	9
701 to 800	10
801 to 900	11
901 to 1000	12
1001 and over	12 plus 1 for each 100 or fraction thereof over 1000

Dispersion

(1) Accessible boat slips shall be dispersed throughout the various types of slips provided.

This provision does not require an increase in the minimum number of boat slips required to be accessible.

15.2.4 Boarding Piers at Boat Launch Ramps

Where boarding piers are provided at boat launch ramps, at least 5 percent, but not less than one of the boarding piers shall comply with *15.2.4 - (below & following page)* and shall be served by an accessible route complying with ADAAG - 4.3 and ADAAG - 4.3.11.

EXCEPTION 1:

Accessible routes serving floating boarding piers shall be permitted to use *Exceptions 1, 2, 5, 6, 7, and 8 in 15.2.2 - (preceding pages)*.

Chapter 71: Recreation Facilities - Federal Final Rule (continued)

EXCEPTION 2:

Where the total length of the gangway or series of gangways serving as part of a required accessible route is at least 30 feet (9144mm), the maximum slope specified by ADAAG - 4.8.2 shall not apply to gangways.

EXCEPTION 3:

Where the accessible route serving a floating boarding pier or skid pier is located within a boat launch ramp, the portion of the accessible route located within the boat launch ramp shall not be required to comply with ADAAG - 4.8.2.

Boarding Pier Clearances

(1) The entire length of the piers shall comply with *15.2.5 - (below & following page)*.

15.2.5 **Accessible Boat Slips**

Accessible boat slips shall comply with *15.2.5 - (below & following page)*.

Clearances

(1) Accessible boat slips shall be served by clear pier space 60 inches (1524mm) wide minimum and at least as long as the accessible boat slips.

Every 10 feet (3048mm) maximum of linear pier edge serving the accessible boat slips shall contain at least one continuous clear opening 60 inches (1524mm) minimum in width.

See Diagram 124 - p. 429.

EXCEPTION 1:

The width of the clear pier space shall be permitted to be 36 inches (914mm) minimum for a length of 24 inches (610mm) maximum, provided that multiple 36-inch (914mm) wide segments are separated by segments that are 60 inches (1524mm) minimum clear in width and 60 inches (1524mm) minimum clear in length.

See Diagram 125(a) - p. 430.

EXCEPTION 2:

Edge protection 4 inches (102mm) high maximum and 2 inches (51mm) deep maximum shall be permitted at the continuous clear openings.

Chapter 71: Recreation Facilities - Federal Final Rule (continued)

See Diagram 125(b) - p. 430.

EXCEPTION 3:

> In alterations to existing facilities, clear pier space shall be permitted to be located perpendicular to the boat slip and shall extend the width of the boat slip, where the facility has at least one boat slip complying with *15.2.5 - (preceding page, above & below),* and further compliance with *15.2.5 - (preceding page, above & below)* would result in a reduction in the number of boat slips available or result in a reduction of the widths of existing slips.

Cleats and other Boat Securement Devices

(2)   Cleats and other boat securement devices shall not be required to comply with ADAAG - 4.27.3.

15.3   **Fishing Piers and Platforms**

15.3.1   **General**

Newly designed or newly constructed and altered fishing piers and platforms shall comply with *15.3 - (below & following pages).*

15.3.2   **Accessible Route**

Accessible routes, including gangways that are part of accessible routes, serving fishing piers and platforms shall comply with ADAAG - 4.3 and ADAAG - 4.3.11.

EXCEPTION 1:

> Accessible routes serving floating fishing piers and platforms shall be permitted to use *Exceptions 1, 2, 5, 6, 7, and 8 in 15.2.2 (this Chapter - pp. 272 & 273).*

EXCEPTION 2:

> Where the total length of the gangway or series of gangways serving as part of a required accessible route is at least 30 feet (9144mm), the maximum slope specified by ADAAG - 4.8.2 shall not apply to the gangways.

15.3.3   **Railings**

Where railings, guards, or handrails are provided, they shall comply with *15.3.3 - (following page).*

Chapter 71: Recreation Facilities - Federal Final Rule (continued)

Edge Protection

(1) Edge protection shall be provided and shall extend 2 inches (51mm) minimum above the ground or deck surface.

EXCEPTION:

Where the railing, guard, or handrail is 34 inches (864mm) or less above the ground or deck surface, edge protection shall not be required if the deck surface extends 12 inches (305mm) minimum beyond the inside face of the railing.

Toe clearance shall be 9 inches (229mm) minimum above the ground or deck surface beyond the railing.

Toe clearance shall be 30 inches (762mm) minimum wide.

See Diagram 126 - p. 431.

Height

(2) At least 25 percent of the railings, guards, or handrails shall be 34 inches (864mm) maximum above the ground or deck surface.

EXCEPTION:

This provision shall not apply to that portion of a fishing pier or platform where a guard which complies with sections 1003.2.12.1 (Height) and 1003.2.12.2 (Opening limitations) of the International Building Code* (incorporated by reference, see ADAAG - 2.3.2) is provided.

Dispersion

(3) Railings required to comply with *15.3.3(2) - (above)* shall be dispersed throughout a fishing pier or platform.

15.3.4 **Clear Floor or Ground Space**

At least one clear floor or ground space complying with ADAAG - 4.2.4 shall be provided where the railing height required by *15.3.3(2) - (above)* is located.

Where no railings are provided, at least one clear floor or ground space complying with ADAAG - 4.2.4 shall be provided.

Chapter 71: Recreation Facilities - Federal Final Rule (continued)

15.3.5 **Maneuvering Space**

At least one maneuvering space complying with ADAAG - 4.2.3 shall be provided on the fishing pier or platform.

15.4 **Golf**

15.4.1 **General**

Newly designed or newly constructed and altered golf courses, driving ranges, practice putting greens, and practice teeing grounds shall comply with *15.4 - (below & following pages)*.

15.4.2 **Accessible Route - Golf Course**

An accessible route shall connect accessible elements and spaces within the boundary of the golf course.

In addition, an accessible route shall connect the golf cart rental area, bag drop areas, practice putting greens, accessible practice teeing grounds, course toilet rooms, and course weather shelters.

The accessible route required by this section shall be 48 inches (1219mm) minimum wide.

Where handrails are provided, the accessible route shall be 60 inches (1524mm) minimum wide.

EXCEPTION 1:

A golf cart passage complying with this *Chapter - 15.4.7 - p. 280* shall be permitted in lieu of all or part of an accessible route required by *15.4.2 - (above)*.

EXCEPTION 2:

The handrail requirements of ADAAG - 4.8.5 shall not apply to an accessible route located within the boundary of a golf course.

15.4.3 **Accessible Route - Driving Ranges**

An accessible route shall connect accessible teeing stations at driving ranges with accessible parking spaces and shall be 48 inches (1219mm) wide minimum.

Where handrails are provided, the accessible route shall be 60 inches (1524mm) wide minimum.

Chapter 71: Recreation Facilities - Federal Final Rule (continued)

EXCEPTION:

> A golf cart passage complying with *15.4.7 - (following page)* shall be permitted in lieu of all or part of an accessible route required by *15.4.3 - (preceding page).*

15.4.4   **Teeing Grounds**

Teeing grounds shall comply with *15.4.4 - (below).*

Number Required

(1) Where one or two teeing grounds are provided for a hole, at least one teeing ground serving the hole shall comply with *15.4.4(3) - (below).*

Where three or more teeing grounds are provided for a hole, at least two teeing grounds shall comply with *15.4.4(3) - (below).*

Forward Teeing Grounds

(2) The forward teeing ground shall be accessible.

EXCEPTION:

> In alterations, the forward teeing ground shall not be required to be accessible where compliance is not feasible due to terrain.

Teeing Grounds

(3) Teeing grounds required by *15.4.4(1) and 15.4.4(2) - (above)* shall be designed and constructed so that a golf cart can enter and exit the teeing ground.

15.4.5   **Teeing Stations at Driving Ranges and Practice Teeing Grounds**

Where teeing stations or practice teeing grounds are provided, at least 5 percent of the practice teeing stations or practice teeing grounds, but not less than one, shall comply with *15.4.4(3) - (above).*

15.4.6   **Weather Shelters**

Where weather shelters are provided on a golf course, each weather shelter shall have a clear floor or ground space 60 inches (1524mm) minimum by 96 inches (2438mm) minimum and shall be designed and constructed so that a golf cart can enter and exit.

15.4.7 Golf Cart Passage

Where curbs or other constructed barriers are provided along a golf cart passage to prohibit golf carts from entering a fairway, openings at least 60 inches (1524mm) wide shall be provided at intervals not to exceed 75 yards (68 580mm).

Width

(1) The golf cart passage shall be 48 inches (1219mm) minimum wide.

15.4.8 Putting Greens

Each putting green shall be designed and constructed so that a golf cart can enter and exit the putting green.

15.5 Miniature Golf

15.5.1 General

Newly designed or newly constructed and altered miniature golf courses shall comply with *15.5 - (below & following pages)*.

15.5.2 Accessible Holes

At least fifty percent of holes on a miniature golf course shall comply with *15.5.3 through 15.5.5 - (below & following pages)* and shall be consecutive.

EXCEPTION:

One break in the sequence of consecutive accessible holes shall be permitted, provided that the last hole on a miniature golf course is the last hole in the sequence.

15.5.3 Accessible Route

An accessible route complying with ADAAG - 4.3 and ADAAG - 4.3.11 shall connect the course entrance with the first accessible hole and the start of play area on each accessible hole.

The course shall be configured to allow exit from the last accessible hole to the course exit or entrance and shall not require travel back through other holes.

Accessible Route - Located on the Playing Surface

(1) Where the accessible route is located on the playing surface of the accessible hole, *Exceptions 1 through 5 - (following page)* shall be permitted.

Chapter 71: Recreation Facilities - Federal Final Rule (continued)

EXCEPTION 1:

Where carpet is provided, the requirements of ADAAG - 4.5.3 shall not apply.

EXCEPTION 2:

Where the accessible route intersects the playing surface of a hole, a 1-inch (25.4mm) maximum curb shall be permitted for a width of 32 inches (813mm) minimum.

EXCEPTION 3:

A slope of 1:4 maximum for a 4-inch (102mm) maximum rise shall be permitted.

EXCEPTION 4:

Landing required by ADAAG - 4.8.4 shall be permitted to be 48 inches (1219mm) in length minimum.

Landing size required by ADAAG - 4.8.4 shall be permitted to be 48 inches (1219mm) minimum by 60 inches (1524mm) minimum.

Landing slopes shall be permitted to be 1:20 maximum.

EXCEPTION 5:

Handrail requirements of ADAAG - 4.8.5 shall not apply.

Accessible Route - Adjacent to the Playing Surface

(2) Where the accessible route is located adjacent to the playing surface, the requirements of ADAAG - 4.3 and ADAAG - 4.3.11 shall apply.

15.5.4 **Start of Play Areas**

Start of play areas at holes required to comply with *15.5.2 - (preceding page)* shall have a slope not steeper than 1:48 and shall be 48 inches (1219mm) minimum by 60 inches (1524mm) minimum.

15.5.5 **Golf Club Reach Range**

All areas within accessible holes where golf balls rest shall be within 36 inches (914mm) maximum of an accessible route having a maximum slope of 1:20 for 48 inches (1219mm) in length.

Chapter 71: Recreation Facilities - Federal Final Rule (continued)

See Diagram 127 - p. 432.

15.6 **Play Areas**

15.6.1 **General**

Newly designed and newly constructed play areas for children ages 2 and over and altered portions of existing play areas shall comply with the applicable provisions of ADAAG - 4.1 through 4.35, and the special application sections ADAAG - 5 through 10, except as modified or otherwise provided in this chapter.

Where separate play areas are provided within a site for specified age groups, each play area shall comply with this section.

Where play areas are designed or constructed in phases, this section shall be applied so that when each successive addition is completed, the entire play area complies with all the applicable provisions of this section.

> EXCEPTION 1:
>
> Play areas located in family child care facilities where the proprietor actually resides shall not be required to comply with *15.6 - (above, below & following pages)*.
>
> EXCEPTION 2:
>
> Where play components are relocated in existing play areas for the purpose of creating safe use zones, *15.6 - (above, below & following pages)* shall not apply, provided that the ground surface is not changed or extended for more than one use zone.
>
> EXCEPTION 3:
>
> Where play components are altered and the ground surface is not altered, the ground surface shall not be required to comply with this *Chapter - 15.6.7 - p. 290,* unless required by ADAAG - 4.1.6(2).
>
> EXCEPTION 4:
>
> The provisions of *15.6.1 through 15.6.7 - (above, below & following pages)* shall not apply to amusement attractions.

Chapter 71: Recreation Facilities - Federal Final Rule (continued)

EXCEPTION 5:

Compliance with ADAAG - 4.4 shall not be required within the boundary of the play area.

EXCEPTION 6:

Stairs shall not be required to comply with ADAAG - 4.9.

15.6.2 **Ground Level Play Components**

Ground level play components shall be provided in the number and types required by *15.6.2(1) and 15.6.2(2) - (below & following page)*.

Ground level play components that are provided to comply with *15.6.2(1) - (below)* shall be permitted to satisfy the number required by *15.6.2(2) - (below & following page)*, provided that the minimum required types of play components are provided.

Where more than one ground level play component required by *15.6.2(1) and 15.6.2(2) - (below & following page)* is provided, the play components shall be integrated in the play area.

General

(1) Where ground level play components are provided, at least one of each type provided shall be located on an accessible route complying with *15.6.4 - (following pages)* and shall comply with this *Chapter - 15.6.6 - pp. 288 & 289*.

Additional Number and Types

(2) Where elevated play components are provided, ground level play components shall be provided in accordance with *Table U - (following page)*.

Ground level play components required by *15.6.2(2) - (above, below & following page)* shall be located on an accessible route complying with *15.6.4 - (following pages)* and shall comply with this *Chapter - 15.6.6 - pp. 288 & 289*.

EXCEPTION:

If at least 50 percent of the elevated play components are connected by a ramp, and if at least 3 of the elevated play components connected by the ramp are different types of play components, *15.6.2(2) - (above & following page)* shall not apply.

Chapter 71: Recreation Facilities - Federal Final Rule (continued)

Table U
Number and Types of Ground Level Play Components
Required to be on Accessible Route

Number of Elevated Play Components Provided	Minimum Number of Ground Level Play Components Required to be on Accessible Route	Minimum Number of Different Types of Ground Level Play Components Required to be on Accessible Route
1	Not Applicable	Not Applicable
2 to 4	*1*	*1*
5 to 7	*2*	*2*
8 to 10	*3*	*3*
11 to 13	*4*	*3*
14 to 16	*5*	*3*
17 to 19	*6*	*3*
20 to 22	*7*	*4*
23 to 25	*8*	*4*
More than 25	8 plus 1 for each additional 3 over 25, or fraction thereof	*5*

15.6.3 **Elevated Play Components**

Where elevated play components are provided, at least 50 percent shall be located on an accessible route complying with *15.6.4 - (below & following pages).*

Elevated play components connected by a ramp shall comply with this *Chapter - 15.6.6 - pp. 288 & 289.*

15.6.4 **Accessible Routes**

At least one accessible route complying with ADAAG - 4.3 and ADAAG - 4.3.11, as modified by *15.6.4 - (following pages),* shall be provided.

Chapter 71: Recreation Facilities - Federal Final Rule (continued)

EXCEPTION 1:

Transfer systems complying with this *Chapter - 15.6.5 - pp. 287 & 288* shall be permitted to connect elevated play components, except where 20 or more elevated play components are provided, no more than 25 percent of the elevated play components shall be permitted to be connected by transfer systems.

EXCEPTION 2:

Where transfer systems are provided, an elevated play component shall be permitted to connect to another elevated play component in lieu of an accessible route.

EXCEPTION 3:

Platform lifts (wheelchair lifts) complying with ADAAG - and applicable State or Local codes shall be permitted to be used as part of an accessible route.

Location

(1) Accessible routes shall be located within the boundary of the play area and shall connect ground level play components as required by *15.6.2(1) and 15.6.2(2) - (preceding pages)* and elevated play components as required by *15.6.3 - (preceding page),* including entry and exit points of the play components.

Protrusions

(2) Objects shall not protrude into ground level accessible routes at or below 80 inches (2032mm) above the ground or floor surface.

Clear Width

(3) The clear width of accessible routes within play areas shall comply with *15.6.4(3) - (below & following page).*

Ground Level

1. The clear width of accessible routes at ground level shall be 60 inches (1524mm) minimum.

EXCEPTION 1:

In play areas less than 1,000 square feet, the clear width of accessible routes shall be permitted to be 44 inches (1118mm) minimum, provided that at least one turning space complying with ADAAG - 4.2.3 is provided where the restricted accessible route exceeds 30 feet (9144mm) in length.

EXCEPTION 2:

The clear width of accessible routes shall be permitted to be 36 inches (914mm) minimum for a distance of 60 inches (1524mm) maximum, provided that multiple reduced width segments are separated by segments that are 60 inches (1524mm) minimum in width and 60 inches (1524mm) minimum in length.

Elevated

2. The clear width of accessible routes connecting elevated play components shall be 36 inches (914mm).

EXCEPTION 1:

The clear width of accessible routes connecting elevated play components shall be permitted to be reduced to 32 inches (813mm) minimum for a distance of 24 inches (610mm), maximum provided that reduced width segments are separated by segments that are 48 inches (1219mm) minimum in length and 36 inches (914mm) minimum in width.

EXCEPTION 2:

The clear width of transfer systems connecting elevated play components shall be permitted to be 24 inches (610 mm) minimum.

Ramp Slope and Rise

(4) Any part of an accessible route with a slope greater than 1:20 shall be considered a ramp and shall comply with ADAAG - 4.8, as modified by *15.6.4(4) - (below & following page)*.

Ground Level

1. The maximum slope for ramps connecting ground level play components within the boundary of a play area shall be 1:16.

Chapter 71: Recreation Facilities - Federal Final Rule (continued)

Elevated

2. Where a ramp connects elevated play components, the maximum rise of any ramp run shall be 12 inches (305mm).

Handrails

(5) Where required on ramps, handrails shall comply with ADAAG - 4.8.5, as modified by *15.6.4(5) - (below)*.

EXCEPTION 1:

Handrails shall not be required at ramps located within ground level use zones.

EXCEPTION 2:

Handrail extensions shall not be required.

Handrail Gripping Surface

1. Handrails shall have a diameter or width of 0.95 inches (24.1mm) minimum to 1.55 inches (39.4mm) maximum, or the shape shall provide an equivalent gripping surface.

Handrail Height

2. The top of handrail gripping surfaces shall be 20 inches (508mm) minimum to 28 inches (711mm) maximum above the ramp surface.

15.6.5 **Transfer Systems**

Where transfer systems are provided to connect elevated play components, the transfer systems shall comply with *15.6.5 - (below & following page)*.

Transfer Platforms

(1) Transfer platforms complying with *15.6.5(1) - (below & following page)* shall be provided where transfer is intended to be from a wheelchair or other mobility device.

See Diagram 128 - p. 433.

Size

1. Platforms shall have a level surface 14 inches (356mm) minimum in depth and 24 inches (610mm) minimum in width.

Chapter 71: Recreation Facilities - Federal Final Rule (continued)

Height

2. Platform surfaces shall be 11 inches (279mm) minimum to 18 inches (457mm) maximum above the ground or floor surface.

Transfer Space

3. A level space complying with ADAAG - 4.2.4 shall be centered on the 48-inch (1219mm) long dimension parallel to the 24-inch (610mm) minimum long unobstructed side of the transfer platform.

Transfer Supports

4. A means of support for transferring shall be provided.

Transfer Steps

(2) Transfer steps complying with *15.6.5(2) - (below)* shall be provided where movement is intended from a transfer platform to a level with elevated play components required to be located on an accessible route.

See Diagram 129 - p. 434.

Size

1. Transfer steps shall have a level surface 14 inches (356mm) minimum in depth and 24 inches (610mm) minimum in width.

Height

2. Each transfer step shall be 8 inches (203mm) maximum high.

Transfer Supports

3. A means of support for transferring shall be provided.

15.6.6 **Play Components**

Ground level play components located on accessible routes and elevated play components connected by ramps shall comply with *15.6.6 - (below & following page)*.

Maneuvering Space

(1) Maneuvering space complying with ADAAG - 4.2.3 shall be provided on the same level as the play components.

Chapter 71: Recreation Facilities - Federal Final Rule (continued)

Maneuvering space shall have a slope not steeper than 1:48 in all directions.

The maneuvering space required for a swing shall be located immediately adjacent to the swing.

Clear Floor or Ground Space

(2) Clear floor or ground space shall be provided at the play components and shall be 30 inches (762mm) by 48 inches (1219mm) minimum.

Clear floor or ground space shall have a slope not steeper than 1:48 in all directions.

Play Tables
Height and Clearances

(3) Where play tables are provided, knee clearance 24 inches (610mm) high minimum, 17 inches deep (432mm) minimum, and 30 inches (762mm) wide minimum shall be provided.

The tops of rims, curbs, or other obstructions shall be 31 inches (787mm) high maximum.

EXCEPTION:

Play tables designed or constructed primarily for children ages 5 and under shall not be required to provide knee clearance if the clear floor or ground space required by *15.6.6(2) - (above)* is arranged for a parallel approach and if the rim surface is 31 inches (787mm) high maximum.

Entry Points and Seats
Height

(4) Where a play component requires transfer to the entry point or seat, the entry point or seat shall be 11 inches (279mm) minimum and 24 inches (610mm) maximum above the clear floor or ground space.

EXCEPTION:

The entry point of a slide shall not be required to comply with *15.6.6(4) - (above)*.

Transfer Supports

(5) Where a play component requires transfer to the entry point or seat, a means of support for transferring shall be provided.

Chapter 71: Recreation Facilities - Federal Final Rule (continued)

15.6.7 **Ground Surfaces**

Ground surfaces along accessible routes, clear floor or ground spaces, and maneuvering spaces within play areas shall comply with ADAAG - 4.5.1 and *15.6.7 - (below)*.

Accessibility

(1) Ground surfaces shall comply with ASTM F 1951* Standard Specification for Determination of Accessibility of Surface Systems Under and Around Playground Equipment (see ADAAG - 2.3.2).

Ground surfaces shall be inspected and maintained ensure continued compliance with ASTM F 1951*.

Use Zones

(2) If located within use zones, ground surfaces shall comply with ASTM F 1992* Standard Specification for Impact Attenuation of Surface Systems Under and Around Playground Equipment (see ADAAG - 2.3.2).

15.6.8 **Soft Contained Play Structures**

Soft contained play structures shall comply with *15.6.8 - (below)*.

Accessible Routes to Entry Points

(1) Where three or fewer entry points are provided, at least one entry point shall be located on an accessible route.

Where four or more entry points are provided, at least two entry points shall be located on an accessible route.

Accessible routes shall comply with ADAAG - 4.3 and ADAAG - 4.3.11.

EXCEPTION:

Transfer systems complying with this *Chapter - 15.6.5 - pp. 287 & 288* or platform lifts (wheelchair lifts) complying with ADAAG - 4.11 and applicable State or Local codes shall be permitted to be used as part of an accessible route.

Chapter 71: Recreation Facilities - Federal Final Rule (continued)

APPENDIX

A15.6 **Play Areas - Children**

A15.6.1 **General**

This section is to be applied during the design, construction, and alteration of play areas for children ages 2 and over.

Play areas are the portion of a site where play components are provided.

This section does not apply to other portions of a site where elements such as sports fields, picnic areas, or other gathering areas are provided.

Those areas are addressed by other sections of ADAAG.

Play areas may be located on exterior sites or within a building.

Where separate play areas are provided within a site for children in specified age groups (e.g., preschool (ages 2 to 5) and school age (ages 5 to 12)), each play area must comply with this section.

Where play areas are provided for the same age group on a site but are geographically separated (e.g., one is located next to a picnic area and another is located next to a softball field), they are considered separate play areas and each play area must comply with this section.

A15.6.2 **Ground Level Play Components**

A ground level play component is a play component approached and exited at the ground level.

Examples of ground level play components include spring rockers, swings, diggers, and stand alone slides.

When distinguishing between the different types of ground level play components, consider the general experience provided by the play component.

Examples of different types of experiences include, but are not limited to, rocking, swinging, climbing, spinning, and sliding.

A spiral slide may provide a slightly different experience from a straight slide, but sliding is the general experience and therefore a spiral slide is not considered a different type of play component than a straight slide.

The number of ground level play components is not dependent on the number of children who can play on the play component.

A large seesaw designed to accommodate ten children at once is considered one ground level play component.

Where a large play area includes two or more composite play structures designed for the same age group, the total number of elevated play components on all the composite play structures must be added to determine the additional number and types of ground level play components that must be provided on an accessible route, and the type of accessible route (e.g., ramps or transfer systems) that must be provided to the elevated play components.

Ground level play components accessed by children with disabilities must be integrated in the play area.

Designers should consider the optimal layout of ground level play components accessed by children with disabilities to foster interaction and socialization among all children.

Grouping all ground level play components accessed by children with disabilities in one location is not considered integrated.

A15.6.3 **Elevated Play Components**

Elevated play components are approached above or below grade and are part of a composite play structure.

A double or triple slide that is part of a composite play structure is one elevated play component.

For purposes of this section, ramps, transfer systems, steps, decks, and roofs are not considered elevated play components.

These elements are generally used to link other elements on a composite play structure.

Although socialization and pretend play can occur on these elements, they are not primarily intended for play.

Some play components that are attached to a composite play structure can be approached or exited at the ground level or above grade from a platform or deck.

For example, a climber attached to a composite play structure can be approached or exited at the ground level or above grade from a platform or deck on a composite play structure.

Play components that are attached to a composite play structure and can be approached from a platform or deck (e.g., climbers and overhead play components), are considered elevated play components.

Chapter 71: Recreation Facilities - Federal Final Rule (continued)

These play components are not considered ground level play components also, and do not count toward the requirements in this *Chapter - 15.6.2 - pp. 283 & 284* regarding the number of ground level play components that must be located on an accessible route.

A15.6.4 **Accessible Routes**

Accessible routes within the boundary of the play area must comply with this *Chapter - 15.6.4 - pp. 284-287*.

Accessible routes connecting the play area to parking, drinking fountains, and other elements on a site must comply with ADAAG - 4.3 and ADAAG - 4.3.11.

Accessible routes provide children who use wheelchairs or other mobility devices the opportunity to access play components.

Accessible routes should coincide with the general circulation path used within the play area.

Careful placement and consideration of the layout of accessible routes will enhance the ability of children with disabilities to socialize and interact with other children.

Where possible, designers and operators are encouraged to provide wider ground level accessible routes within the play area or consider designing the entire ground surface to be accessible.

Providing more accessible spaces will enhance the integration of all children within the play area and provide access to more play components.

A maximum slope of 1:16 is required for ground level ramps; however, a lesser slope will enhance access for those children who have difficulty negotiating the 1:16 maximum slope.

Handrails are not required on ramps located within ground level use zones.

Where a stand alone slide is provided, an accessible route must connect the base of the stairs at the entry point, and the exit point of the slide.

A ramp or transfer system to the top of the slide is not required.

Where a sand box is provided, an accessible route must connect to the border of the sand box.

Accessibility to the sand box would be enhanced by providing a transfer system into the sand or by providing a raised sand table with knee clearance complying with this *Chapter - 15.6.6(3) - p. 289*.

Elevated accessible routes must connect the entry and exit points of 50 percent of elevated play components.

Chapter 71: Recreation Facilities - Federal Final Rule (continued)

Ramps are preferred over transfer systems since not all children who use wheelchairs or other mobility devices may be able to use or may choose not to use transfer systems.

Where ramps connect elevated play components, the maximum rise of any ramp run is limited to 12 inches (305mm).

Where possible, designers and operators are encouraged to provide ramps with a lesser slope than the 1:12 maximum.

Berms or sculpted dirt may be used to provide elevation and may be part of an accessible route to composite play structures.

Platform lifts complying with ADAAG - 4.11 and applicable State and Local codes are permitted as a part of an accessible route.

Because lifts must be independently operable, operators should carefully consider the appropriateness of their use in unsupervised settings.

A15.6.5 **Transfer Systems**

Transfer systems are a means of accessing composite play structures.

Transfer systems generally include a transfer platform and a series of transfer steps.

Children who use wheelchairs or other mobility devices transfer from their wheelchair or mobility devices onto the transfer platform and lift themselves up or down the transfer steps and scoot along the decks or platforms to access elevated play components.

Some children may be unable or may choose not to use transfer systems.

Where transfer systems are provided, consideration should be given to the distance between the transfer system and the elevated play components.

Moving between a transfer platform and a series of transfer steps requires extensive exertion for some children.

Designers should minimize the distance between the points where a child transfers from a wheelchair or mobility device and where the elevated play components are located.

Where elevated play components are used to connect to another elevated play component in lieu of an accessible route, careful consideration should be used in the selection of the play components used for this purpose.

Transfer supports are required on transfer platforms and transfer steps to assist children when transferring.

Chapter 71: Recreation Facilities - Federal Final Rule (continued)

Some examples of supports include a rope loop, a loop type handle, a slot in the edge of a flat horizontal or vertical member, poles or bars, or D rings on the corner posts.

A15.6.6 **Play Components**

Clear floor or ground spaces, maneuvering spaces, and accessible routes may overlap within play areas.

A specific location has not been designated for the clear floor or ground spaces or maneuvering spaces, except swings, because each play component may require that the spaces be placed in a unique location.

Where play components include a seat or entry point, designs that provide for an unobstructed transfer from a wheelchair or other mobility device are recommended.

This will enhance the ability of children with disabilities to independently use the play component.

When designing play components with manipulative or interactive features, consider appropriate reach ranges for children seated in wheelchairs.

Table V - (below) provides guidance on reach ranges for children seated in wheelchairs.

These dimensions apply to either forward or side reaches.

The reach ranges are appropriate for use with those play components that children seated in wheelchairs may access and reach.

Where transfer systems provide access to elevated play components, the reach ranges are not appropriate.

Table V
Children's Reach Ranges

Forward or Side Reach	*Ages 3 and 4*	*Ages 5 through 8*	*Ages 9 through 12*
High (maximum)	36 inches (914mm)	40 inches (1016mm)	44 inches (1118mm)
Low (minimum)	20 inches (508mm)	18 inches (457mm)	16 inches (406mm)

Where a climber is located on a ground level accessible route, some of the climbing rings should be within the reach ranges.

A careful balance of providing access to play components but not eliminating the challenge and nature of the activity is encouraged.

Chapter 71: Recreation Facilities - Federal Final Rule (continued)

A15.6.7   **Ground Surfaces**

Ground surfaces along clear floor or ground spaces, maneuvering spaces, and accessible routes must comply with the ASTM F 1951* Standard Specification for Determination of Accessibility of Surface Systems Under and Around Playground Equipment.

The ASTM F 1951* standard is available from the American Society for Testing and Materials (ASTM), 100 Barr Harbor Drive, West Conshohocken, PA 19428-2959, telephone (610) 832-9585.

The ASTM F 1951* standard may be ordered online from ASTM (http://www.astm.org).

The ASTM 1951* standard determines the accessibility of a surface by measuring the work required to propel a wheelchair across the surface.

The standard includes tests of effort for: both straight ahead and turning movement, using a force wheel on a rehabilitation wheelchair as the measuring device.

To meet the standard, the force required must be less than that required to propel the wheelchair up a ramp with a 1:14 slope.

When evaluating ground surfaces, operators should request information about compliance with the ASTM F 1951* standard.

Ground surfaces must be inspected and maintained regularly and frequently to ensure continued compliance with the ASTM F 1951* standard.

The type of surface material selected and play area use levels will determine the frequency of inspection and maintenance activities.

When using a combination of surface materials, careful design is necessary to provide appropriate transitions between the surfaces.

Where a rubber surface is installed on top of asphalt to provide impact attenuation, the edges of the rubber surface may create a change in level between the adjoining ground surfaces.

Where the change in level is greater than 1/2-inch (12.7mm), a sloped surface with a maximum slope of 1:12 must be provided.

Products are commercially available that provide a 1:12 slope at transitions.

Transitions are also necessary where the combination of surface materials include loose fill products.

Chapter 71: Recreation Facilities - Federal Final Rule (continued)

Where edging is used to prevent the loose surface from moving onto the firmer surface, the edging may create a tripping hazard.

Where possible, the transition should be designed to allow for a smooth and gradual transition between the two surfaces.

15.7 Exercise Equipment and Machines - Bowling Lanes - Shooting Facilities

15.7.1 General

Newly designed or newly constructed and altered exercise equipment and machines, bowling lanes, and shooting facilities shall comply with *15.7 - (below)*.

15.7.2 Exercise Equipment and Machines

At least one of each type of exercise equipment and machines shall be provided with clear floor or ground space complying with ADAAG - 4.2.4 and shall be served by an accessible route.

Clear floor or ground space shall be positioned for transfer or for use by an individual seated in a wheelchair.

Clear floor or ground spaces for more than one piece of equipment shall be permitted to overlap.

15.7.3 Bowling Lanes

Where bowling lanes are provided, at least 5 percent, but not less than one of each type of lane shall be served by an accessible route.

15.7.4 Shooting Facilities

Where fixed firing positions are provided at a site, at least 5 percent, but not less than one, of each type of firing position shall comply with *15.7.4(1) - (below)*.

Fixed Firing Position

(1) Fixed firing positions shall contain a 60-inch (1524mm) diameter space and shall have a slope not steeper than 1:48.

15.8 Swimming Pools - Wading Pools - Spas

15.8.1 General

Newly designed or newly constructed and altered swimming pools, wading pools, and spas shall comply with *15.8 - (following pages)*.

Chapter 71: Recreation Facilities - Federal Final Rule (continued)

EXCEPTION:

> An accessible route shall not be required to serve raised diving boards or diving platforms.

15.8.2 **Swimming Pools**

At least two accessible means of entry shall be provided for each public use and common use swimming pool.

The primary means of entry shall comply with *15.8.5 - (Swimming Pool Lifts) - (following pages) or this Chapter - 15.8.6 - (Sloped Entries) - pp. 301 & 302.*

The secondary means of entry shall comply with one of the following: *15.8.5 (Swimming Pool Lifts) - (following pages), this Chapter - 15.8.6 - (Sloped Entries) - pp. 301 & 302, this Chapter - 15.8.7 - (Transfer Walls) - pp. 302 & 303, this Chapter - 15.8.8 - (Transfer Systems) - pp. 303-305, or this Chapter - 15.8.9 - (Pool Stairs) - p. 305.*

EXCEPTION 1:

> Where a swimming pool has less than 300 linear feet (91 440mm) of swimming pool wall, at least one accessible means of entry shall be provided and shall comply with *15.8.5 (Swimming Pool Lifts - (following pages) or this Chapter - 15.8.6 - (Sloped Entries) - pp. 301 & 302.*

EXCEPTION 2:

> Wave action pools, leisure rivers, sand bottom pools, and other pools where user access is limited to one area, shall provide at least one accessible means of entry that complies with *15.8.5 - (Swimming Pool Lifts) - (following pages), this Chapter - 15.8.6 - (Sloped Entries) - pp. 301 & 302, or this Chapter - 15.8.8 - (Transfer Systems) - pp. 303-305.*

EXCEPTION 3:

> Catch pools shall be required only to be served by an accessible route that connects to the pool edge.

15.8.3 **Wading Pools**

At least one accessible means of entry complying with this *Chapter - 15.8.6 - (Sloped Entries) - pp. 301 & 302* shall be provided for each wading pool.

Chapter 71: Recreation Facilities - Federal Final Rule (continued)

15.8.4 **Spas**

At least one accessible means of entry complying with *15.8.5 - (Swimming Pool Lifts) - (below & following pages), this Chapter - 15.8.7 - (Transfer Walls) - pp. 302 & 303, or this Chapter - 15.8.8 - (Transfer Systems) - pp. 303-305* shall be provided for each spa.

EXCEPTION:

Where spas are provided in a cluster, 5 percent, but not less than one, in each cluster shall be accessible.

15.8.5 **Pool Lifts**

Pool lifts shall comply with *15.8.5 - (below & following pages)*.

Pool Lift Location

(1) Pool lifts shall be located where the water level does not exceed 48 inches (1219mm).

EXCEPTION 1:

Where the entire pool depth is greater than 48 inches (1219mm), *15.8.5(1) - (above)* shall not apply.

EXCEPTION 2:

Where multiple pool lift locations are provided, no more than one shall be required to be located in an area where the water level does not exceed 48 inches (1219mm).

Seat Location

(2) In the raised position, the centerline of the seat shall be located over the deck and 16 inches (406mm) minimum from the edge of the pool.

The deck surface between the centerline of the seat and the pool edge shall have a slope not greater than 1:48.

See Diagram 130(a) - p. 435.

Clear Deck Space

(3) On the side of the seat opposite the water, a clear deck space shall be provided parallel with the seat.

Chapter 71: Recreation Facilities - Federal Final Rule (continued)

The space shall be 36 inches (914mm) wide minimum and shall extend forward 48 inches (1219mm) minimum from a line located 12 inches (305mm) behind the rear edge of the seat.

The clear deck space shall have a slope not greater than 1:48.

See Diagram 130(b) - p. 435.

Seat Height

(4) The height of the lift seat shall be designed to allow a stop at 16 inches (406mm) minimum to 19 inches (483mm) maximum measured from the deck to the top of the seat surface when in the raised (load) position.

See Diagram 130(c) - p. 435.

Seat Width

(5) The seat shall be 16 inches (406mm) minimum wide.

Footrests and Armrests

(6) Footrests shall be provided and shall move with the seat.

If provided, armrests positioned opposite the water shall be removable or shall fold clear of the seat when the seat is in the raised (load) position.

EXCEPTION:

Footrests shall not be required on pool lifts provided in spas.

Operation

(7) The lift shall be capable of unassisted operation from both the deck and water levels.

Controls and operating mechanisms shall be unobstructed when the lift is in use and shall comply with ADAAG - 4.27.4.

Submerged Depth

(8) The lift shall be designed so that the seat will submerge to a water depth of 18 inches (457mm) minimum below the stationary water level.

See Diagram 131(a) - p. 436.

Chapter 71: Recreation Facilities - Federal Final Rule (continued)

Lifting Capacity

(9) Single person pool lifts shall have a minimum weight capacity of 300 lbs. (136kg) and be capable of sustaining a static load of at least one and a half times the rated load.

15.8.6 **Sloped Entries**

Sloped entries designed to provide access into the water shall comply with *15.8.6 - (below & following page)*.

Sloped Entries

(1) Sloped entries shall comply with ADAAG - 4.3 and ADAAG - 4.3.11, except as modified below.

EXCEPTION:

Where sloped entries are provided, the surfaces shall not be required to be slip-resistant.

Submerged Depth

(2) Sloped entries shall extend to a depth of 24 inches (610mm) minimum to 30 inches (762mm) maximum below the stationary water level.

Where landings are required by ADAAG - 4.8, at least one landing shall be located 24 inches (610mm) minimum to 30 inches (762mm) maximum below the stationary water level.

See Diagram 131(b) - p. 436.

EXCEPTION:

In wading pools, the sloped entry and landings, if provided, shall extend to the deepest part of the wading pool.

Handrails

(3) Handrails shall be provided on both sides of the sloped entry and shall comply with ADAAG - 4.8.5.

The clear width between handrails shall be 33 inches (838mm) minimum and 38 inches (965mm) maximum.

See Diagram 132 - p. 437.

Chapter 71: Recreation Facilities - Federal Final Rule (continued)

EXCEPTION 1:

Handrail extensions specified by ADAAG - 4.8.5 shall not be required at the bottom landing serving a sloped entry.

EXCEPTION 2:

Where a sloped entry is provided for wave action pools, leisure rivers, sand bottom pools, and other pools where user access is limited to one area, the required clear width between handrails shall not apply.

EXCEPTION 3:

The handrail requirements of ADAAG - 4.8.5 and *15.8.6(3) - (preceding page & above)* shall not be required on sloped entries in wading pools.

15.8.7 **Transfer Walls**

Transfer walls shall comply with *15.8.7 - (below & following page)*.

Clear Deck Space

(1) A clear deck space of 60 inches (1524mm) minimum by 60 inches (1524mm) minimum with a slope not steeper than 1:48 shall be provided at the base of the transfer wall.

Where one grab bar is provided, the clear deck space shall be centered on the grab bar.

Where two grab bars are provided, the clear deck space shall be centered on the clearance between the grab bars.

See Diagram 133 - p. 438.

Height

(2) The height of the transfer wall shall be 16 inches (406mm) minimum to 19 inches (483mm) maximum measured from the deck.

See Diagram 134(a) - p. 439.

Wall Depth and Length

(3) The depth of the transfer wall shall be 12 inches (305mm) minimum to 16 inches (406mm) maximum.

Chapter 71: Recreation Facilities - Federal Final Rule (continued)

The length of the transfer wall shall be 60 inches (1524mm) minimum and shall be centered on the clear deck space.

See Diagram 134(b) - p. 439.

Surface

(4) Surfaces of transfer walls shall not be sharp and shall have rounded edges.

Grab Bars

(5) At least one grab bar shall be provided on the transfer wall.

Grab bars shall be perpendicular to the pool wall and shall extend the full depth of the transfer wall.

The top of the gripping surface shall be 4 inches (102mm) minimum and 6 inches (152mm) maximum above walls.

Where one grab bar is provided, clearance shall be 24 inches (610mm) minimum on both sides of the grab bar.

Where two grab bars are provided, clearance between grab bars shall be 24 inches (610mm) minimum.

Grab bars shall comply with ADAAG - 4.26.

See Diagram 134(c) - p. 439.

15.8.8 **Transfer Systems**

Transfer systems shall comply with *15.8.8 - (below & following page).*

Transfer Platform

(1) A transfer platform 19 inches (483mm) minimum clear depth by 24 inches (610mm) minimum clear width shall be provided at the head of each transfer system.

See Diagram 135(a) - p. 440.

Chapter 71: Recreation Facilities - Federal Final Rule (continued)

Clear Deck Space

(2) A clear deck space of 60 inches (1524mm) minimum by 60 inches (1524mm) minimum with a slope not steeper than 1:48 shall be provided at the base of the transfer platform surface and shall be centered along a 24-inch (610mm) minimum unobstructed side of the transfer platform.

See Diagram 135(b) - p. 440.

Height

(3) The height of the transfer platform shall comply with *15.8.7(2) - (preceding page)*.

Transfer Steps

(4) Transfer step height shall be 8 inches (203mm) maximum.

Transfer steps shall extend to a water depth of 18 inches (457mm) minimum below the stationary water level.

See Diagram 136(a) - p. 441.

Surface

(5) The surface of the transfer system shall not be sharp and shall have rounded edges.

Size

(6) Each transfer step shall have a tread clear depth of 14 inches (356mm) minimum and 17 inches (432mm) maximum and shall have a tread clear width of 24 inches (610mm) minimum.

See Diagram 136(b) - p. 441.

Grab Bars

(7) At least one grab bar on each transfer step and the transfer platform, or a continuous grab bar serving each transfer step and the transfer platform, shall be provided.

Where provided, the top of the gripping surface shall be 4 inches (102mm) minimum and 6 inches (152mm) maximum above each step and transfer platform.

Where a continuous grab bar is provided, the top of the gripping surface shall be 4 inches (102mm) minimum and 6 inches (152mm) maximum above the step nosing and transfer platform.

Grab bars shall comply with ADAAG - 4.26 and be located on at least one side of the transfer system.

The grab bar located at the transfer platform shall not obstruct transfer.

See Diagram 136(c) - p. 441.

15.8.9 **Pool Stairs**

Pool stairs shall comply with *15.8.9 - (below).*

(1) Pool stairs shall comply with ADAAG - 4.9, except as modified below.

Handrails

(2) The width between handrails shall be 20 inches (508mm) minimum and 24 inches (610mm) maximum.

Handrail extensions required by ADAAG - 4.9.4 shall not be required at the bottom landing serving a pool stair.

15.8.10 **Water Play Components**

Where water play components are provided, the provisions of this *Chapter - 15.6 - pp. 282-289,* ADAAG - 4.3 and ADAAG - 4.3.11 shall apply, except as modified or otherwise provided in this section.

EXCEPTION 1:

Where the surface of the accessible route, clear floor or ground spaces and maneuvering spaces connecting play components is submerged, the provisions of this *Chapter 15.6 - pp. 282-289,* ADAAG - 4.3 and ADAAG - 4.3.11 for cross slope, running slope, and surface shall not apply.

EXCEPTION 2:

Transfer systems complying with this *Chapter - 15.6.5 - pp. 287 & 288* shall be permitted to be used in lieu of ramps to connect elevated play components.

Diagram 1

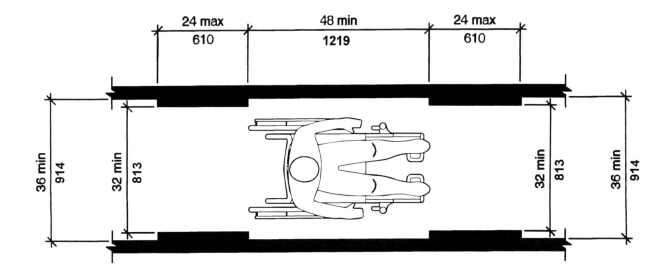

Clear Width of an Accessible Route

Diagram 2

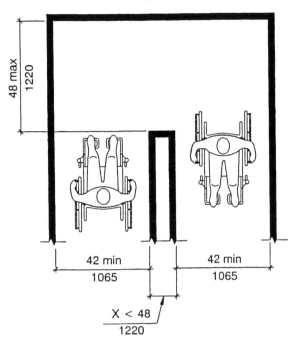

(a)
180 Degree Turn

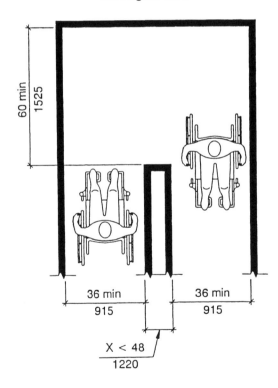

(b)
180 Degree Turn
(Exception)

Clear Width at Turn

Diagram 3

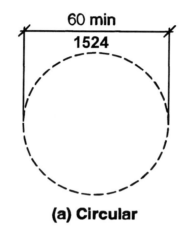

(a) Circular

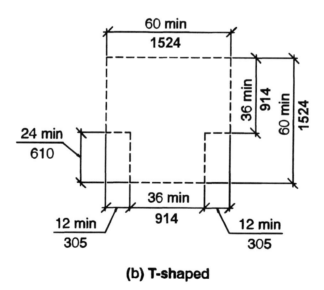

(b) T-shaped

Size of Wheelchair Turning Space

Diagram 4

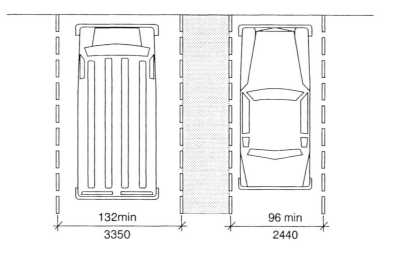

Vehicle Parking Space Size

Diagram 5

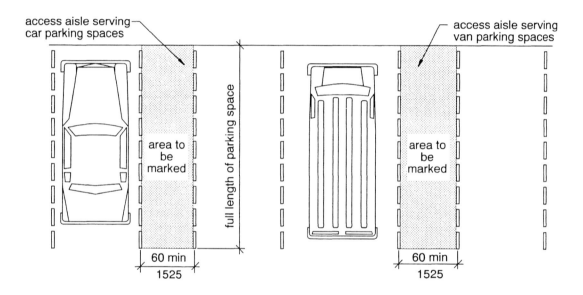

Parking Space Access Aisles

Diagram 6

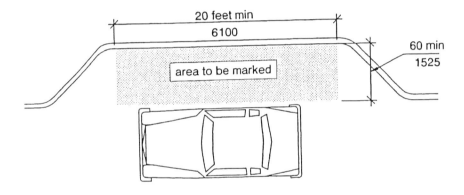

Passenger Loading Zone Access Aisle

Diagram 7

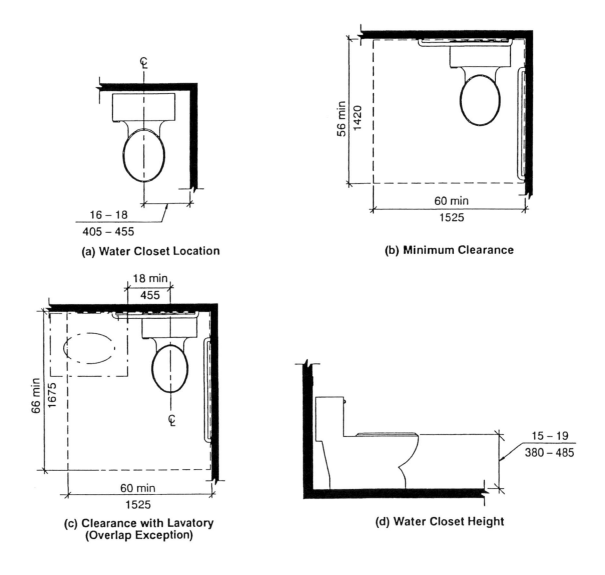

(a) Water Closet Location

(b) Minimum Clearance

(c) Clearance with Lavatory (Overlap Exception)

(d) Water Closet Height

Water Closets in Type A Units

Diagram 8

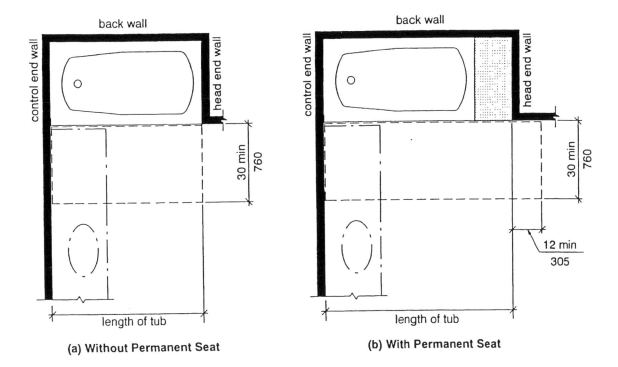

Clearance for Bathtubs in Type A Units

Diagram 9

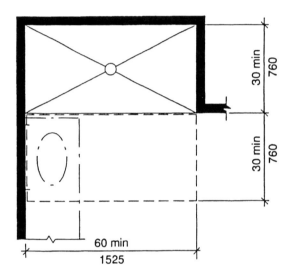

Note: Sink permitted per *Chapter 61: Shower Compartments - 608.2.2 - pp. 228 & 229*.

Standard Roll-in-Type Shower Compartment in Type A Units

Diagram 10

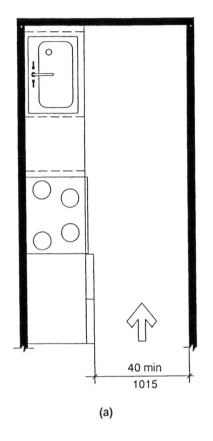
(a)

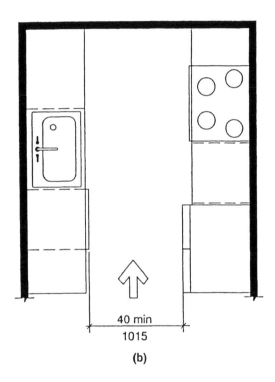
(b)

40 min
1015

40 min
1015

Minimum Kitchen Clearance in Type A Units

Diagram 11

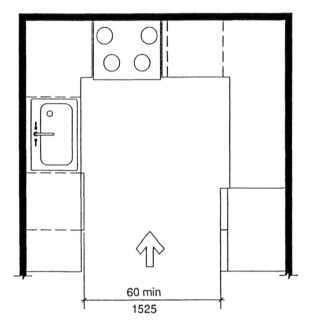

U-Shaped Kitchen Clearance in Type A Units

Diagram 12

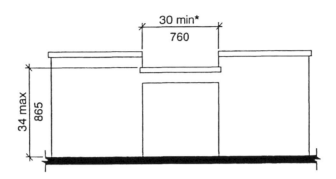

* 36 inches (914mm) minimum if part of T-shaped turning space per *Chapter 50: Turning Space - 304.3.2 - pp. 198 & 199 and Chapter 13: Type A Units - 1003.3.2 - p. 44.*

(a) Work Surface in Kitchen for Type A Units

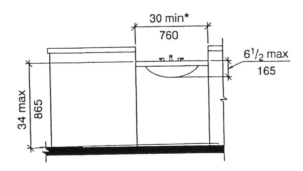

* 36 inches (914mm) minimum if part of T-shaped turning space per *Chapter 50: Turning Space - 304.3.2 - pp. 198 & 199 and Chapter 13: Type A Units - 1003.3.2 - p. 44.*

(b) Kitchen Sink for Type A Units

Work Surface and Sink in Kitchen for Type A Units

Diagram 13

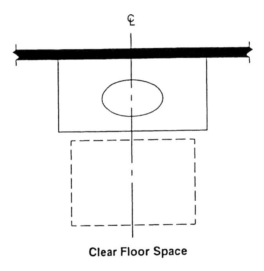

Clear Floor Space

Lavatory in Type B Units - Option A Bathrooms

Diagram 14

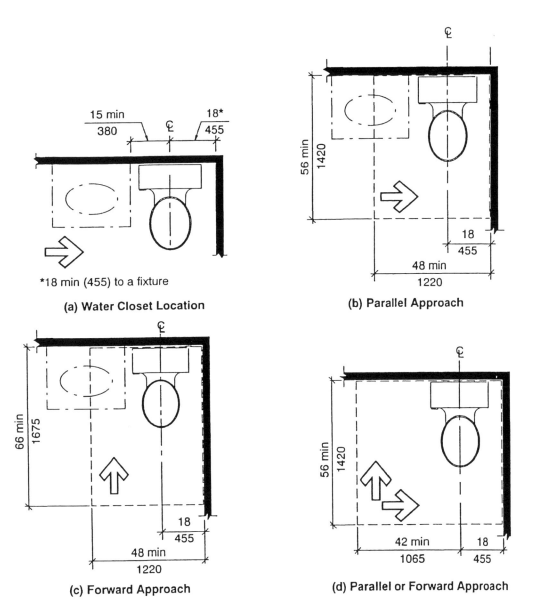

Water Closets in Type B Units

Diagram 15

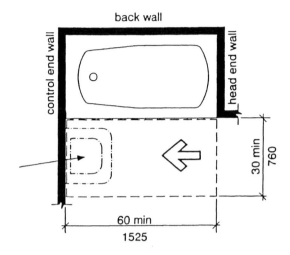

Lavatory complying with *Chapter 28: Sinks - 606 - pp. 118-120.*

(a)

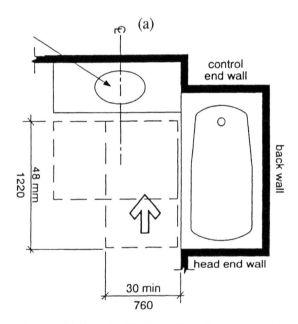

Lavatory complying with *Chapter 14: Type B Units - 1004.11.3.1.1 - p. 60.*

(b)

Parallel Approach Bathtub in Type B Units - Option A Bathrooms

Diagram 16

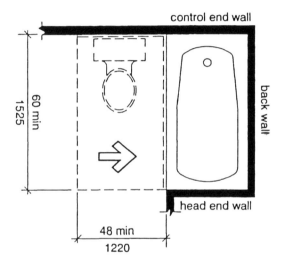

**Forward Approach Bathtub in Type B Units
Option A Bathrooms**

Diagram 17

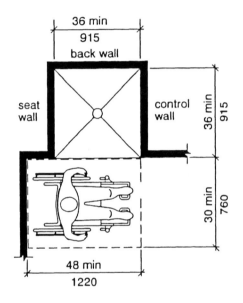

Transfer-Type Shower Compartment in Type B Units

Diagram 18

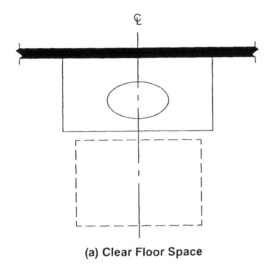

(a) Clear Floor Space

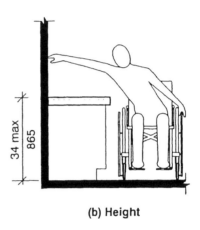

(b) Height

Lavatory in Type B Units - Option B Bathrooms

Diagram 19

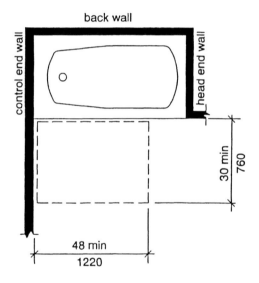

Bathtub Clearance in Type B Units - Option B Bathrooms

Diagram 20

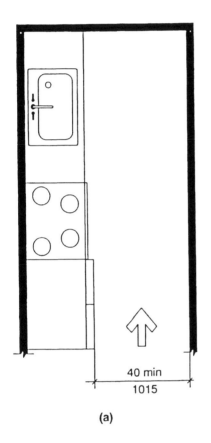
(a)

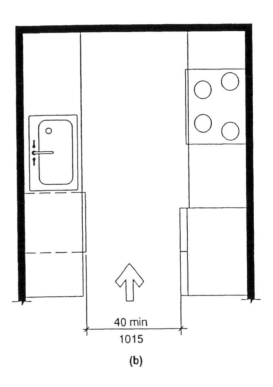
(b)

Minimum Kitchen Clearance in Type B Units

Diagram 21

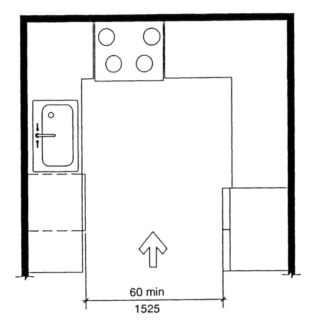

U-Shaped Kitchen Clearance in Type B Units

Diagram 22

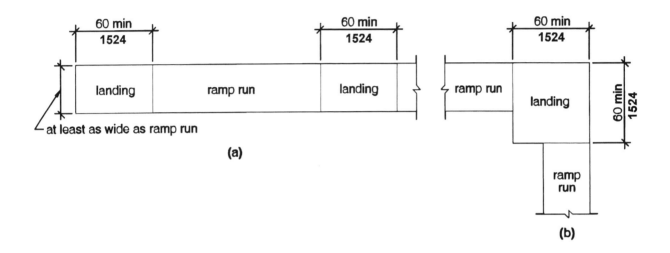

Ramp Landings

Diagram 23

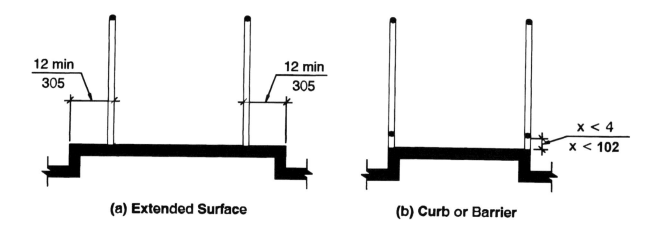

(a) Extended Surface

(b) Curb or Barrier

Ramp Edge Protection

Diagram 24

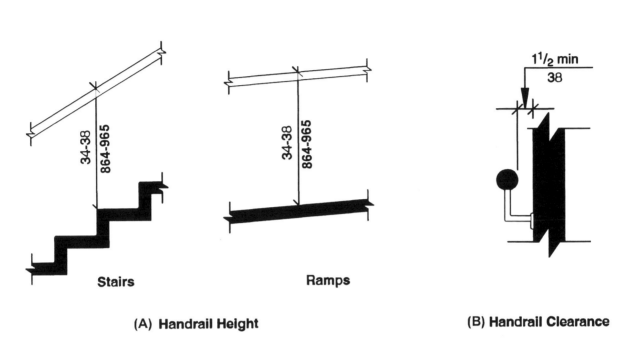

(A) Handrail Height (B) Handrail Clearance

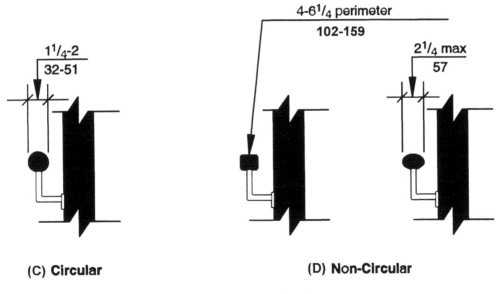

(C) Circular (D) Non-Circular

Handrail Cross Section

Handrails at Stairs and Ramps

Diagram 25

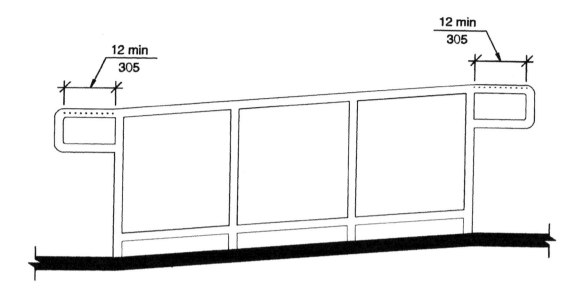

(A) Top and Bottom Handrail Extensions at Ramps

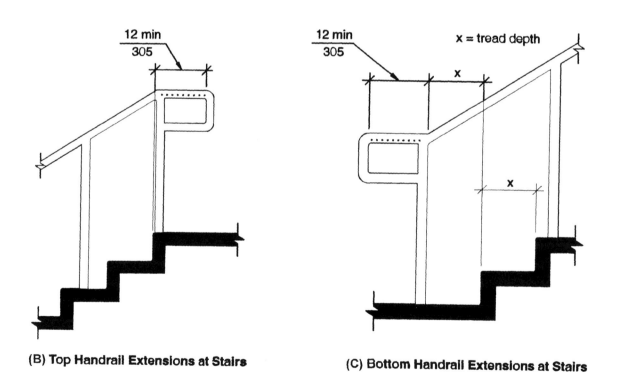

(B) Top Handrail Extensions at Stairs

(C) Bottom Handrail Extensions at Stairs

Handrail Extensions at Ramps and Stairs

Diagram 26

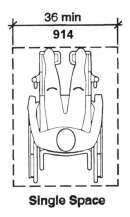
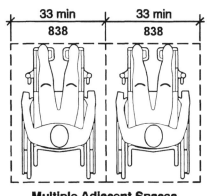

(A) **Width of a Wheelchair Space in Auditorium and Assembly Areas**

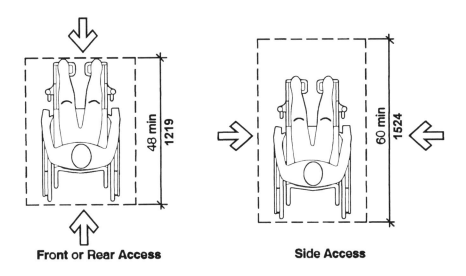

(B) **Depth of a Wheelchair Space in Auditorium and Assembly Areas**

Wheelchair Spaces in Auditorium and Assembly Areas

Diagram 27

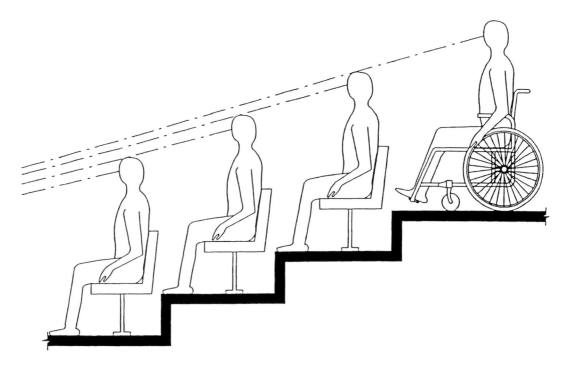

(a) Lines of Sight over the Heads of Seated Spectators

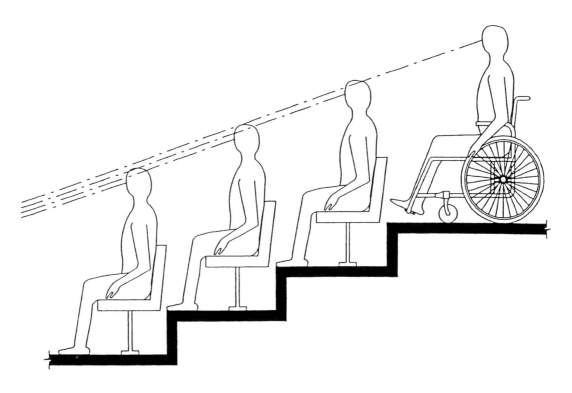

(b) Lines of Sight between the Heads of Seated Spectators

Lines of Sight Over and Between the Heads of Seated Spectators

Diagram 28

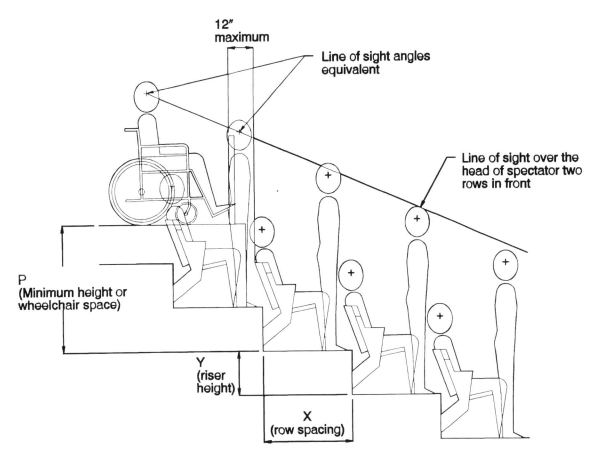

Calculation:
$P = [(2X + 34)(Y - 2.25)/X] + (20.2 - Y)$

Wheelchair Space Elevation

Diagram 29

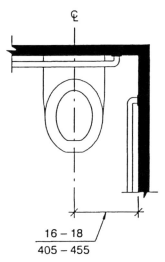

(a) Accessible Water Closets

16 – 18
405 – 455

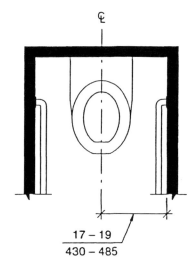

(b) Ambulatory Accessible Water Closets

17 – 19
430 – 485

Water Closet Location

Diagram 30

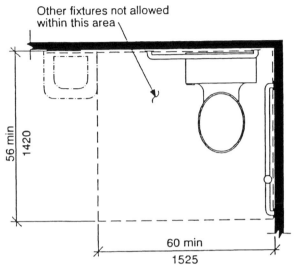

(a) Size of Clearance for Water Closet

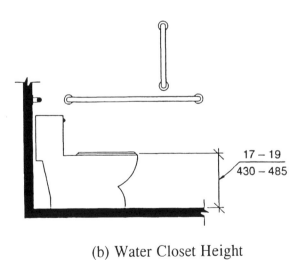

(b) Water Closet Height

Clearance and Height for Water Closet

Diagram 31

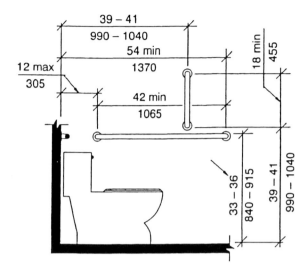

For Position, *see Chapter 62: Grab Bars - 609.4 - p. 235.*

(a) Side Wall Grab Bar for Water Closet

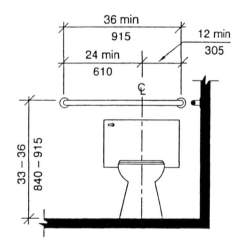

For Position, *see Chapter 62: Grab Bars - 609.4 - p. 235.*

(b) Rear Wall Grab Bar for Water Closet

Side Wall and Rear Wall Grab Bar for Water Closet

Diagram 32

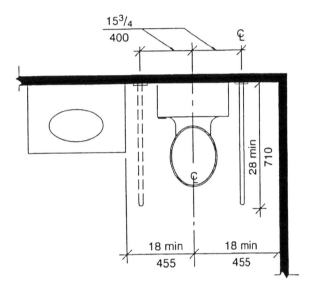

Swing-up Grab Bar for Water Closet

Diagram 33

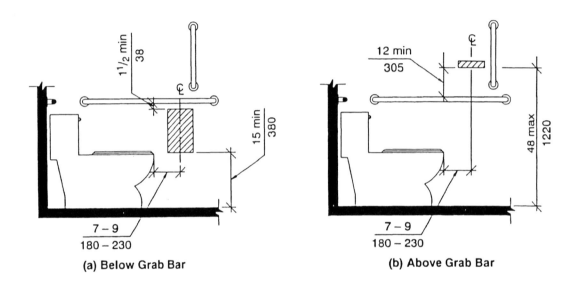

(a) Below Grab Bar

(b) Above Grab Bar

For Spacing, *see Chapter 62: Grab Bars - 609.3 - pp. 234 & 235.*

Dispenser Location

Diagram 34

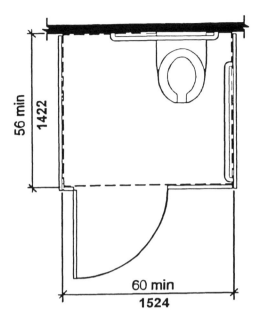

(a) Wall-Hung Water Closet – Adult

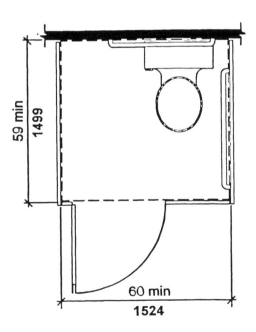

(b) Floor-Mounted Water Closet – Adult
Wall-Hung and
Floor-Mounted Water Closet – Children

Wheelchair Accessible Toilet Compartments

Diagram 35

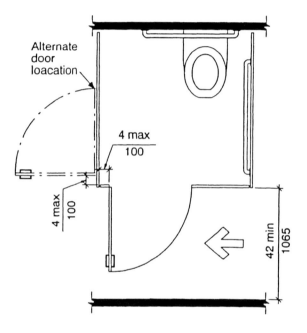

Wheelchair Accessible Compartment Doors

Diagram 36

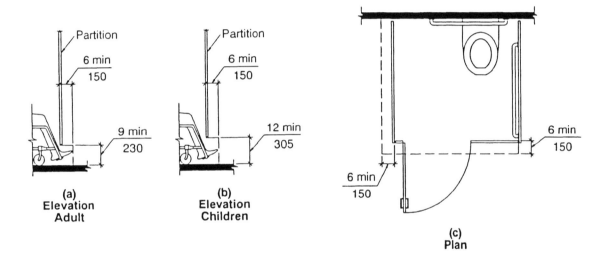

Wheelchair Accessible Compartment Toe Clearance

Diagram 37

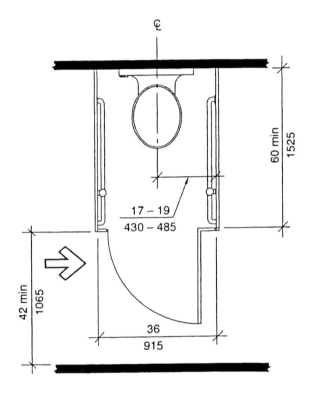

For Location, *see Chapter 27: Water Closet Compartment - 604.2 - p. 110.*

Ambulatory Accessible Compartment

Diagram 38

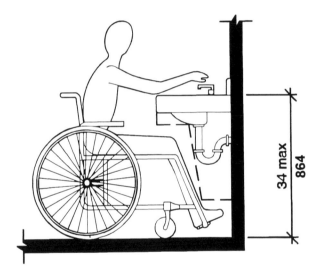

Height of Lavatories and Sinks

Diagram 39

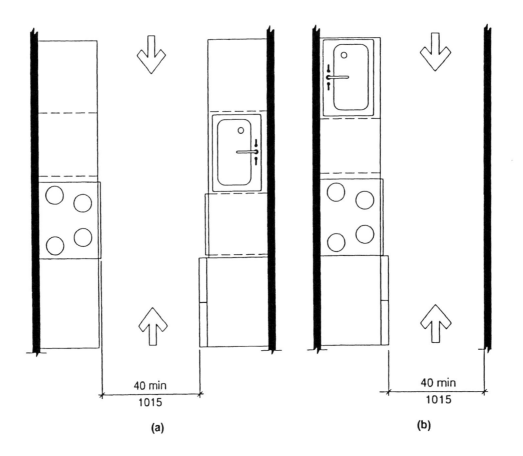

Pass-through Kitchen Clearance

Diagram 40

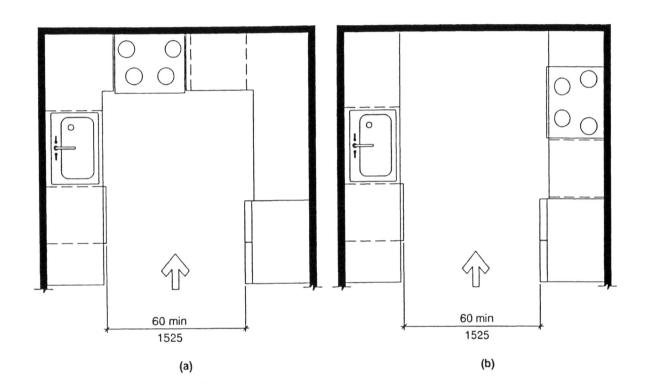

U-Shaped Kitchen Clearance

Diagram 41

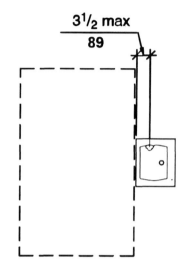

(a) Parallel Approach

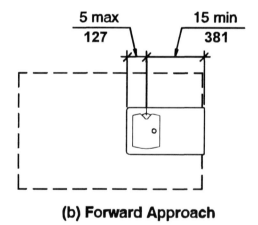

(b) Forward Approach

Drinking Fountain Spout Location

Diagram 42

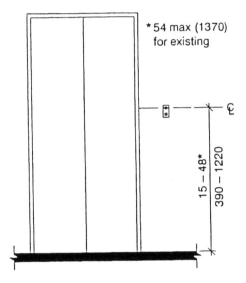

See Chapter 54: Reach Ranges - 308 - pp. 206 & 207.

Height of Elevator Call Buttons

Diagram 43

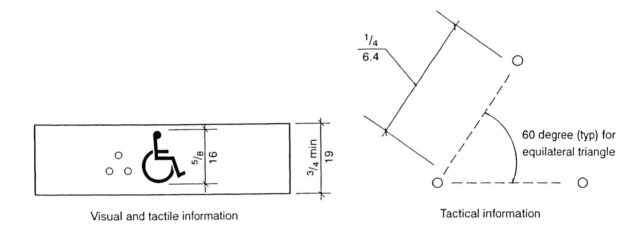

Visual and tactile information

Tactical information

Destination-Oriented Elevator Indication

Diagram 44

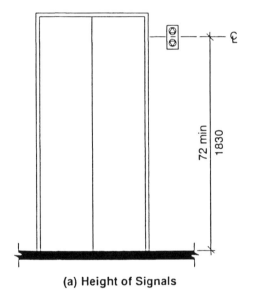
(a) Height of Signals

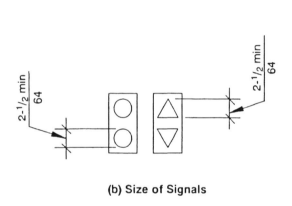
(b) Size of Signals

Elevator Visible Signals

Diagram 45

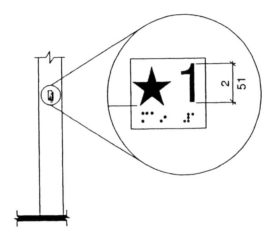

Elevator Floor Designation

Diagram 46

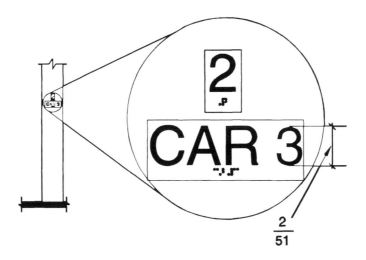

Destination-Oriented Elevator Car Identification

Diagram 47

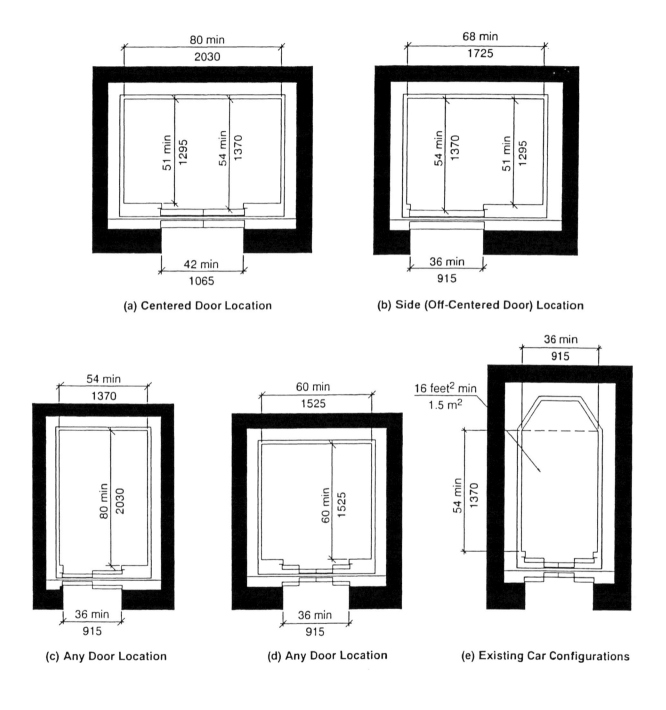

Inside Dimensions of Elevator Cars

Diagram 48

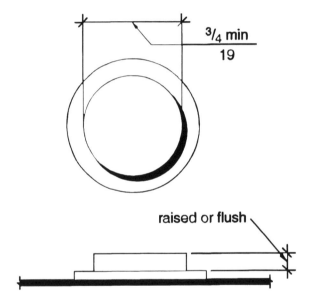

Elevator Car Control Buttons

Diagram 49

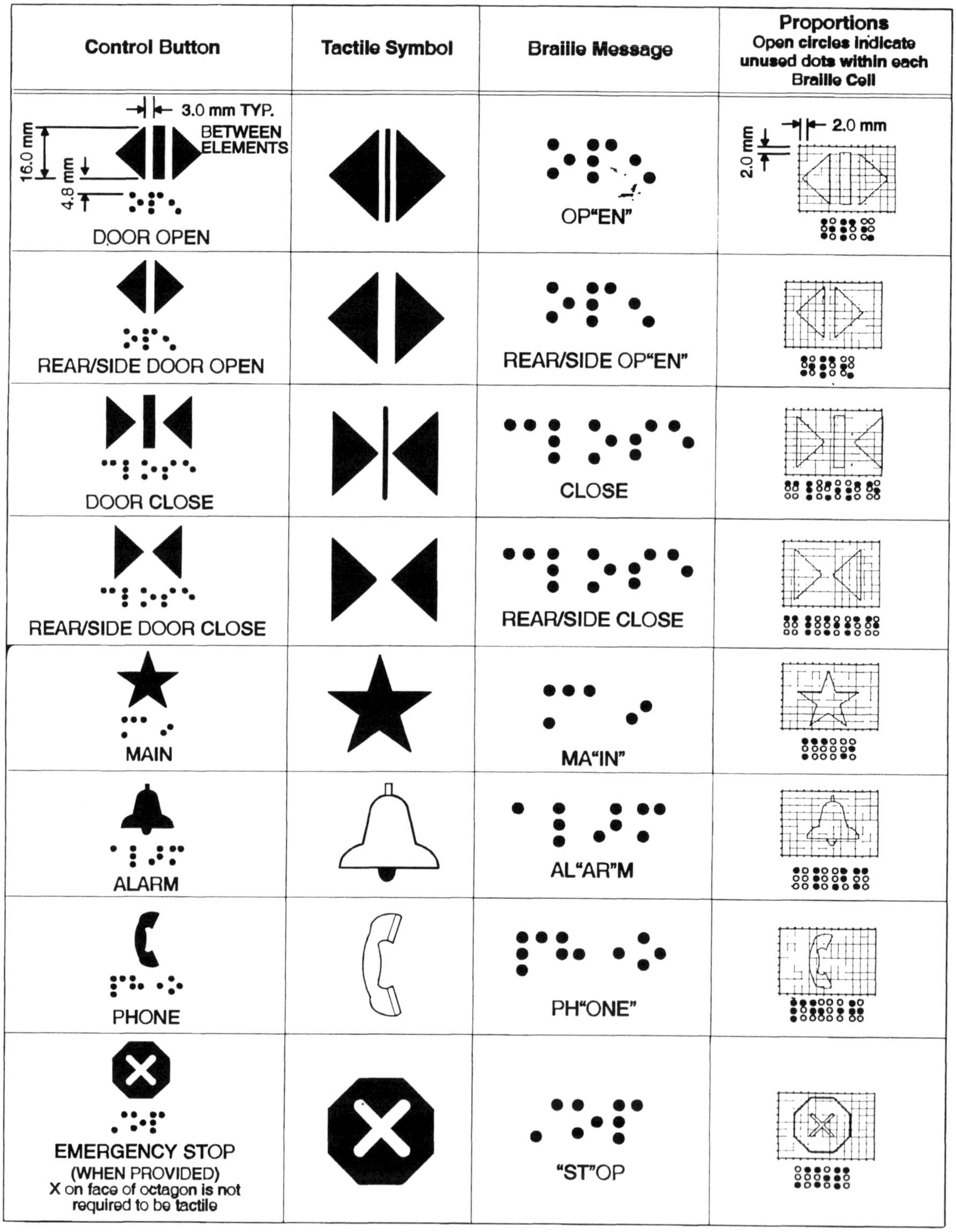

Control Button	Tactile Symbol	Braille Message	Proportions Open circles indicate unused dots within each Braille Cell
DOOR OPEN (16.0 mm, 4.8 mm, 3.0 mm TYP. BETWEEN ELEMENTS)	◆❘◆	OP"EN"	(2.0 mm, 2.0 mm)
REAR/SIDE DOOR OPEN	◆❘▶	REAR/SIDE OP"EN"	
DOOR CLOSE	▶❘◀	CLOSE	
REAR/SIDE DOOR CLOSE	▶◀	REAR/SIDE CLOSE	
MAIN	★	MA"IN"	
ALARM	🔔	AL"AR"M	
PHONE	☎	PH"ONE"	
EMERGENCY STOP (WHEN PROVIDED) X on face of octagon is not required to be tactile	⊗	"ST"OP	

Control Button Identification

Diagram 50

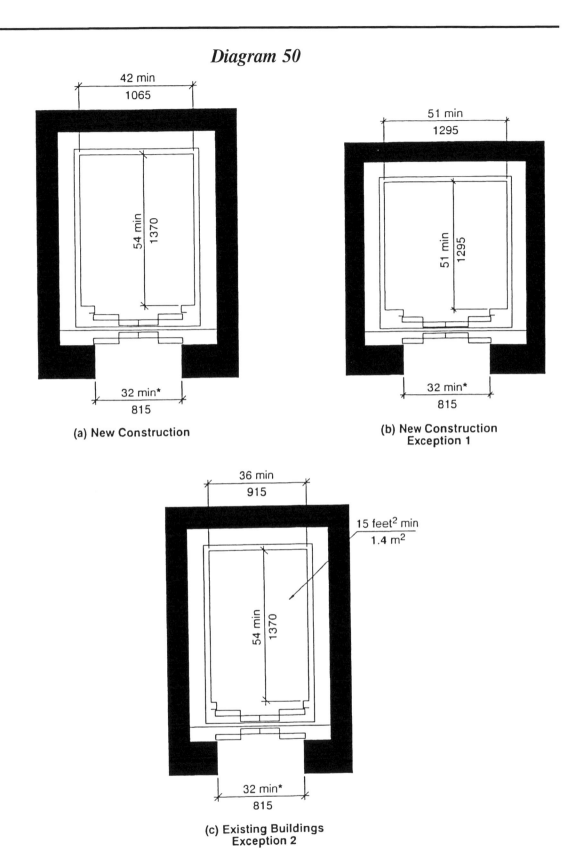

(a) New Construction

(b) New Construction Exception 1

(c) Existing Buildings Exception 2

*Door opening size from Chapter 32: Limited-Use/Limited-Application Elevators - 408.3.3 - p. 143.

Inside Dimensions of Limited-Use/Limited-Application (LULA) Elevator Cars

Diagram 51

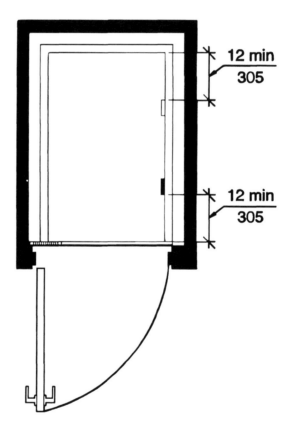

Location of Controls in Private Residence Elevators

Diagram 52

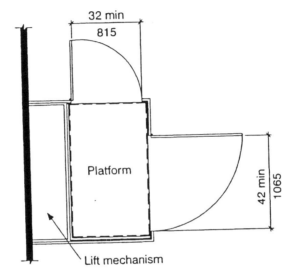

Platform Lift Doors and Gates

Diagram 53

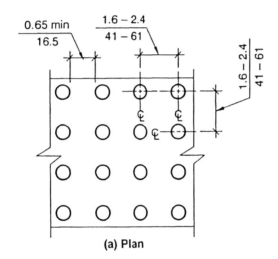
(a) Plan

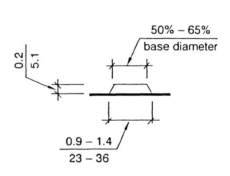
(b) Elevation (Enlarged)

Truncated Dome Size and Spacing

Diagram 54

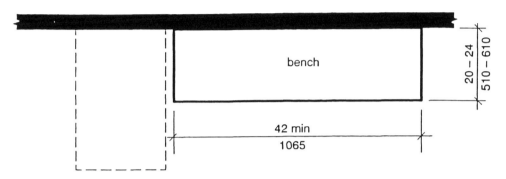

(a) Clear Floor Space and Size

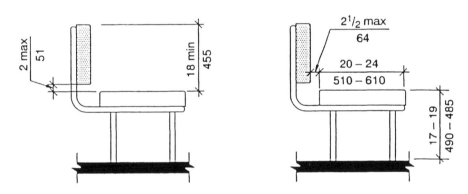

(b) Bench Back Support and Seat Height

Benches

Diagram 55

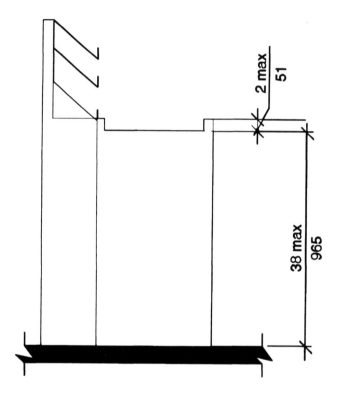

Height of Checkout Counters

Diagram 56

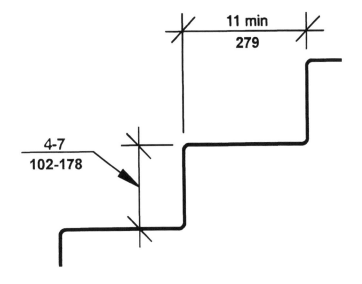

Treads and Risers for Accessible Stairways

Diagram 57

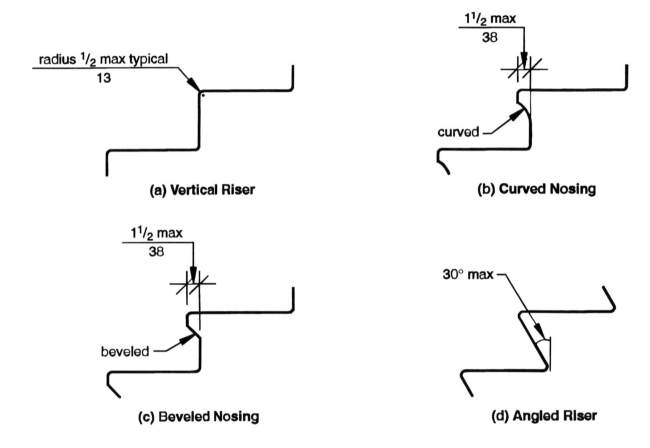

Stair Nosings

Diagram 58

(A)
International Symbol of Accessibility

(B)
International TTY Symbol

(C)
Volume-Controlled Telephone

(D)
International Symbol of Access for Hearing Loss

Signage Symbols of Accessibility

Diagram 59

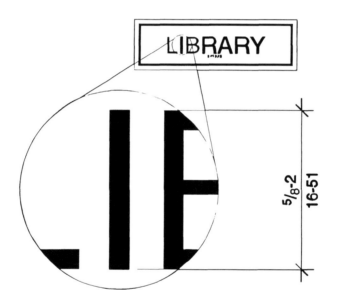

Character Height

Diagram 60

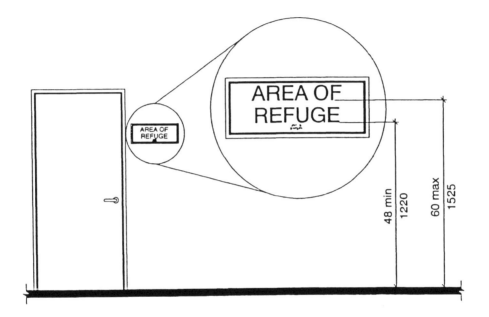

Note: For Braille mounting height *see **Chapter 44: Signage - 703.4.5 - p. 180.***

Height of Tactile Characters above Floor or Ground

365

Diagram 61

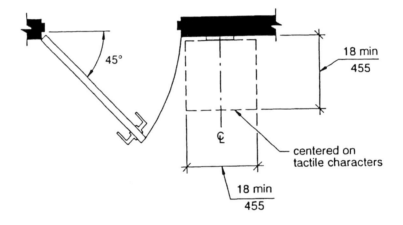

Location of Tactile Signs at Doors

Diagram 62

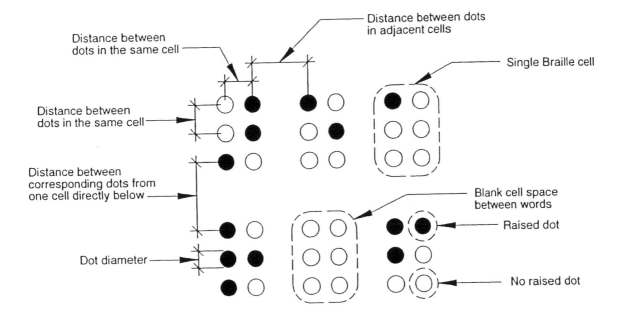

Braille Measurement

Diagram 63

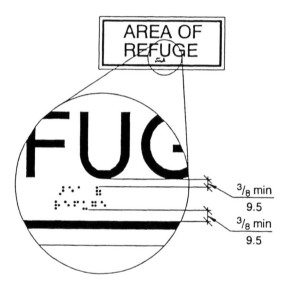

Position of Braille

Diagram 64

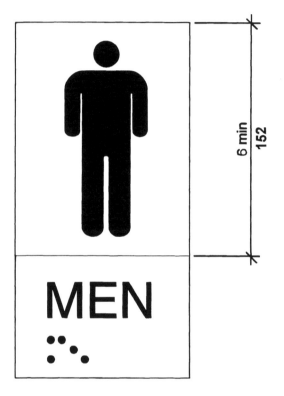

Pictogram Field

Diagram 65

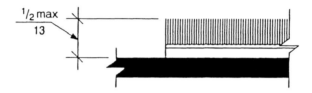

(a) Carpet on Floor Surfaces

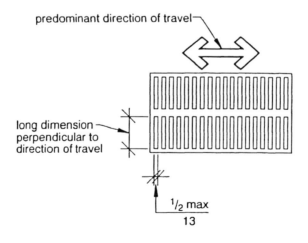

(b) Openings in Floor Surfaces

Carpet on and Openings in Floor Surfaces

Diagram 66

Vertical Changes in Level

Diagram 67

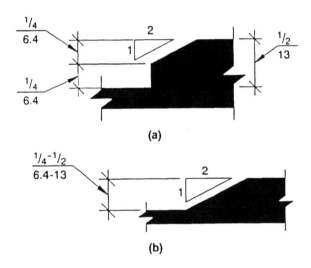

Beveled Changes in Level

Diagram 68

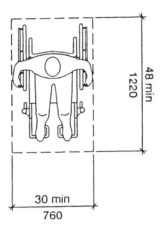

Size of Clear Floor Space

Diagram 69

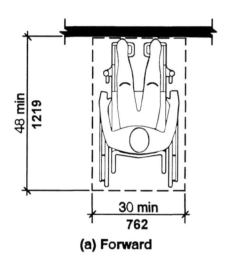

(a) Forward

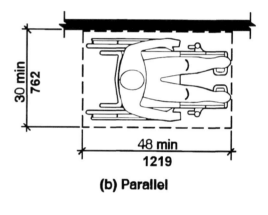

(b) Parallel

Position of Clear Floor Space

Diagram 70

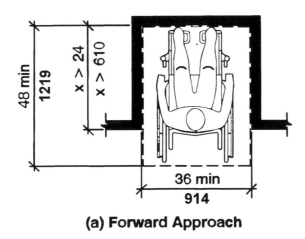

(a) Forward Approach

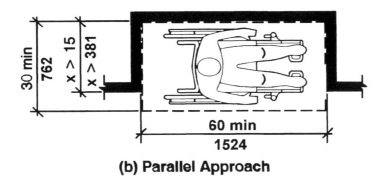

(b) Parallel Approach

Maneuvering Clearance in an Alcove

Diagram 71

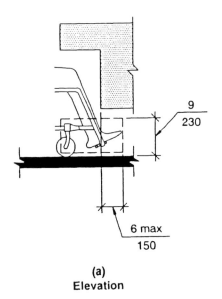
(a) Elevation

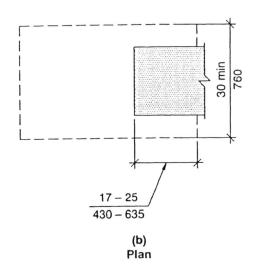
(b) Plan

Toe Clearance

Diagram 72

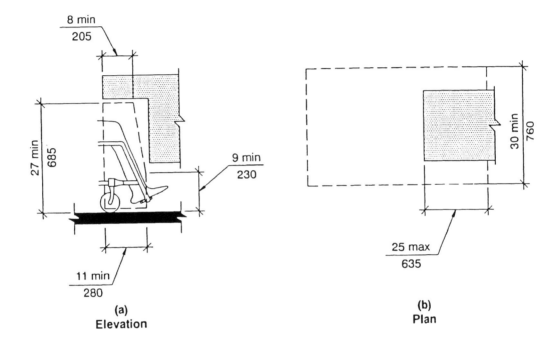

(a) Elevation

(b) Plan

Knee Clearance

Diagram 73

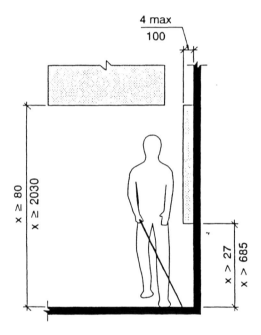

Limits of Protruding Objects

Diagram 74

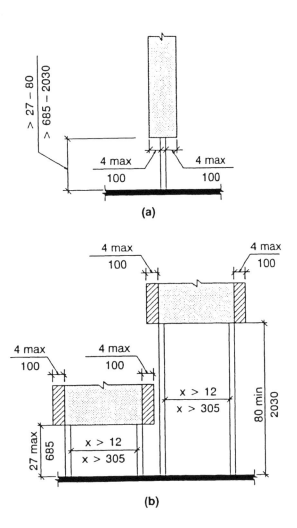

Post-Mounted Protruding Objects

Diagram 75

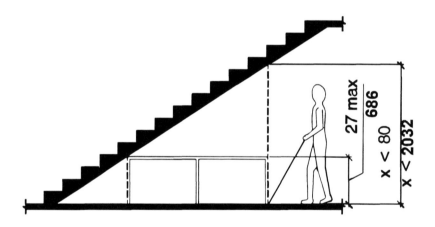

Reduced Vertical Clearance

Diagram 76

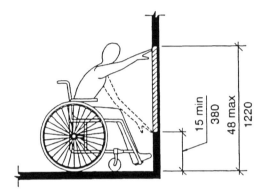

Unobstructed Forward Reach

Diagram 77

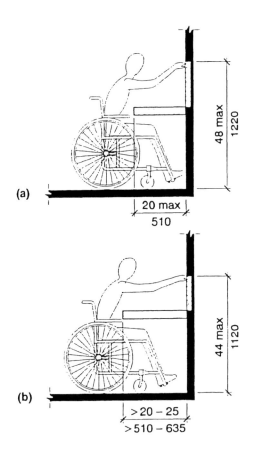

Obstructed High Forward Reach

Diagram 78

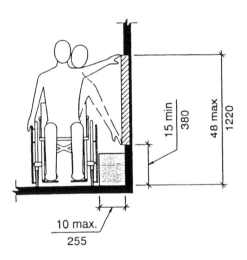

Unobstructed Side Reach

Diagram 79

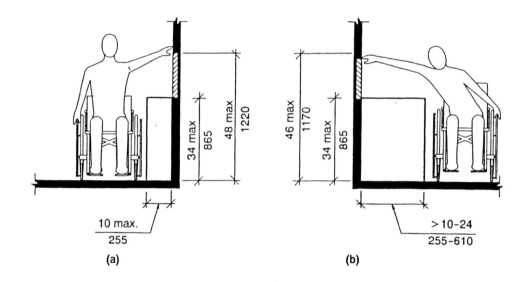

Obstructed High Side Reach

Diagram 80

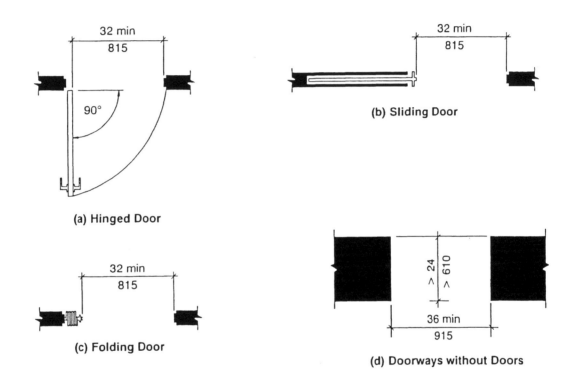

Clear Width of Doorways

Diagram 81

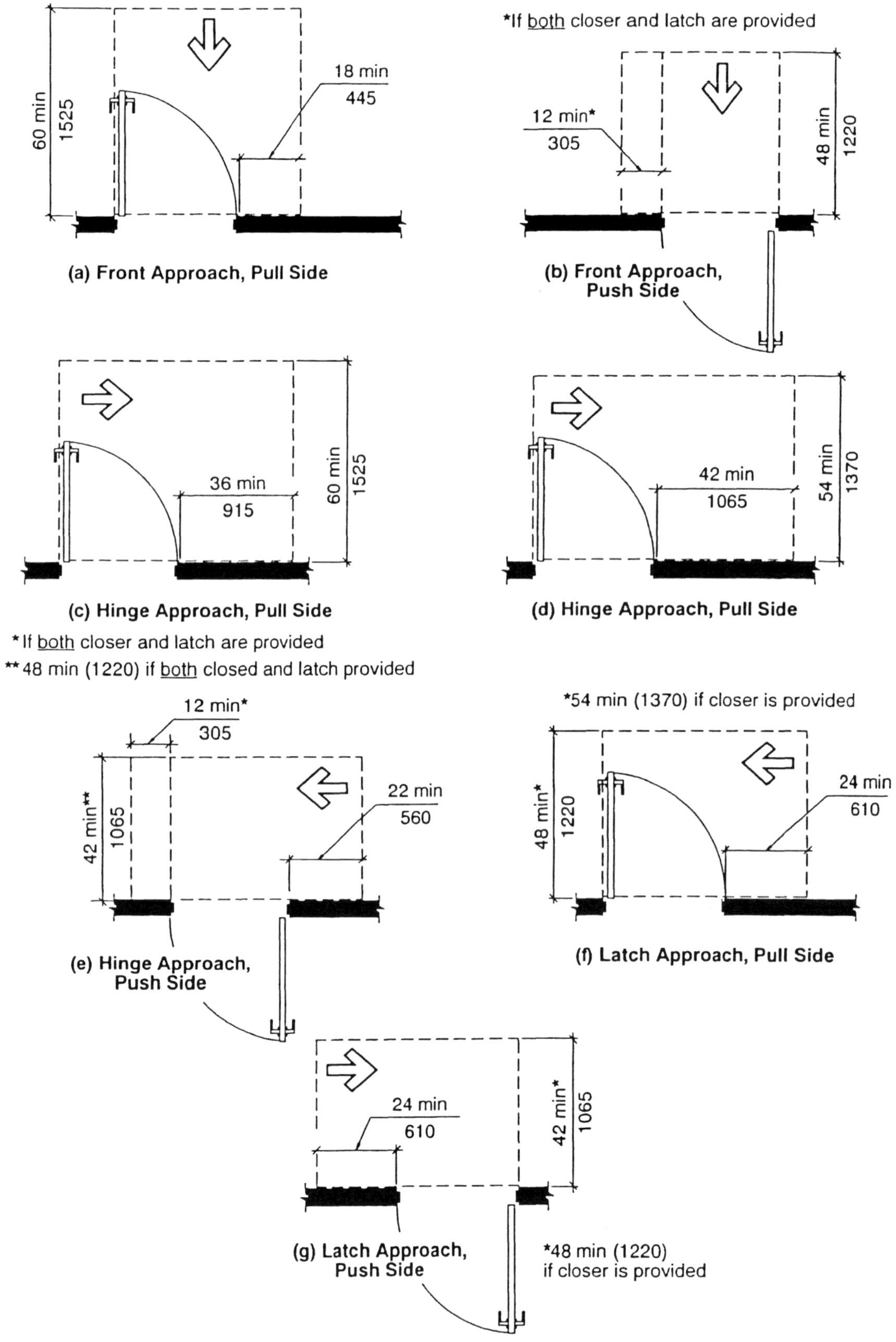

(a) Front Approach, Pull Side
- 60 min / 1525
- 18 min / 445

(b) Front Approach, Push Side
- *If both closer and latch are provided
- 12 min* / 305
- 48 min / 1220

(c) Hinge Approach, Pull Side
- 36 min / 915
- 60 min / 1525

(d) Hinge Approach, Pull Side
- 42 min / 1065
- 54 min / 1370

*If both closer and latch are provided
**48 min (1220) if both closed and latch provided

(e) Hinge Approach, Push Side
- 12 min* / 305
- 42 min** / 1065
- 22 min / 560

(f) Latch Approach, Pull Side
- *54 min (1370) if closer is provided
- 48 min* / 1220
- 24 min / 610

(g) Latch Approach, Push Side
- 24 min / 610
- 42 min* / 1065
- *48 min (1220) if closer is provided

Maneuvering Clearance at Manual Swinging Doors

Diagram 82

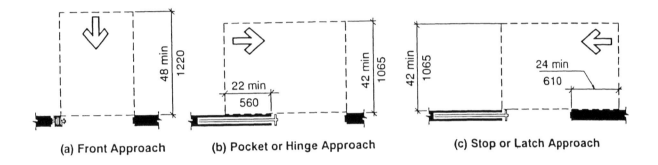

(a) Front Approach (b) Pocket or Hinge Approach (c) Stop or Latch Approach

Maneuvering Clearance at Sliding and Folding Doors

Diagram 83

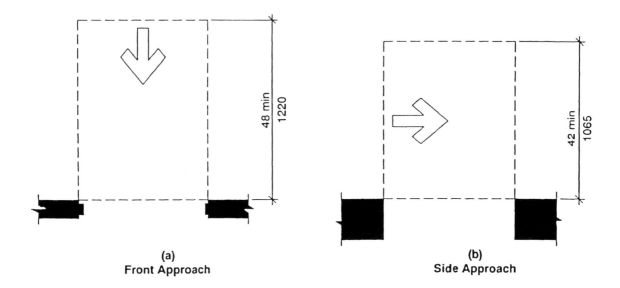

(a) Front Approach

(b) Side Approach

Maneuvering Clearance at Doorways without Doors

Diagram 84

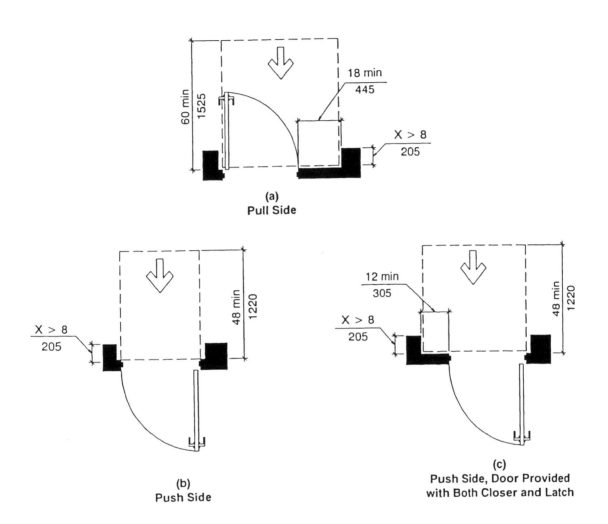

Maneuvering Clearance at Recessed Doors

Diagram 85

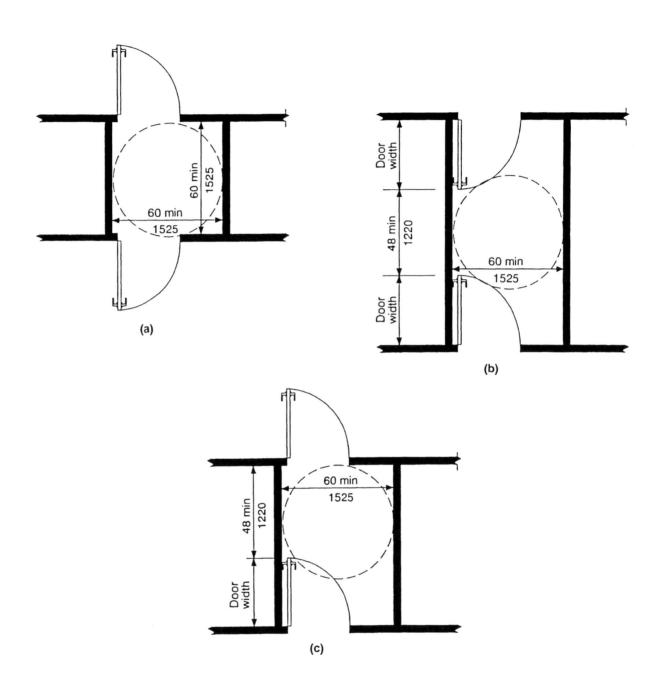

Two Doors in Series

Diagram 86

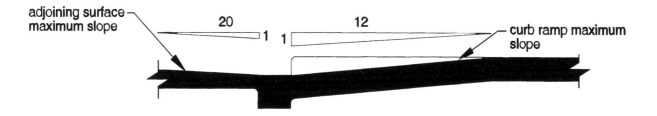

Counter Slope of Surfaces Adjacent to Curb Ramps

Diagram 87

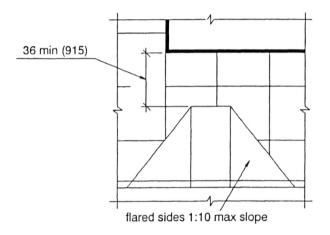

For Landings, *see Chapter 57: Curb Ramps - 406.7 - p. 218.*

Sides of Curb Ramps

Diagram 88

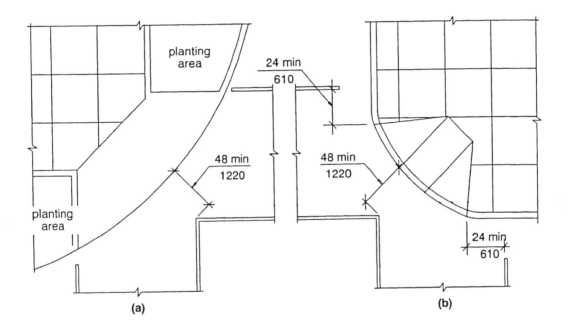

Diagonal Curb Ramps

Diagram 89

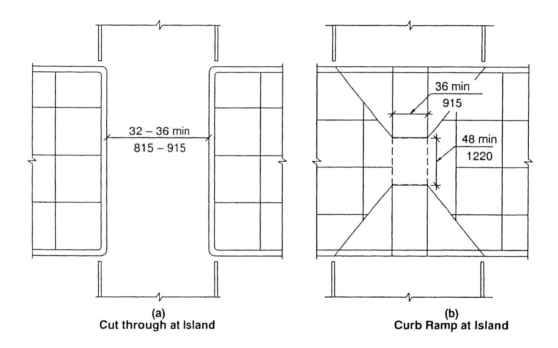

(a)
Cut through at Island

(b)
Curb Ramp at Island

For Clear Width, *see Chapter 4: Accessible Route - 403.5 - pp. 13 & 14.*

Islands

Diagram 90

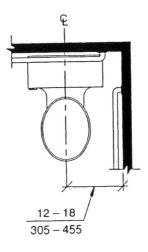

Children's Water Closet Location

Diagram 91

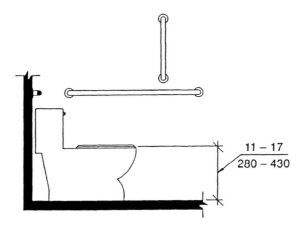

(a) Children's Water Closet Height

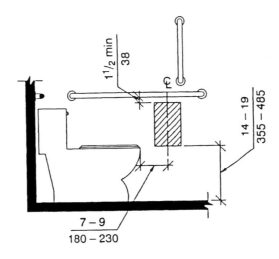

(b) Children's Dispenser Location

Children's Water Closet Height and Dispenser Location

Diagram 92

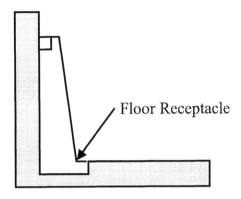

(a) Stall Type

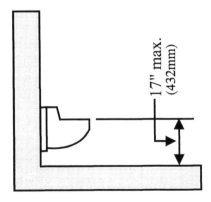

(b) Elongated Wall-Hung

Urinals

Diagram 93

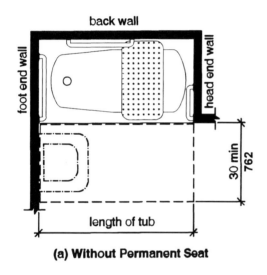

(a) Without Permanent Seat

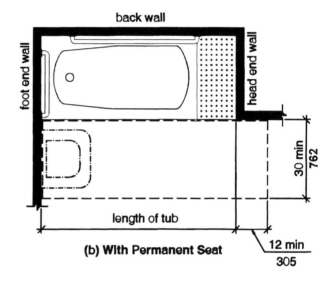

(b) With Permanent Seat

Clearance for Bathtubs

Diagram 94

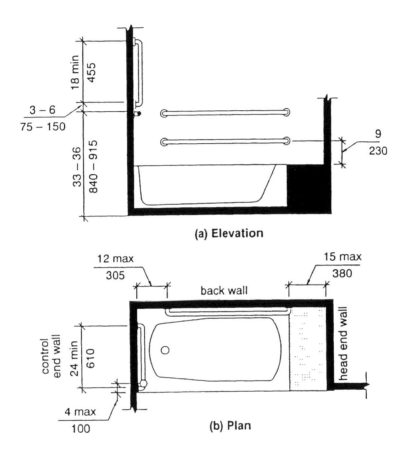

(a) Elevation

(b) Plan

For position of Grab Bars, *see Chapter 62: Grab Bars - 609.4 - p. 235.*

Grab Bars for Bathtubs with Permanent Seats

Diagram 95

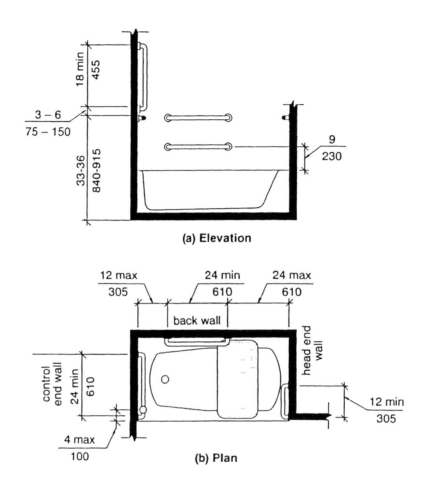

(a) Elevation

(b) Plan

For position of Grab Bars, *see Chapter 62: Grab Bars - 609.4 - p. 235.*

Grab Bars for Bathtubs without Permanent Seats

Diagram 96

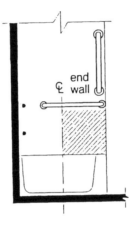

Location of Bathtub Controls

Diagram 97

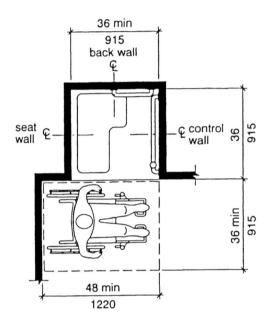

Note: Inside finished dimensions measured at the center points of opposing sides.

Transfer-Type Shower Compartment Size and Clearance

Diagram 98

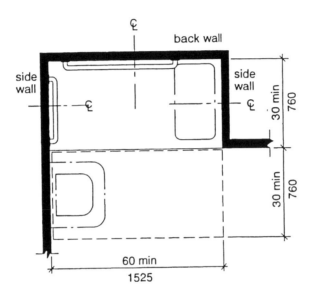

Note: Inside finished dimensions measured at the center points of opposing sides.

Standard Roll-in-Type Shower Compartment Size and Clearance

Diagram 99

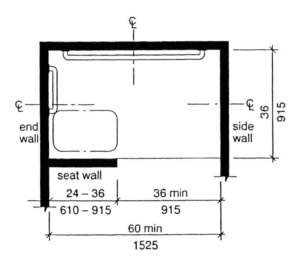

Note: Inside finished dimensions measured at the center points of opposing sides.

Alternate Roll-in-Type Shower Compartment Size and Clearance

Diagram 100

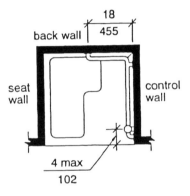

Grab Bars in Transfer-Type Showers

Diagram 101

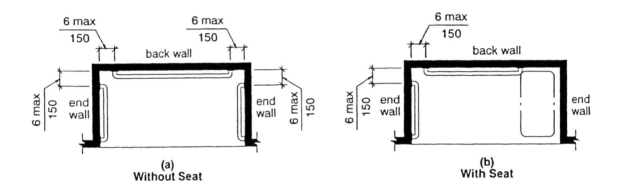

(a) Without Seat

(b) With Seat

Grab Bars in Standard Roll-in-Type Showers

Diagram 102

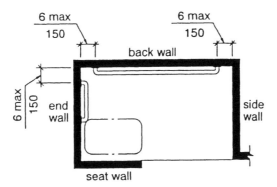

Grab Bars in Alternate Roll-in-Type Showers

Diagram 103

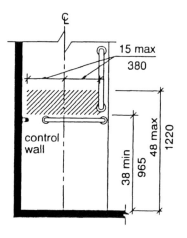

Transfer-Type Shower Controls and Hand Shower Location

Diagram 104

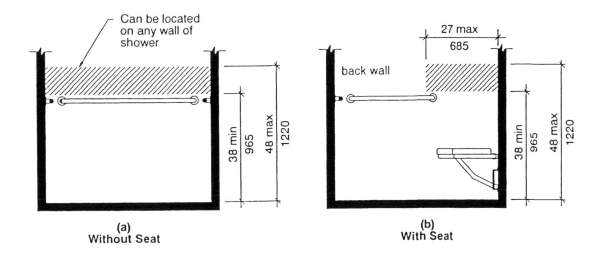

Standard Roll-in-Type Shower Control and Hand Shower Location

Diagram 105

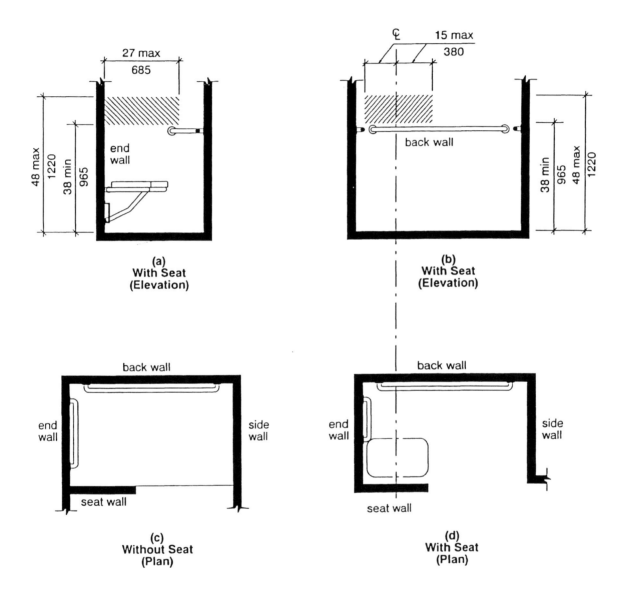

Alternate Roll-in-Type Shower Control and Hand Shower Location

Diagram 106

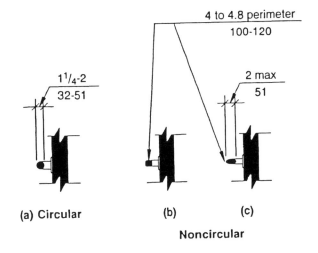

(a) Circular

(b) (c)
Noncircular

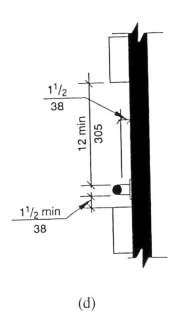

(d)

Size and Spacing of Grab Bars

Diagram 107

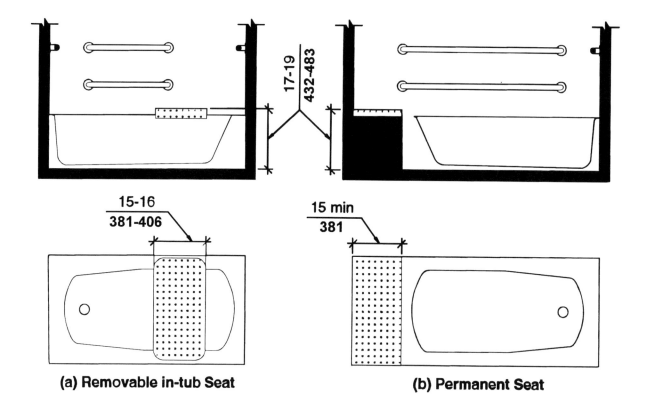

(a) Removable in-tub Seat

(b) Permanent Seat

Bathtub Seats

Diagram 108

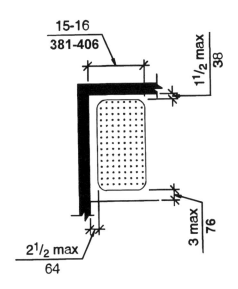

(A) Rectangular Shower Compartment Seat

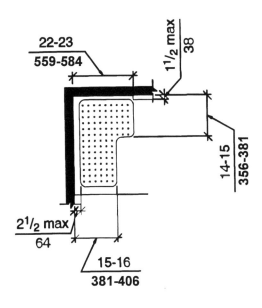

(B) L-Shaped Shower Compartment Seat

Shower Compartment Seats

Diagram 109

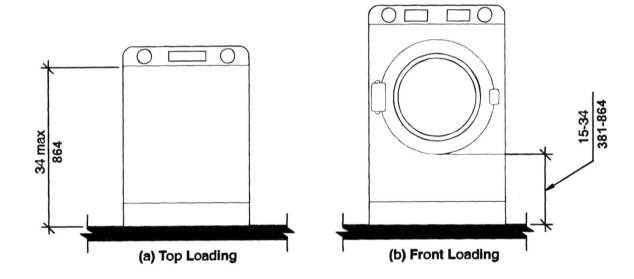

Height of Laundry Equipment

Diagram 110

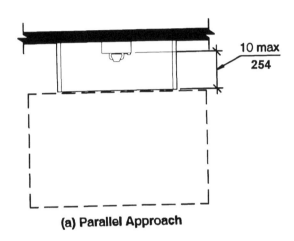
(a) Parallel Approach

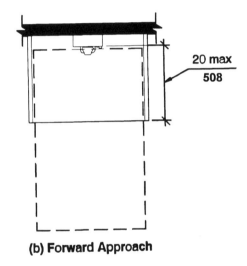
(b) Forward Approach

Clear Floor Space for Telephones

Diagram 111

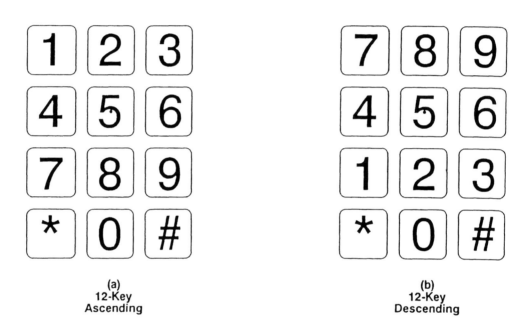

(a)
12-Key
Ascending

(b)
12-Key
Descending

Numeric Key Layout

Diagram 112

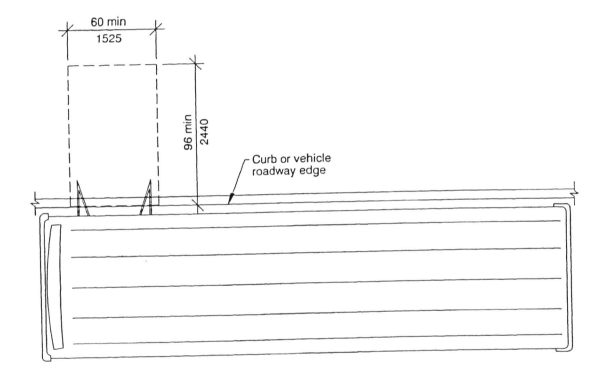

Size of Bus Boarding and Alighting Areas

Diagram 113

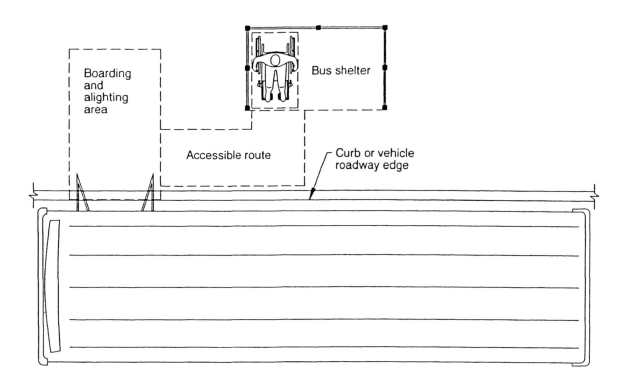

Bus Shelters

Diagram 114

Track Crossings

Diagram 115

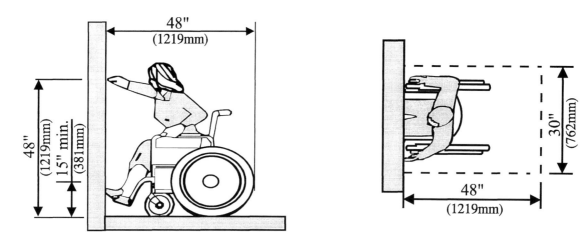

(a) Forward Reach Limit

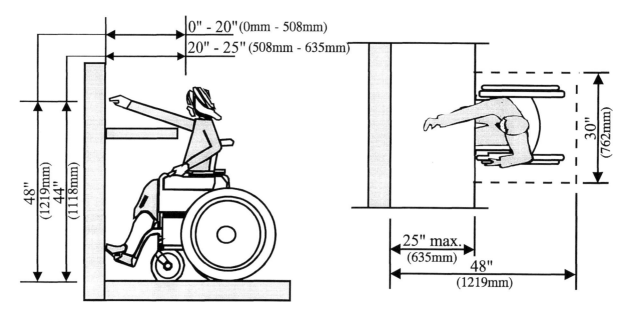

Note: Clear knee space should be as deep as the reach distance.

(b) Maximum Forward Reach Over and Obstruction

Reach Ranges - FHAG

Diagram 116

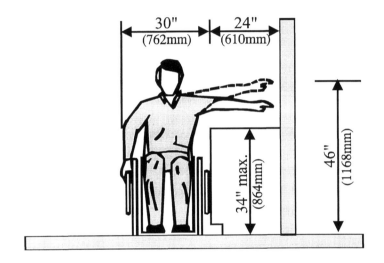

Maximum Side Reach Over an Obstruction

Maximum Side Reach over an Obstruction - FHAG

Diagram 117

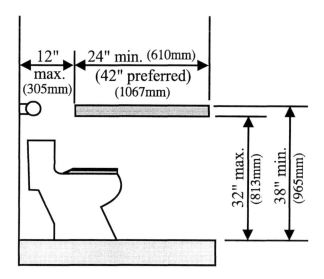

(a) Side Wall View

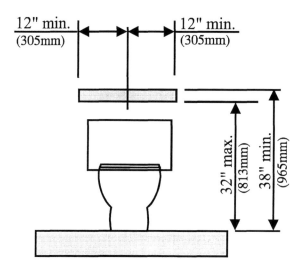

(b) Back Wall View

Note: The lightly shaded areas are reinforced for installation of grab bars.

Water Closets in Adaptable Bathrooms - FHAG

Diagram 118

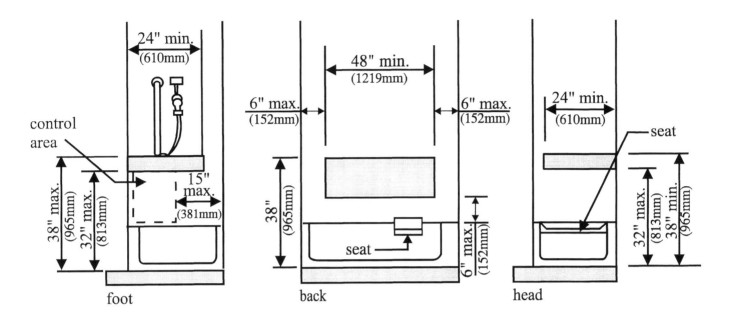

(a) With Seat in Tub

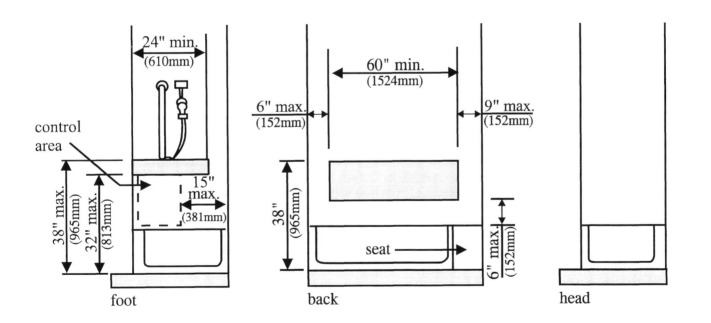

(b) With Seat at Head of Tub

Grab Bar Reinforcements for Adaptable Bathtubs - FHAG

Diagram 119

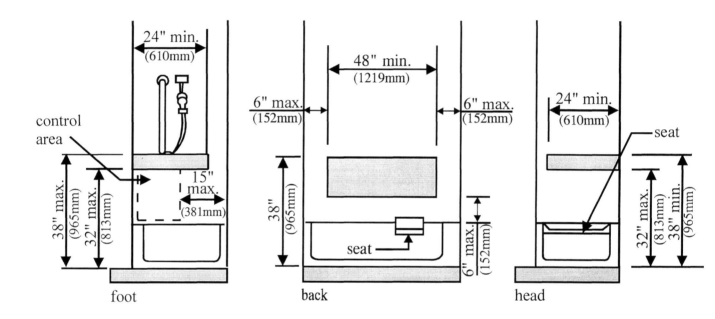

Note: The lightly shaded areas are reinforced for installation of grab bars.

Grab Bar Reinforcements for Adaptable Showers - FHAG

Diagram 120

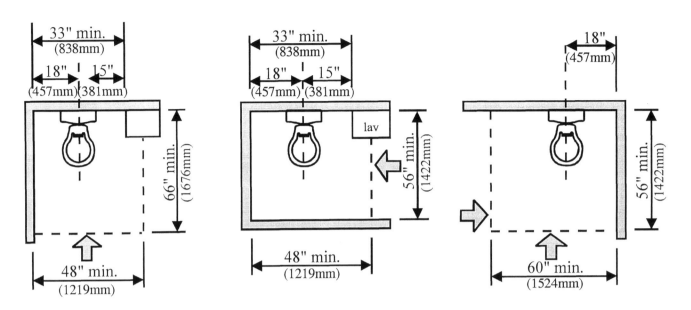

(a) Clear Floor Space for Water Closets

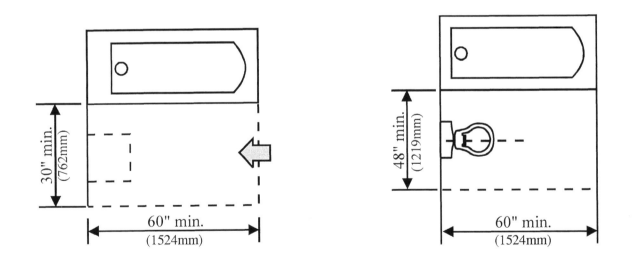

(b) Clear Floor Space at Bathtubs

Clear Floor Space for Adaptable Bathrooms - FHAG

425

Diagram 121

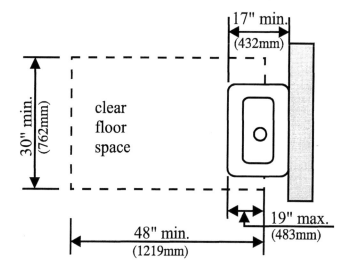

(a) Lavatory With Knee Space

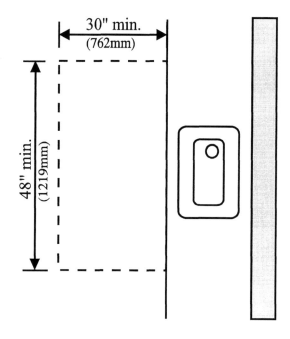

(b) Lavatory Without Knee Space

Clear Floor Space at Lavatories - FHAG

Diagram 122

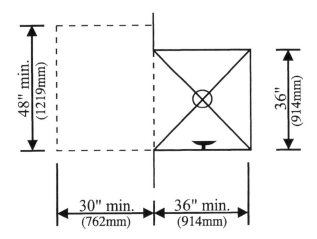

(a) Clear Floor Space at Shower

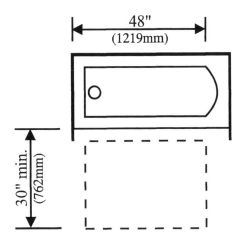

(b) Clear Floor Space at Bathtub

Note: Clear floor space beside tub may overlap with clear floor space beneath adjacent fixtures.

Clear Floor Space at Showers and Bathtubs - FHAG

Diagram 123

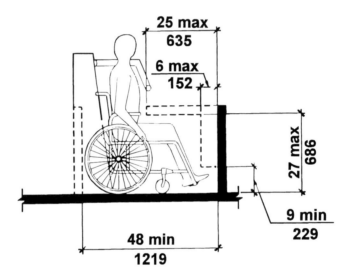

Protrusions in Wheelchair Spaces

Diagram 124

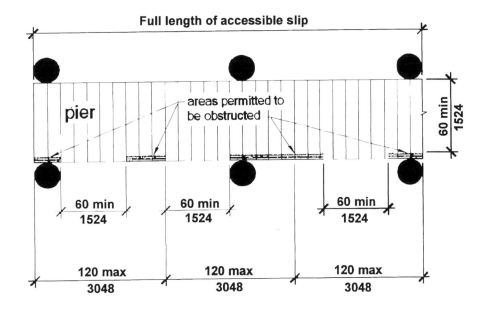

Pier Clearances

Diagram 125

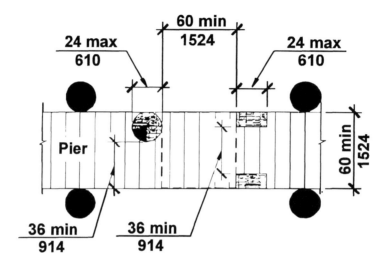

(a) Pier Clear Space Reduction

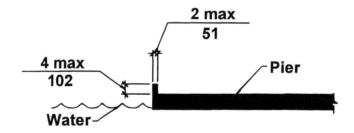

(b) Edge Protection at Pier

Clear Space and Edge Protection at Piers

Diagram 126

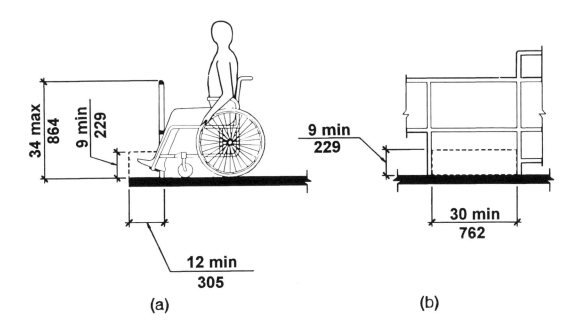

Edge Protection at Fishing Piers

Diagram 127

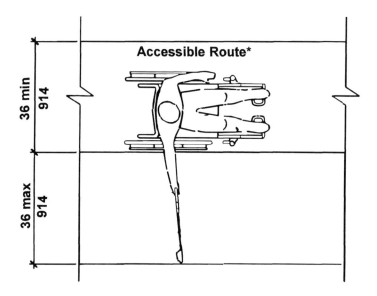

* Note: 1:20 maximum Slope

Golf Club Reach Range

Diagram 128

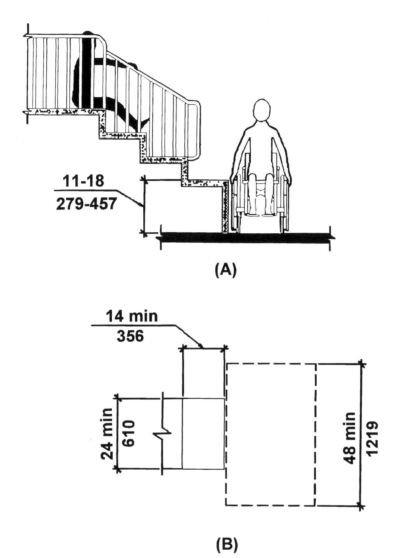

Transfer Platforms

Diagram 129

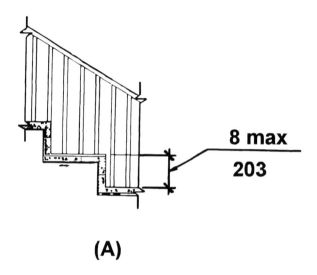

(A)

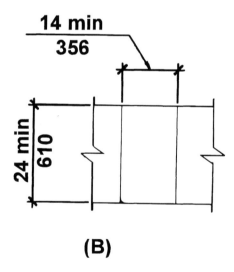

(B)

Transfer Steps

Diagram 130

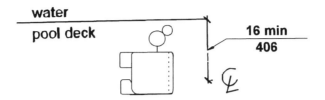

(a) Pool Lift Seat Location

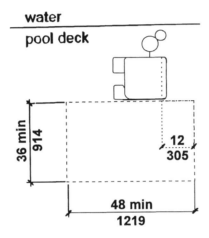

(b) Clear Deck Space at Pool Lifts

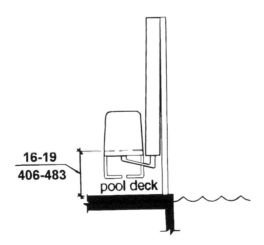

(c) Pool Lift Seat Height

Pool Lifts

Diagram 131

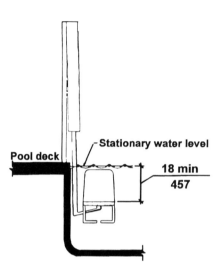

(a) Pool Lift Submerged Depth

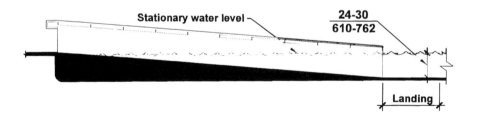

(b) Sloped Entry Submerged Depth

Pool Lift and Sloped Entry - Submerged Depth

Diagram 132

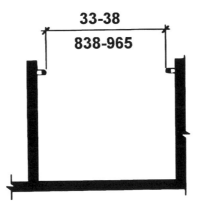

Slope Entry Handrails

Diagram 133

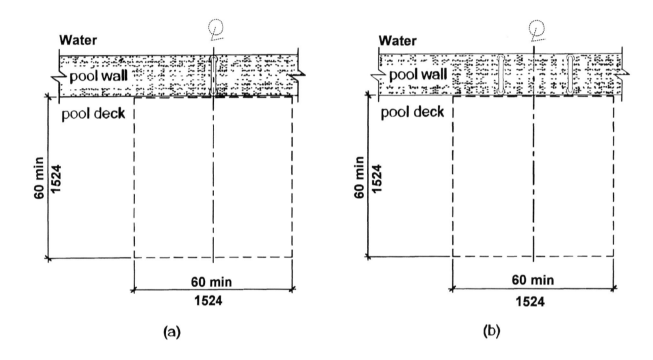

Clear Deck Space at Transfer Walls

Diagram 134

(a) Transfer Wall Height

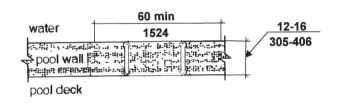

(b) Transfer Wall Depth and Length

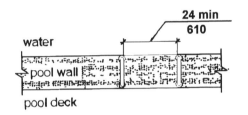

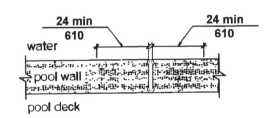

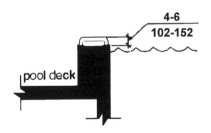

(c) Grab Bars at Transfer Walls

Transfer Walls

Diagram 135

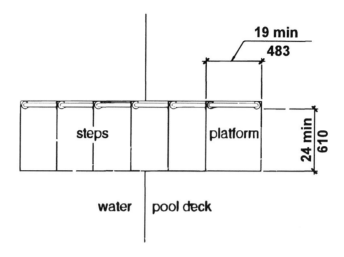

(a) Transfer System Platform

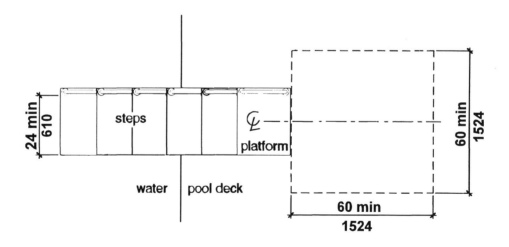

(b) Clear Deck Space at Transfer Systems

Transfer Systems

Diagram 136

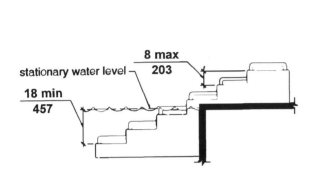

(A) Transfer System Steps

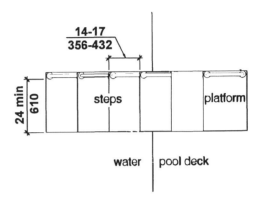

(B) Size of Transfer System Steps

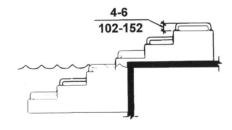
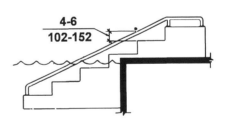

(C) Grab Bars at Transfer Systems

Transfer Systems

BIBLIOGRAPHY

Washington State Building Code Council. International Building Code. 2003 Edition. July 1, 2005. Chapter 51-50. Second Edition. 2005 and 2006 Amendments.

International Code Council, Inc.. 2003 International Building Code. Falls Church, VA.

International Code Council, Inc.. ICC/ANSI A117.1-2003. Country Club Hills, Illinois.

Department of Housing and Urban Development. Office of the Assistant Secretary for Fair Housing and Equal Opportunity. Part VI. 24 CFR Section 1. Final Fair Housing Accessibility Guidelines. Wednesday, March 6, 1991.

Architectural and Transportation Barriers Compliance Board. Federal Register. 36 CFR Parts 1190 and 1191. Americans with Disabilities Act (ADA). Accessibility Guidelines for Buildings and Facilities; Recreation Facilities. September 3, 2002. USA.

INDEX

above grade 8, 10, 292
access aisles viii, 21-23, 25, 26, 218, 265
accessibility iv, vi, vii, x, 1, 3-6, 9, 16, 18, 23, 24, 27, 29, 32, 36, 84, 85, 95, 98, 99, 103, 104, 107, 109, 118, 121, 125, 128, 130, 149, 152, 154, 156-158, 164-167, 170-172, 181, 184, 185, 187-189, 193, 257, 258, 290, 293, 296
accessible boat slips 274, 275
accessible counters 159
accessible entrances iv, 16, 20, 24, 170, 190
accessible holding cells 157
accessible routes iv, viii, 1, 2, 4, 6-14, 20, 22, 23, 25, 28, 37, 39, 40, 43, 44, 48, 55, 56, 69, 73, 86, 89, 90, 95, 104, 108, 110, 128, 142, 145, 149, 150, 152, 162-164, 167, 171, 187-191, 193, 201, 205, 209, 214, 217, 219, 251, 253-263, 268, 271-276, 278-281, 283-286, 288, 290, 292-298, 305
accessible toilet compartments ix, 152, 221
accessible units iv, 17, 27, 29-35, 39, 42, 43, 55, 66
accessible windows 165
acoustic coupler 241
active leaves 178, 209
ADA i, ii
ADAAG 258, 259, 267, 268, 270-278, 280-288, 290, 291, 293, 294, 297, 300-303, 305
adaptable bathrooms xi
adaptable bathtubs xi
adaptable showers xi
additions 187, 188
adjustable-height shower head 232
adult females 99
adult males 99
agricultural buildings 7
air traffic control towers 11

airports 11, 108, 185, 186
aisle stairs 77, 79
aisle width 79
alarm notification appliances 81-83
alarms v, viii, 6, 66, 81-83, 101, 191
alcoves x, 201
alighting areas xi, 250, 251
allowable stresses 161, 236, 238
alterations 81, 102, 187-191, 193, 210, 218, 267, 276, 279, 291
altered boating facilities 272
alternate roll-in-type showers xi, 229-231, 238
alternative grab bars 262
ambient noise 83
ambulatory accessible compartments v, 110, 113, 116, 222
Amendments iii, 254
amusement attractions 282
amusement ride seats 267, 268, 271, 272
amusement rides vii, 267-272
apartment houses 34
appliance controls 41, 45, 52, 123
appliances 41, 45, 49, 52, 58, 59, 64, 66, 67, 81-83, 122, 123, 164, 191, 239, 263
areas of refuge 170-172
armrests 91, 300
arrival points 9, 36-38, 193, 256, 257
assembly v, vi, ix, 5, 10, 69, 73, 84-89, 107, 149, 156, 171, 184, 243, 259
assembly area seating v, vi, 69, 84, 85, 149, 156, 171
assembly areas v, ix, 10, 85-89, 156, 184, 243
assisted rescue 171, 172
assistive listening systems vii, viii, 87, 88, 171, 181, 243
attics 40, 44
audible alarm notification appliances 82, 83
audible alarms viii, 82
audible communications 87

443

INDEX

audible emergency alarm systems	101
audible indicators	140
audible signals	130-132, 249
audible signs	186, 252
audio amplification system	87
auditorium	ix
automatic door systems	215
automatic doors	57, 215
automatic gates	215
automatic reset	241
automatic teller machines	vii, 244, 246
bag drop areas	278
balconies	27, 28, 56, 260
balcony surfaces	260
balusters	78
barriers	i, ii, 12, 28, 73, 76, 77, 205, 258, 280
bars	vii, xi, xii, 31, 46, 48, 59-61, 77, 104, 110-114, 116, 119, 121, 222, 224-227, 229-232, 234-236, 262, 264, 295, 302-305
base cabinets	49, 64, 122, 263
base flood elevation	257
bases	240
bathing facilities	v, 2, 41, 46, 59, 61, 63, 101, 104, 105, 109, 171, 184, 192, 194, 234
bathing rooms	v, 27, 60, 105, 107, 108, 170, 171, 194
bathroom fixtures	264
bathtub controls	xi
bathtub enclosures	227
bathtub fixture	107, 108
bathtub rim	227
bathtub seats	xi, 227, 237
bathtubs	vii, viii, ix, xi, xii, 46, 48, 59, 60-63, 107, 108, 224-227, 235, 237, 262, 265
bathtubs with permanent seats	xi, 225
bathtubs without permanent seats	xi, 226
beds	101
bell	191
benches	vi, x, 101, 102, 149, 160, 161, 262
berms	294
beveled changes in level	x
bleachers	10, 85
boarding area	186, 252
boarding pier clearances	275
boarding piers	274
boarding platforms	253
boat launch ramps	274
boat securement devices	276
boat slip edge	274
boat slips	viii, 273-276
bottom rail height	215
brackets	78
Braille	viii, x, 138, 176, 179, 180, 248
Braille dots	179
Braille measurement	x
brick	260, 261
bridging	7
building directories	184, 185
building elevator	258, 260
building entrance	9, 20, 36, 37, 187, 254, 257-259, 261-263
bumpers	126
burners	53, 123
bus	xi, 154, 185, 250, 251
bus bay	185, 251
bus boarding	xi, 250
bus route identification signs	185, 251
bus schedules	185, 251
bus shelters	xi, 251
bus stops	154, 185, 250, 251
buttons	ix, x, 129-131, 137-139, 142, 145, 147
cabinetry	47, 49-51, 60, 63
cabinets	42, 49-52, 54, 64, 122, 152, 263, 264
call buttons	ix, 129-131, 142, 145
car controls	136, 138, 144, 147, 175, 178, 180
car gates	133, 146

INDEX

car parking spaces 21
car platform sill 136, 144, 146
car position indicators 139
car threshold 136, 147
carpet x, 195, 281
carpet edge trim 195
carpet tile 195
carports 7
case 173, 176, 255, 256, 258, 260
catch pools 298
catwalks 7
cavities 214
cells v, 8, 31, 99-101, 111, 157, 180
central holding cells 99
change in direction 71, 75
changes in level vi, x, 13, 39, 43, 56, 57, 70, 195, 197, 213, 216, 232, 260
character height viii, x, 174-177
character spacing 175, 177
character width 175, 176
characters x, 132, 133, 138-141, 169, 173-178, 180, 184-186, 245, 246, 251-253
checkout counters x
check-out aisles viii, 157-159, 162, 170, 192
check-writing surfaces 157
child care facilities 282
children vii, 96, 105, 118, 119, 267, 282, 289, 291-295
children's dispenser xi
children's use vii, 96, 110, 114, 115, 117, 126, 221, 235
children's water closet xi
circular cross section ix, 78, 234
circular space 198
circulation path 4, 11, 89, 204, 253, 293
clear deck space xii, 299, 300, 302-304

clear floor space vi, x-xii, 46, 48-54, 59, 60, 63-65, 96, 101, 102, 104, 106, 108, 110, 118, 119, 122-126, 129, 151, 153, 160-162, 200-203, 206-208, 216, 223, 236, 239, 240, 244, 246, 251, 259, 263, 264, 266
clear opening 57, 135, 143, 150, 209, 210, 215, 259, 270, 275
clear opening width 135, 143, 150, 209, 210, 215
clear pier space 275, 276
clear width viii, xi, 1, 13, 14, 23, 56, 57, 70, 74, 75, 205, 209, 218, 250, 253, 260, 270, 285, 286, 301-304
clear width at turn viii, 14
clear width of doorways xi
cleats 276
clerk's stations 149
clock face 253
clocks 253
closed compartment 147
closed-circuit communication system 68
closets v, vii-ix, xi, 3, 9, 39, 43, 46, 47, 55, 59, 107, 109-111, 113, 114, 117, 152, 192, 221, 222, 235
closing speed 214
clothes dryers vii, 41, 46, 58, 239
clusters 255
clusters of dwelling units 255
coastal high-hazard area 257
coat hooks 2, 48, 106, 110, 117, 152, 160
common use 4, 5, 8, 10, 28, 55, 106, 111, 119, 225, 229, 231, 258, 259, 298
common use areas 8, 55, 258, 259
common use facility 28, 258
common-use system interface 68
communication features iv, 39, 43, 55, 66-68, 101
communications equipment rooms 7
communications systems 147
companion seats 87, 90, 271

INDEX

compartment doors　　　　　ix, 114-116
complex　　　　　　　　　　　　154
composite play structures　　292, 294
construction sites　　　　　　　　7
construction trailers　　　　　　　7
continuity　　　　　　　　　　　78
continuous grab bar　　　225, 226, 304
control button identification　　　　x
control switches　　　　　　　3, 216
control wall　　　228, 230, 231, 238
controls　　vi, x, xi, 2, 3, 41, 45, 48,
　　52, 53, 58, 101, 106, 113, 117,
　　120, 123, 124, 129, 136-138, 142,
　　144, 147, 151, 164, 169, 175, 178,
　　180, 181, 189, 191, 216, 222, 223,
　　227, 229, 231-233, 235, 237, 241,
　　247, 261, 300
cooktop　　　　　53, 65, 121-123, 263
cord　　　　　　　　　　　148, 241
cord length　　　　　　　　　　241
corner posts　　　　　　　　　　295
corner-type curb ramps　　　　　218
correctional facilities　　　　　　8, 17
corridors　　　　　　　　　　　5, 70
counter edge protection　　　　　163
counter slope　　　　　　　　xi, 217
counter surface　　　51, 63, 119, 162, 163
counters　　vi, 10, 49, 50, 64, 97, 100,
　　106, 122, 157, 159, 162, 163, 263
countertops　　　　　　49, 64, 122, 263
courtrooms　　　　　　　v, 87, 99, 102
court-floor holding cells　　　　　99
covered dwelling unit　　255, 259, 264, 266
covered units　　　　　　　　　259
crawl spaces　　　　　　　　　　7
critical-care　　　　　　　　　　105
cross slope　　　　　13, 69, 74, 273, 305
crossings　　　　　　　xi, 218, 219, 253
cubicles　　　　　　　　　　　100
curb　　vii, xi, 12, 69, 72, 73, 76,
　　154, 197, 217-219, 250, 258, 281
curb ramps　　　vii, xi, 12, 69, 72,
　　76, 154, 197, 217-219, 258

D rings　　　　　　　　　　　295
day care　　　　　　　　8, 105, 118
day care facilities　　　　　　　　8
deck surface　　　　　　　　277, 299
decks　　　xii, 28, 56, 77, 260, 277,
　　292, 294, 299, 300, 302-304
definitions　　　　　　　　　iv, 4
destination-oriented elevators
　　130-134, 140, 141
detainees　　　　　　8, 17, 100, 101
detectable warnings　　　vi, 4, 154,
　　155, 219, 220, 252
detention and correctional facilities　　8
detergent and bleach compartments　239
detoxification facilities　　　　　　30
diagonal curb ramps　　　　　xi, 218
diggers　　　　　　　　　　　291
digits　　　　　　　　　　　　253
dining　　v, 27, 42, 54-56, 84, 85, 95,
　　96, 102, 122, 149, 163, 188
dining areas　　v, 27, 42, 84, 85, 95,
　　102, 122, 163, 188
dining surfaces　　　　　　v, 95, 96
dining terraces　　　　　　　　149
direct exterior access　　　　　　261
direction of travel　　　1, 15, 69, 71,
　　131, 196, 219
directional and informational signs　184
directional signage　　　　　　　170
dishwasher　　　　　　52, 65, 123, 263
dispenser location　　　　　　ix, xi
dispensers　　　2, 48, 106, 110, 114,
　　117, 120, 222
dispersion　　86, 98, 149, 157, 274, 277
display units　　　　　　　　　152
diving boards　　　　　　　　　298
diving platforms　　　　　　　　298
door closers　　　　　　204, 210, 214
door delay　　　　　　　　　　135
door hardware　　　　114, 116, 147, 213
door knock　　　　　　　　　　191
door pull　　　　　　　　　115, 116
door spring hinges　　　　　　　214
door surface　　　　　　　　　214

INDEX

door swing 46, 59, 104, 106, 108, 160, 178, 199, 216
doorbell 67
doors vii-xi, 2, 3, 12, 13, 40, 44, 46, 50-52, 56, 57, 59, 70, 71, 75, 104, 106, 108, 114-116, 123, 133-135, 142, 143, 145, 146, 150, 160, 178, 199, 209-216, 239, 259, 260, 263, 264
doors and doorways vii, 2, 3, 12, 40, 44, 56, 57, 71, 75, 104, 114-116, 133, 135, 143, 145, 150, 209, 259
doors in series xi, 213, 216
doorways vii, viii, xi, 2, 3, 12, 40, 44, 56, 57, 71, 75, 104, 114-116, 133, 135, 143, 145, 150, 192, 209, 212, 213, 215, 216, 259
doorways without doors viii, xi, 209, 212
door-opening force 2, 214
dot 139, 179, 245
double doors 178
double or triple slide 292
drain pipes 51, 52, 120
drain stoppers 227
drawers 152
dressing vi, 152, 158, 160, 170, 192
drinking fountain spout ix
drinking fountains v, ix, 125-127, 189, 293
driving ranges 278, 279
drop-off 76, 154
dwelling units iv, 12, 17, 27, 29-32, 34-36, 39, 43, 55, 66, 71, 77, 78, 82, 105, 254, 255, 257-263
dwellings 7, 254, 255, 257-259, 261-263

edge protection ix, xii, 72, 75, 163, 275, 277
edging 297
egress iv, 12, 14, 40, 44, 57, 69, 70, 72, 75-78, 101, 102, 149, 168, 171-173, 188, 190, 191, 197, 217, 272
electric substations 7
electrical 7, 41, 45, 53, 58, 65, 123, 164, 189, 191, 242, 261
electrical convenience outlets 164
electrical outlets 189, 191, 242, 261
electrical receptacles 164
elevated play components 283-288, 292-295, 305
elevated walkways 16, 37, 258
elevator call buttons ix, 129, 142
elevator car control buttons x
elevator car controls 136, 144, 147, 175, 178, 180
elevator cars viii, x, 135, 136, 139, 143, 144, 146
elevator doors 133-135
elevator operation 128, 142, 145
elevator penthouses 7
elevator pits 7
elevator service 36, 37
elevators v, x, 2, 7, 12, 40, 44, 45, 56, 57, 128-138, 140-146, 171, 172, 190, 254, 255, 260, 268, 273
elongated openings 196
emergency alarm 101, 138
emergency communications 141, 144, 147, 172
emergency controls 137, 138
employee work area 5
enclosures 71, 227, 233, 240, 242
entrance door 40, 44, 56, 57
entrances iv, 9, 16, 17, 20, 24, 28, 38, 132, 170, 185, 186, 190, 193, 252, 254-256, 258
entry points 256, 289, 290, 293, 295
environmental controls 41, 45, 58, 261
equipment catwalks 7

INDEX

equipment spaces 7
escalators 190, 253
exceptions iv, 6, 10, 11, 16, 17, 28-30, 33-36, 41, 44, 45, 48, 51, 52, 58, 60, 63, 69, 72, 76-81, 87, 95, 104, 106, 111, 112, 115, 118, 119, 123, 126, 129-132, 134, 137, 138, 144, 157, 164, 184, 186, 188, 189, 193, 204, 210, 215, 225, 229, 231, 235, 246, 247, 257, 274, 276, 280
existing amusement ride 267
existing buildings vi, viii, 6, 74, 126, 144, 187-191, 193
existing elements 207
existing elevators 129-132, 134-138, 190
existing facilities 233, 276
existing natural grade 257
existing play areas 282
existing slope 256
exit 6, 23, 26, 69, 71, 150, 169, 171-173, 264, 265, 270, 279, 280, 285, 293
exit points 285, 293
exit stairway 172
exits 16, 70, 81, 171, 172
exposed edges 195
exposed pipes and surfaces 52, 120
extensions ix, 79, 273, 287, 302, 305
exterior decks 28, 56, 260
exterior doors 2, 214, 260
exterior entrance 255
exterior signs 3, 181, 184
exterior sliding doors 44, 57
exterior spaces 27, 39, 43

Fair Housing Accessibility Guidelines vii
Fair Housing Amendments 254
fairway 280
fare machines vii, 244, 246
fastener mounting device 161, 236, 238
Federal Final Rule vii, 166
FHAG vii, xi, xii, 254, 258-264

finish and contrast 175, 178, 180, 181, 185
finished grade 37, 256-258
finished grade elevation 257
finished surface 261, 265
fire alarm notification 67
fire alarm system 66, 81, 82
fire doors 2, 214
fire protection systems v, 6, 66, 81, 101
fire safety 7
fire towers 7
firewalls 254
fishing piers vii, xii, 276-278
fittings vi, 152, 158, 160, 170, 192, 235
fixed facilities 185
fixed firing position 297
fixed seating 10, 73, 85, 156
fixed shower head 227, 232
fixed transportation facilities 185
fixtures 2, 46, 48, 56, 59, 62, 105-107, 110, 111, 117, 131, 264, 265
flared sides 12, 72, 217, 218
floating boarding pier 275
floating piers 273
floodplain 257
floor designations 132, 137-139, 147
floor landings 136
floor level 20, 28, 56, 86, 104, 169, 260, 261
floor surfaces vi, x, 13, 22, 25, 39, 43, 74, 75, 89, 136, 144, 146, 151, 168, 195, 197, 198, 200, 212, 213, 217
floor-mounted 114, 115, 262
floor-mounted grab bars 262
floor-mounted water closets 114
fluoroscopes 12
flush controls 3, 48, 113, 222, 223
folding shelves 152
folding shower seat 32
food service lines 159, 163
footcandles 136, 147, 168
footrests 300

INDEX

footrests and armrests 300
force 2, 161, 208, 214, 236, 238, 296
forward approach ix, 50-54, 61, 62, 64, 65, 96, 118, 123, 125, 162, 201, 212, 223, 240, 261, 263, 264
forward or side reaches 295
forward reach x, 2, 106, 117, 160, 206
forward teeing grounds 279
freezers 53, 124
free-standing press boxes 10
freight elevators 7
front loading machines 239
fuel-dispensing devices 8
fuel-dispensing systems 8
function keys 245
functional areas 260

gangways 272, 273, 275, 276
gaps 269
garages 7, 12, 69
gates x, 13, 133, 145, 146, 150, 209, 215
general exceptions iv, 6, 29, 30, 33-36
general purpose hospitals 30
glass doors 215
glass-walled stalls 262
glazing panels 215
golf vii, xii, 278-281
golf cart 278-280
golf cart passage 278-280
golf cart rental area 278
golf club reach range xii, 281
golf courses 278-280
grab bars vii, ix, xi, xii, 31, 46, 48, 59-61, 77, 104, 110-114, 116, 222, 224-227, 229-232, 234-236, 262, 264, 265, 302-305
grandstands 85, 86, 88
graspability 78, 80
gripping surfaces 78, 235, 236, 287, 303, 304
ground floor 254, 255, 257, 258, 260
ground floor unit 254, 260

ground level play components viii, 283-286, 288, 291-293
ground level use zones 287, 293
ground space 271, 272, 277, 279, 289, 297
ground surfaces 73, 269, 270, 282, 290, 293, 296
Group A-5 149
Group I occupancies iv, 19, 20, 24, 29-31, 36, 81-83, 157, 165
Group I-1 19, 20, 29, 81, 82
Group I-2 24, 29, 30, 83
Group I-3 31, 157
Group R occupancies iv, 8, 32-36, 71, 72, 77, 81, 82, 165, 166
Group R-1 8, 32, 81
Group R-2 19, 33, 34, 71, 77, 82, 166, 191
Group R-3 8, 19, 35, 71, 72, 77, 166
Group R-4 35
Group U 7, 72
guardrails 205
guards 73, 77, 154, 252, 276, 277
gutters 217

hall call buttons 129, 131-134
hall signals 131, 142
hand showers xi, 227, 231, 232
handles 213
handrail clearance ix
handrail extensions ix, 79, 273, 287, 302, 305
handrail height ix, 77, 79, 287
handrails iv, xii, 14, 69-72, 74-80, 168, 204, 218, 268, 273, 276-278, 287, 293, 301, 302, 305
hands 253
handset 163, 181, 241, 242, 246, 249
hand-held receivers 186, 252
hand-held shower 227, 232
hand-operated 3, 48, 113, 120, 222, 223
hand-operated flush controls 3, 48, 113, 222, 223

INDEX

hardware   vi, 41, 45, 114, 116, 147, 164, 189, 213
health care providers   11
hearing-aid   88, 241, 243
hearing-aid compatibility   241, 243
high forward reach   x, 206
high side reach   x, 207
highway and tunnel utility facilities   7
hinged or pivoted doors   213
historic buildings   vi, 6, 187-189, 193
historic significance   193
historic structures   193
hoistway door   133, 134
hoistway entrances   131, 132
holding cells   v, 8, 31, 99, 100, 111, 157
horizontal gap   269
horizontal or vertical joints   214
hospitals   30
housing   v, vii, 5, 8, 31, 100, 111, 254
housing cells   v, 8, 31, 100
HVAC diffusers   41, 45, 58, 164

IBC   1, 4, 6, 9, 16, 18, 20, 24, 27, 29, 32, 36, 69, 77, 81, 84, 85, 95, 98, 99, 103, 104, 107, 109, 118, 121, 125, 128, 149, 152, 154, 156-158, 164-167, 170, 184, 187, 193
ICC/ANSI   iii-vi, 1-3, 12, 13, 15, 21, 24, 25, 27, 39, 43, 55, 66, 73, 77, 83, 85, 87, 89, 95, 96, 100, 102, 103, 105-107, 109, 113, 117, 118, 121, 125, 128, 136, 137, 141-146, 150, 152-154, 159-162, 165, 167, 172, 173, 181, 182, 184, 185, 188, 190, 191, 195, 197, 198, 200, 202, 204, 206, 208, 209, 214-217, 221, 223, 224, 228, 234, 236, 237, 239, 240, 243, 244, 249, 250, 253
ICC/ANSI a117.1-2003   iii, 66, 83, 136, 141-146, 150, 182, 195, 197, 198, 200, 202, 204, 206, 208, 215, 236

identification   x, 23, 67, 91, 133, 141, 169, 170, 172, 185, 186, 246, 251, 252
identification signs   169, 185, 186, 251, 252
illumination   136, 144, 147, 172, 173, 182
impervious surface   56
inactive leaf   57, 178
individual building test   255, 256
individual dwelling units   71, 255, 259
informational signs   184, 186
inmates   8, 17, 101
input   244, 246, 247
input verification   246
installation   28, 46, 59-61, 104, 111, 189, 225, 229, 231, 236, 258, 262, 266
installation of grab bars   46, 59-61, 111, 225, 229, 231, 262
instructions   172, 246, 248
integration   86, 90, 293
intensive-care   105
intercom systems   41, 45, 58
interior and exterior signs   3, 181, 184
interior hinged door   2, 214
interior rooms and spaces   184
interior spaces   28, 56, 184
International Building Code   i, iii-vi, 1, 4, 6-8, 27, 69-71, 73, 77, 79, 81, 82, 84, 167, 170, 188, 189, 191, 277
International Symbol of Access for Hearing Loss   x, 181
International Symbol of Accessibility   x, 3, 23, 170, 172, 181, 184
International TTY Symbol   x
in-car signals   131
in-room smoke alarm   81
in-tub seat   48, 224
islands   xi, 219

INDEX

jambs	132, 133
judge's benches	149
judicial facilities	v, 17, 84, 99
jury boxes	102, 149, 191
juvenile females	99
juvenile males	99
key surfaces	245, 247
keypads	129, 130, 137, 139, 142, 241
keys	245, 247
kick plates	214
kitchen appliances	52, 122
kitchen base cabinet	261
kitchen cabinets	42, 52, 54
kitchen clearance	viii, ix
kitchen sink	ix, 119
kitchen storage	52
kitchen work areas	49, 64, 122
kitchenettes	v, 5, 42, 121
kitchens	v, 9, 42, 49, 64, 121, 122, 165, 260, 263
knee and toe clearance	vi, 50, 51, 53, 59, 65, 96, 104, 119, 123, 125, 162, 198-200, 202
knee clearance	x, 97, 119, 202, 203, 264, 289, 293
knee space	263-265
ladders	7
landing length	71
landing sill	136, 147
landing slopes	281
landing surfaces	168, 261
landings	ix, 1, 15, 70-72, 74-76, 128, 133, 136, 142, 145, 150, 168, 169, 218, 273, 301
latch	2, 40, 53, 114-116, 123, 178, 210-212, 214
latch side	40, 53, 114, 116, 123, 178, 210-212
latches	213
laundry compartment	239
laundry equipment	xi, 41, 46, 58
lavatories	v, ix, xii, 42, 46-48, 60-63, 104, 106-108, 118-120, 122, 229, 264, 265
legal restrictions	258
leisure rivers	298, 302
level	vi, viii, x, 1, 5, 10, 11, 13, 15, 20, 21, 23, 25, 28, 39, 43, 47, 56, 57, 60, 70, 82, 83, 85-87, 104, 132, 136, 141, 147, 168, 169, 192, 193, 195, 197, 213, 216, 217, 219, 232, 243, 256, 257, 260-263, 266, 283-288, 291-293, 295, 296, 299-301, 304
level cut pile	195
level loop	195
life safety	7
lifeguard stands	7
lift seat	300
lifting capacity	301
lifts	vi, x, xii, 12, 40, 44, 45, 56, 58, 102, 149-151, 189-191, 268, 273, 285, 290, 294, 298-301
light switches	41, 45, 164, 261
lighting	41, 45, 58, 164, 168, 169
limited access spaces	7
limited-use/limited-application elevators	v, 40, 45, 57, 142, 273
line spacing	175, 177
lines of sight	ix, 91
lint screens	239
living and dining areas	27
load and unload area	268, 269, 271, 272
loading and service entrances	16
locker rooms	vi, 152, 158, 160, 170, 192
lockers	152
locks	213
loft	260
logos	184, 185
long-term care facilities	24
loop type handle	295
LULA	x
L-shaped seats	238

INDEX

main entry level	132
main floor level	86
maneuvering clearance	x, xi
maneuvering space	264, 268-270, 278, 288, 289
manual doors	150, 209
manual gates	209
manual swinging doors	viii, xi, 211
manually operated doors	134
maps	185, 251
marked crossings	218, 219
marking	21, 22, 25
materials hoists	7
materials storage	7
means of access	9, 258, 260
means of egress	iv, 12, 14, 40, 44, 57, 69, 70, 72, 75-77, 101, 102, 149, 168, 171, 172, 188, 190, 191, 197, 217, 272
means of entry	298, 299
mechanical	i, 7, 82, 189
mechanical equipment rooms	82
medical facilities	24
medicine cabinets	152
menus	184, 185
mercantile occupancies	107
metal detectors	12
mezzanine levels	86
mezzanine seating	95
mezzanines	10, 11, 56, 86, 87, 95, 186, 252
miniature golf	vii, 280
miniature golf course	280
mirrors	47, 106
mixed occupancy	107
mobile or portable amusement rides	267
mobility aid	264, 265
mobility device	270, 271, 287, 294, 295
mop or service sinks	118
mounting height	180
multibuilding facility	98
multifamily dwellings	254, 255, 257-259, 261-263
multilevel assembly seating	5, 86, 87
multilevel assembly seating areas	86
multilevel assembly spaces	87
multilevel buildings and facilities	11, 193
multilevel parking structures	21
multiple accessible entrances	20
multiple buildings	166, 254, 256
multiple entrances	255, 256
multiple pool lift locations	299
multiple posts or pylons	204
multiple tenant facilities	11
multistory	4, 37, 260, 262, 263, 266
multistory units	37
new construction	149, 188, 189, 254
newel posts	78
nonoccupiable spaces	7
non-circular cross section	ix, 234
non-elevator buildings	37, 38, 255, 260
non-glare	175, 178, 180, 181
nosings	x, 77, 168
notification devices	191
numerals	253
numeric key layout	xi
nursing homes	29
observation galleries	7
obstructed high forward reach	x
obstructed high side reach	x
obstructions	xi, 48, 78, 110, 113, 114, 116, 134, 174, 198, 206, 207, 212, 218, 261, 289
offices	11, 171
offset hinges	259
open risers	168
openings	x, 137, 195, 196, 209, 253, 259, 270, 271, 275, 280
operable parts	vii, 8, 41, 42, 45, 52, 54, 57, 58, 113, 114, 119, 120, 123, 126, 129, 136, 145, 147, 151, 153, 164, 165, 208, 213, 216, 222, 223, 227, 231, 239, 241, 244, 261
operable windows	vi, 41, 42, 45, 54, 165

INDEX

operating controls 2, 106, 117, 189
operating instructions 246
operating mechanisms vi, 164, 300
opposing base cabinets 49, 64, 122, 263
Option A bathrooms ix
Option B bathrooms ix
outdoor approaches 72
outdoor conditions 72
outdoor dining terraces 149
outlets 41, 45, 58, 126, 164, 189, 261
outpatient 19, 20
output 182, 244, 246, 247
ovens 53, 65, 123, 124, 263
overflow 119
overhead play components 292

pad 195
parallel approach ix, 53, 59-64, 96, 101, 119, 124, 126, 137, 161, 162, 200, 201, 207, 239, 240, 263, 264, 289
parked vehicles 218
parking iv, viii, 7, 9, 12, 16, 18-25, 28, 69, 170, 184, 187, 218, 256-258, 278, 293
parking garage entrances 16
parking spaces iv, viii, 18-23, 69, 170, 218, 258, 278
partition support members 115
partitions 10, 100, 110, 114, 115, 221
passageways 7, 8
passenger elevators 128
passenger loading zones iv, 9, 18, 20, 24, 25, 28, 170, 187, 256
passenger transportation facilities 11, 108
passing spaces 14
pass-through kitchen ix, 121
patios 27, 28, 56, 77, 259, 260
paved work areas 7
pay telephones 188, 242
pedestrian access 9
pedestrian arrival points 36-38, 256, 257
pedestrian entrance 20

pedestrian paths 251
pedestrian walkways 9
pedestrians 4, 16
permanent interior spaces 184
permanent seats xi, 225, 226, 237
permanently installed telephones 191
physical barriers 28, 258
picnic area 291
pictogram field x, 180
pictograms 180, 184
pier edge 275
piers vii, xii, 273-276
piping 7
planned entrance 36, 37, 256, 257
planned finished grade 256
platform lifts vi, x, 12, 40, 44, 45, 56, 58, 102, 150, 151, 189, 190, 268, 273, 285, 290, 294
platform screens 154, 252
platform surfaces 288
platforms vii, xii, 149, 186, 251-253, 276, 287, 294, 298
play areas vii, 280-282, 283, 285, 286, 290-293, 295, 296
play components viii, 282-289, 291-295, 305
play structures 290, 292, 294
play tables 289
playground equipment 290, 296
playing surface 280, 281
plumbing fixtures 56, 105
plywood or wood blocking 262
pocket or sliding doors 259
point of sales 159
poles 295
pool depth 299
pool edge 298, 299
pool lift location 299
pool lifts xii, 298-301
pool stairs 298, 305
pools vii, 18, 297, 298, 301, 302
portable toilets and bathing facilities 184
posts 78, 204, 295
post-mounted protruding objects x

453

INDEX

powder rooms	260, 262-264
power-assisted doors	215
power-operated	2, 135, 143, 146, 150, 214
power-operated doors	2, 146, 150, 214
power-operated swinging doors	143
practice putting greens	278
practice teeing grounds	278, 279
prerecorded text messages	88
preschool	291
press boxes	10
primary entrance	28, 39, 40, 43, 44, 55-57, 67, 194
primary entrance door	40, 44, 56, 57
primary entry doors	259
primary school occupancies	105, 118
prison guard towers	7
privacy	108, 244
private garages	7
private office	104, 106, 111, 119, 225, 229, 231
private residence elevators	v, x, 40, 45, 57, 145
projecting objects	234, 235
projections	70, 79, 210
protruding objects	vi, x, 125, 204, 205, 242
protrusion limits	204
protrusions	xii, 31, 111, 270, 285
psychiatric facilities	30
public address systems	88, 253
public entrance	5
public or common-use system	68
public pay telephones	188
public streets	9, 256
public telephones	240, 241
public toilets	171
public transportation stops	9, 256
public way	9, 149
public-use areas	5
pulls	213
push button controls	241
push side	145, 178, 214
putting greens	278, 280
pylons	204
radiating sound waves	181
railings	72, 276, 277
raised areas	7
raised borders	177, 180
raised floor area	55
raised islands	219
raised thresholds	213
ramp dimensions	viii, 74
ramp edge protection	ix
ramp landings	ix, 72, 75, 76
ramp runs	70-76, 194, 287, 294
ramp slope	69, 77, 286
ramps	iv, vii-ix, xi, 12, 40, 44, 56, 57, 69-77, 102, 150, 151, 154, 190, 191, 193, 194, 197, 217-219, 258, 269, 274, 286-288, 292-294, 305
range	xii, 50, 51, 53, 65, 67, 119-123, 132, 152, 179, 182, 243, 263, 281
reach depth	viii, 120, 206, 207
reach ranges	vii, viii, xi, 2, 8, 54, 106, 117, 129, 136, 141, 153, 160, 163, 206, 208, 241, 295
rear wall grab bar	ix, 112, 116
receiver volume control	241
receivers	viii, 87, 88, 182, 186, 243, 252
recessed doors	xi, 212
recreational facilities	vi, vii, 27, 107, 166, 267
rectangular seats	238
reduced vertical clearance	x, 205
refrigerator/freezer	53, 65, 124, 263
refrigerators	53, 124
rehabilitation facilities	30
reinforced walls	262, 264
reinforcement	xi, 46, 47, 59, 60, 104, 111, 225, 229, 231, 233, 262, 264
removable in-tub seat	48, 224
reopening device	134
resident parking areas	256

INDEX

residents	27	screening devices	12
restricted entrances	5, 16	sculpted dirt	294
restricted use areas	257	seat and row designations	184
restrooms	9	seat location	299
returned curbs	218	seat surface	161, 300
revolving doors	13	seated spectators	ix, 91

rise 1, 15, 70, 72, 74, 75, 191, 273, 281, 286, 287, 294

riser height 93, 94, 167

risers x, 73, 93, 167, 168

road surfaces 217

roadway 218, 250, 251

roll-in-type shower compartments viii, xi, 228, 229, 231, 232

roofs 292

rope loop 295

route of travel 2, 20, 214

rubber surface 296

running slope 13, 69, 74, 219, 305

safe use zones 282

sales vi, 159, 162

sales and service counters vi, 159, 162

sand bottom pools 298, 302

sand box 293

scaffolding 7

scope 1, 12, 13, 21, 24, 69, 73, 83, 89, 95, 100, 102, 105, 109, 118, 121, 125, 128, 142, 145, 150, 152, 154, 159-161, 165, 167, 173, 187, 193, 195, 197, 198, 200, 202, 204, 206, 208, 209, 217, 221, 223, 224, 228, 234, 237, 239, 240, 243, 244, 249, 250

scoping iv, 6, 12, 13, 21, 24, 39, 43, 55, 66, 73, 83, 89, 95, 100, 102, 105, 109, 118, 121, 125, 128, 142, 145, 150, 152, 154, 159-161, 165, 167, 173, 189, 195, 197, 198, 200, 202, 204, 206, 208, 209, 217, 221, 223, 224, 228, 232, 234, 237, 239, 240, 243, 244, 249, 250

scoping requirements iv, 6

seating v, vi, 5, 10, 69, 73, 77, 80, 84-95, 149, 156, 157, 171, 188, 271

seating areas 86, 188

seats vii, xi, 5, 10, 46, 59, 60, 87, 88, 90, 91, 93, 110, 111, 161, 221, 222, 224-227, 230, 231, 233, 237, 238, 240, 242, 267, 271, 272, 289

securement devices 270, 276

security 7, 8, 12, 17, 41, 45, 58, 100, 108, 158, 163, 209, 213, 246

security barriers 12

security bollards 12

security checkpoints 12, 108

security devices 158

security glazing 100, 163

security personnel 8, 17, 209

security screening devices 12

seesaw 292

self-service shelves 152, 159, 163

self-service storage facilities v, viii, 84, 98

selling space 158

separate buildings 254

separate entrance 254

separate-sex bathing rooms 107, 108

separate-sex toilet room 108

service counters vi, 159, 162

service entrances 5, 16, 17

service facilities vi, 101, 157, 158, 192

service sinks 118

shelters xi, 251, 278, 279

shelving 152

shoulder-to-shoulder seating 271

shower compartment seats xi, 237

INDEX

shower compartments vii-ix, xi, 46, 49, 59, 60-64, 228, 229, 231-233, 235, 237
shower controls xi, 229, 235
shower enclosures 233
shower fittings 235
shower seat 32, 62, 231, 262
showers vii-ix, xi, xii, 32, 33, 46, 49, 59-64, 107, 108, 227-233, 235, 237, 238, 262, 264-266
side entry 270
side reach x, xi, 2, 106, 117, 160, 207, 295
side wall grab bar ix, 112
sidelites 215
sides of curb ramps xi, 217, 218
sidewalks 9, 251, 256
sidewall 147
sightlines 186, 252
signage vi, 3, 23, 130, 132, 133, 138, 139, 141, 169-172, 184-187, 190, 194, 248, 251-253, 269
signals x, 130-132, 142, 172, 182, 183, 249
signs vi, x, 3, 23, 88, 132, 133, 142, 169-171, 173, 178, 181, 184-186, 189, 190, 194, 251, 252
single occupant 8, 104, 106, 111, 119, 225, 229, 231
single occupant structures 8
single person pool lifts 301
single structure 34, 35, 254
single-story dwelling units 260
single-user 105, 170
sink bowl 51, 64
sinks v, ix, 47, 51, 52, 60, 62-64, 106, 118-120, 122, 229
site 4, 5, 9, 21, 24, 32, 34, 36-38, 67, 149, 154, 165-167, 184, 193, 254-258, 282, 291, 293, 297
site analysis test 255, 256
site arrival points 9, 193
site impracticality 37, 255-257

skid pier 275
sleeping rooms 40, 105, 191
sleeping units iv, 8, 17, 19, 27, 29-37, 39, 42, 43, 55, 66, 77, 81, 82, 103, 105, 157, 187, 191
slide 289, 291-293
sliding and folding doors viii, xi, 211, 212
sliding door tracks 260
sliding patio door assembly 259
slope xi-13, 28, 37, 38, 40, 44, 56, 57, 69, 70, 73-75, 77, 79, 80, 89, 168, 190, 191, 194, 197, 198, 200, 212, 213, 217, 219, 250, 251, 256-258, 260, 268, 269, 273, 275, 276, 281, 286, 289, 293, 294, 296, 297, 299, 300, 302, 304, 305
sloped entries xii, 298, 301, 302
smoke detection 66, 67
soft contained play structures 290
softball field 291
solid partitions 100
sound pressure 82, 83, 243
sound-on-cane contact 155
spacing x, xi, 93, 155, 175, 177, 234
spas vii, 297, 299, 300
special occupancies v, 84, 85, 95, 98, 99
spectators viii, ix, 91-93
spiral slide 291
spout location ix, 126
spout outlets 126
spouts ix, 126, 127
spring hinges 214
spring rockers 291
stadiums 85, 86, 88
stair flight 79, 169
stair nosings x
stair treads 168
stairs ix, 77-79, 167, 168, 172, 190, 283, 293, 298, 305
stairways vi, x, 77, 167-169
stall showers 266
stall-type 223
stand alone slides 291, 293

INDEX

standard roll-in-type shower compartment v, iii, xi
standard roll-in-type showers viii, xi, 228, 230, 238
stationary water level 300, 301, 304
stations 7, 102, 149, 185, 186, 252, 278, 279
steps xii, 167, 253, 256, 288, 292, 294, 304
storage v, vi, viii, 5, 7, 9, 10, 42, 52, 54, 84, 98, 108, 122, 152, 153, 272
storage facilities v, vi, viii, 42, 54, 84, 98, 108, 153
storage rooms 9
story 4, 10, 11, 36, 37, 108, 260
straight slide 291
streets 9, 217, 251, 256
structural strength 161, 236, 238
style 174, 176
submerged depth xii, 300, 301
sunken floor area 56
sunken living room 260
sunken tub 262
surface hazards 235
swimming pool wall 298
swinging doors viii, xi, 57, 143, 145, 209-211
swings 264, 265, 291, 295
swing-up grab bar ix, 111-113
switches 3, 41, 45, 58, 164, 216, 261
symbols of accessibility 181

tables i, iv, vi, viii, 95, 97, 157, 289
tactile viii, x, 130, 132, 133, 138, 139, 141, 169, 172, 173, 176-178, 180, 184-186, 245, 252
tactile characters x, 132, 133, 138, 141, 169, 176-178, 180, 184, 252
tactile signage 172
tactile signs x, 169, 173, 178, 185, 186, 252
tactile star 132
tactile symbols viii, 139, 245
tactile text descriptors 184
teeing grounds 278, 279
teeing stations 278, 279
telephone cord 148, 241
telephone directories 241
telephone enclosure 240-242
telephone handset 163, 181, 241, 242, 246
telephone handset devices 163
telephone jack 68
telephone keypad 130, 137, 245
telephones vii, x, xi, 68, 101, 130, 137, 147, 148, 163, 171, 181, 188, 189, 191, 240-242, 245, 246, 296
tempered glass doors 215
tenant spaces 11, 17
terminal information systems 185, 186
terminals 185, 186
terraces 27, 149
textured loop 195
theaters 85
thermostats 261
thresholds 44, 57, 136, 147, 192, 213, 216, 232, 233, 260
ticket gates 209
ticket offices 171
timetables 185, 251
toe clearance vi, ix, x, 50, 51, 53, 59, 65, 96, 104, 115, 119, 123, 125, 162, 198-200, 202, 203, 277
toe space 53, 65, 123, 125, 264
toilet and bathing facilities v, 2, 41, 46, 59, 101, 104, 105, 109, 192, 194
toilet and bathing rooms v, 27, 60, 105, 107, 108, 170, 171, 194
toilet compartments v, vii, ix, 109, 110, 114-117, 152, 221, 222, 235
toilet paper dispensers 114, 222
toilet room fixtures 105

INDEX

toilet rooms　　　5, 39, 44, 55, 104, 105, 107, 108, 152, 192, 194, 278
toll booths　　　8
top loading machines　　　239
track crossings　　　xi, 253
traffic control devices　　　158, 182
traffic lanes　　　20, 218
train　　　186
transaction prompts　　　246
transfer devices　　　272
transfer entry　　　271
transfer height　　　271, 272
transfer platforms　　　xii, 287, 288, 294, 303-305
transfer space　　　288
transfer steps　　　xii, 288, 294, 304
transfer systems　　　xii, 285-287, 290, 292, 294, 295, 298, 299, 303, 305
transfer walls　　　xii, 298, 299, 302, 303
transfer-type shower compartments　　　ix, xi, 228, 231-233
transfer-type showers　　　ix, xi, 228, 231-233, 238
transformer vaults　　　7
transit platform edges　　　154
transit system　　　186
transition plates　　　273
transitions　　　217, 296
transportation　　　vii, 9, 11, 108, 185, 189, 195, 250, 256
transportation facilities　　　vii, 11, 108, 185, 195, 250
trash compactor　　　53, 65, 263
tray slides　　　163
tread　　　77-79, 92-94, 167, 168, 304
tread depth　　　94, 167
tread surface　　　168
treads　　　x, 73, 93, 167, 168
truncated domes　　　x, 155
TTY　　　x, 68, 181, 191, 241, 242
TTY communication　　　68
tub and shower fixtures　　　265
tunnels　　　8, 16

turning space　　　vi, viii, 14, 40, 44, 48, 75, 101, 102, 105, 110, 135, 160, 198, 199, 202, 213, 286
turnstiles　　　13, 158
two doors in series　　　xi, 213, 216
two-way communication systems　　　vii, 141, 249
Type A units　　　iv, viii, ix, 17, 19, 27, 32, 34, 36, 39, 43, 55, 66, 111, 191, 225, 229, 231
Type B units　　　iv, ix, 17, 19, 27-30, 33-39, 43, 55, 66, 111, 112, 120, 166
T-shaped turning space　　　14

underground tunnels　　　8
undisturbed site　　　36, 256, 257
unisex　　　v, 107, 108, 170, 171, 192, 194
unisex bathing room　　　107
unisex toilet and bathing rooms　　　v, 107, 108, 170, 171, 194
unisex toilet room　　　107, 108
unobstructed forward reach　　　x
unobstructed side reach　　　x
unusual characteristics　　　254, 255, 257
urinals　　　vii, xi, 109, 223
usable bathrooms　　　263
usable doors　　　259, 263
usable kitchens　　　260, 263
usable kitchens and bathrooms　　　260, 263
use zones　　　282, 287, 290, 293
utility buildings　　　7
u-shaped areas　　　122
u-shaped kitchen　　　ix, 121

valet parking　　　24
van parking spaces　　　21-23
vanities　　　61, 265
vans　　　23
vehicle pull-up space　　　25
vehicle roadway　　　250
vehicle roadway edge　　　250

INDEX

vehicular arrival point 37, 257
vehicular or pedestrian arrival points 36, 37, 256, 257
vehicular route 26, 28, 258
vehicular traffic lanes 218
vehicular way 9, 22, 25
ventilation 164
verbal announcement 132, 140
verbal annunciators 132
vertical bar 227, 232
vertical changes in level x
vertical clearance x, 23, 26, 78, 205, 242
vertical difference 269
vertical support 126
viewing distance 174
visible alarm notification appliances 81-83
visible alarms 81, 191
visible and audible alarms viii, 82
visible indicators 139, 140
visible notification appliances 66, 67
visible signal elements 131
visible signals x, 130, 131, 172
vision lites 215
visiting areas 100, 157
visual alarm signal appliances 191
visual alarms 83, 101, 191
visual characters 139, 173, 175, 176, 178, 184-186, 251-253
voice communication 67, 163
volume controls 101, 181, 191, 241
volume-controlled telephones x, 241

WAC iii-vii, 1, 8, 11, 13, 15, 16, 19, 20, 24, 32, 34, 72, 73, 79, 106, 113, 117, 125, 128, 137, 154, 166, 181, 188-192, 214, 216
wading pools vii, 297, 298, 301, 302
waiting lines 159
walking surfaces iv, 1, 4, 12-15, 40, 44, 56, 72, 155
walkways 9, 16, 77

wall depth and length xii, 302
walls xii, 46, 47, 49-51, 60, 64, 104, 111, 122, 225, 229-231, 262-265, 298, 299, 302, 303
wall-hung 114, 115, 223
wall-hung water closets 114
washing machines vii, 41, 46, 58, 239
Washington State Building Code iii
water closet compartments v, 2, 3, 46, 60, 104, 109, 221, 222, 235
water closet height ix, xi
water closet seats 110, 221
water closets v, vii-ix, xi, 2, 3, 46-48, 59, 60-63, 104, 107-117, 192, 221, 222, 235
water coolers v, 125
water flow 126
water level 299-301, 304
water or sewage treatment pump rooms 7
water play components 305
water stream 127
water supply and drain pipes 52, 120
wave action pools 298, 302
weather shelters 278, 279
weight capacity 301
wet bars 119, 121
wet locations 161
wheel flanges 253
wheelchair accessible compartment doors ix
wheelchair accessible compartment toe clearance ix
wheelchair accessible compartments v, 109, 114, 115
wheelchair accessible telephones 240
wheelchair accessible toilet compartments ix
wheelchair space elevation ix
wheelchair spaces viii, ix, xii, 5, 10, 85-87, 89-94, 102, 149, 191, 268, 269-271
wheelchair storage space 272
wheelchair turning space viii, 48

INDEX

windows   vi, 41, 42, 45, 54, 163, 165, 171, 189
witness stands   102, 149, 191
work areas   5-7, 10, 49, 64, 81, 122
work surfaces   v, vi, ix, 42, 50, 96, 122-124, 157